N' in Rome—
the sacrifices
laughters . . .

READ

and her mother left home

harder, just before Sophia was born. I went to the Naples Conservatory of Music and got my diploma when I was 17.

"Today, my mother is dead, but my father is still alive. He is 78 now and he still lives in the little house where we were raised with my sister. He stopped work only eight years ago.

"The little house is still rented. When my father does die, we are hoping to buy that house for my sister to live in and to serve as a permanent memory of those difficult days, and make us all thankful for the good fortune we have had since."

How was your life when Sophia was born?

She took a deep breath: "That period of my life was a little difficult and I do not wish to speak of it much now. As I said, just before Sophia was born I was supporting myself giving piano lessons and I returned to my parents' home to have Sophia.

OVERCROWDED

"IT did not help to ease the crowded conditions at home. Already living there were my father, mother, two brothers, and sister. Then I went there to have Sophia. In 1938, I was visiting some cousins in Naples, and while I was there, Maria was born.

"By this time, one of my brothers had been married, too, and his wife later had a baby, so life there had become almost impossible during the early days of the war. We had only three rooms to live in, and at one time there were nine people in them."

Couldn't you find yourself another place to live?

"No. People were fleeing from the extreme south and a lot more people wanted to leave Rome because they feared bombing and were trying to stay with relatives in the mid-south, too. Also money and work were short."

You must have had many problems having two baby girls.

"I found clothing them very difficult because the war had made us so poor.

"I would take some of my clothes and whatever scraps of material I could get ing up and from time to time she would suddenly spring up an inch or two very quickly.

"She would have to wear a dress with a strip of completely different material round the waist, to make it longer, or a strip downwards to make it wider."

How was Sophia's personality as a child, and did she or Maria ever get upset by the way they had to live?

"No. Maria was too young to appreciate the conditions at first, and Sophia was never a greedy or petulant child. She was always modest in her demands. She appreciated the situation even at the age of six.

"You know, I have always thought how lucky I have been with both my daughters, because they were both adult in so many ways, even when they were quite little. Neither of them was ever a silly, playful little girl. They were always very considerate and serious-minded, almost like little women when they were born."

What was the worst period in the whole war for yourself and your two girls?

the worst time. Perhaps it was when we were all evacuated from Pozzuoli to Naples.

"You see, Pozzuoli was in the line of the Allied advance. It was chaos and confusion. The Germans were retreating and were being chased by the English and Americans.

THE LONG WALK

"WE all had to walk the 10 kilometres [*more than six miles*] from Pozzuoli to Naples and both my girls had fever. I had to carry little Maria in my arms all the way. Never, as long as I live, will I forget that walk, or the walk back from Naples 10 days later, when the Americans had liberated the area. I never thought 10 kilometres would seem so far."

Is it true you actually begged for food in the streets of Naples?

"The only time during this terrible period when I actually begged for food was when we were in Naples. The Germans were

My Wicked First Life

My Wicked First Life

Before the Wilderness

Mike Tomkies

Whittles Publishing

Published by
Whittles Publishing Ltd.,
Dunbeath Mains Cottages,
Dunbeath,
Caithness, KW6 6EY,
Scotland, UK
www.whittlespublishing.com

ISBN 1-904445-35-7

Printed by Bell & Bain Ltd., Glasgow

Also by Mike Tomkies

Books

Biography
The Big Man (The John Wayne story)
It Sure Beats Working (The Robert Mitchum story)

Nature
Alone in the Wilderness
Between Earth and Paradise
A Last Wild Place
My Wilderness Wildcats
Liane – A Cat from the Wild
Wildcat Haven
Out of the Wild
Golden Eagle Years
On Wing and Wild Water
Moobli
Last Wild Years
In Spain's Secret Wilderness
Wildcats

Novel
Let Ape and Tiger Die (unpublished)

Videos
Eagle Mountain Year
At Home with Eagles
Forest Phantoms
My Barn Owl Family
River Dancing Year
Wildest Spain
Wildest Spain Revisited
Last Eagle Years
My Bird Table Theatres
My Wild 75th Summer

Contents

Foreword

This is the autobiography I swore I would never write. Twelve years ago the editorial chiefs at Jonathan Cape offered me my highest ever advance of £10,000 to write it. I started making notes, then turned the offer down flat, replying that 'Only an egotist would write an autobiography – trying to tell the world what a great guy he has been.' I had not been a great guy. In fact, I had been a rather *bad* guy, and maybe I should keep quiet about that. However, after publishing seventeen books, mostly about rare and dramatic wildlife in the wildest parts of Canada, Scotland and Spain, I had run out of species I wanted to write about. And then, after making ten wildlife films, I had run out of species I wanted to film. In my mid-seventies I was faced, day after interminable day, with nothing to do. And as I looked through my old notes again I had a new thought: If I can't tell the world what a great guy I've been, or what a bad guy I've been, I could at least tell it what a fool I've been. And maybe that world, or rather a very small part of it, might have a few belly laughs. I hope no one ever accuses me of *not* having a misspent youth. So, here it is – my wicked first life before I went into the wilderness. I hope you enjoy reading about it as much as I enjoyed living it.

Mike Tomkies

1
Born a Runt

'You were a real runt when you were born, Michael.' Your skull and features were all twisted, your face so grey and ugly, that when the doctor and midwife weren't looking, I straightened your skull and got your eyes level, with my hands.

I stared at my father in astonishment. He was now seventy-five years old and I was fifty, and I was looking after him in Spain when he had become incapable following the death of his second wife. As he lapsed into one of the 'sudden slumbers' to which he was prone, I found myself looking back on what seemed to me an incredible life. And I had been born a runt?

I had run for my school and for my battalion in the Guards. I had boxed at school and in the Army. One of my jobs had entailed toiling in a timber yard, working a giant hand crane on trees weighing many tons. I had been a cup- and medal-winning racing cyclist. I had been one of a crew sailing across the Bay of Biscay in winter without an engine... and had hiked most of the 500 miles from Lisbon to Madrid on the way home to Britain when that yacht trip foundered.

Had I not also been a crime reporter in Fleet Street, and then a show-business columnist travelling the major capitals of the world, mixing drinks, copy and romance with the world's top movie stars? And when I had cut out from that hedonistic life to write the 'Great Novel' in Canada, I had tried to raise money to live on by working on the rough sea-salmon fishing boats along British Columbia's rugged coast, and as a logger with the lusty men of the wild forests, dealing with felled trees over six feet across the butt. I had also worked as an assistant blaster, blowing huge stumps apart with dynamite to make the road into Simon Fraser University.

On a trip around Mexico, at the request of the *Daily Express* to report on it, I was the first man to run round the new Tartan track for the 1968 Olympic Games before it was completely laid. I can still hear the irate yells of the Mexican workmen!

Even now, before flying out to Spain to look after my father, I was living halfway up a roadless loch with no mod cons whatever, and toting heavy camera packs over 300 square miles of the wild Scottish Highlands for my studies on golden eagles, wildcats, pine martens, badgers, foxes, peregrines, rare divers and herds of wild red deer. I had to fetch supplies in thirteen-mile return trips in a small open boat through all seasons. In summer, just for exercise, I sometimes rowed the full distance.

And I was born a runt?

After he woke from his brief slumber, my father filled in more details about my birth.

'You had a forceps delivery and I recall the doctor trying to smooth out with his fingers the marks the tongs had made. You only weighed five and a quarter pounds and you lay on the bed all screwed up, wizened like a prune and grey-looking. I was sure you would not live. Your face was all twisted too and I was quite horrified at how you looked. Having heard that a newborn baby's skull was malleable, I waited until the doctor and midwife weren't looking, and with my hands I straightened out your features before the bones set. I twisted the left side of your face up until it was level with your right.'

Now I knew why I've always had a bumpy skull and have dreaded going bald. It also dawned on me right then that my adventurous physical life had possibly been the result of my subconsciously trying to prove to the world that I was not a runt, while knowing in my heart that I really was. Now, too, I had an inkling of why as a child I had often felt my father was displeased with me, that I was never quite 'up to standard' in his eyes. But to begin at the beginning...

Both my grandfathers had unusual lives. My mother's father, John Stewart, known as Jack, was a Highlander who came from Islay and was reputed to be a descendant of the Lords of the Isles. A man of stocky build with powerful 'hill' legs, he had been a renowned amateur boxer in his youth yet held strong religious beliefs. Unable to find work at home, he had ended up in Nottingham where he worked as an estate agent and sold religious artefacts as a secondary career. He became a local preacher and for twenty-five years was Sunday School Superintendent of the West Bridgeford Baptist Church. There is a testimonial plaque to him on the wall there to this day. Apparently he had an eye for the ladies, for he had three wives, the first of whom, another Scot, Alice McKinlay, was the mother of my mother, Adela McKinlay Stewart, and another daughter, Dee, and a son Jack, who emigrated to Canada and became lost to the family. 'Grandpa Jack' was living with his second wife, Gladys, when Alice McKinlay was killed in dramatic circumstances near the Trent Bridge cricket ground in Ladybay Road by a runaway horse-drawn bus which mounted the pavement and ploughed into the bus queue.

My father's father, David Tomkies, came from the Bilston area of Staffordshire and claimed to have a Scot – a Campbell – among his grannies. As a young man he travelled all over Canada, was ambushed by Indians, returned to Britain to have his injuries treated and married Florence Singleton, a beautiful young Yorkshire woman who, on 3 March, 1903, gave birth to my father, Vincent Tomkies. Vincent told me of the years before I was born.

When he was a boy one of his worst memories was of the lace and net-making factory in Lenton Boulevard, Nottingham, where his father David worked, slaving all day, working long net machines which he rented from the franchise owner, Sir Ernest Jardine, who was a hard taskmaster. Mostly, he made mosquito netting for the South American market.

'I'll never forget those great machines – they were noisy and kept grinding, grinding, grinding, making tiny fine threads. They had a system in those days which they called "Twist hands". I can see him now, shoving his hands into the great machines and twisting the thread ends together when they broke under the tension, doing "twist hands". The only way you could oil the machines was with black lead because oil would have stained the net. I would cycle over and immediately hear these terrible grinding machines, see my dad with a pencil in his ear, up to the armpits in black lead. He often worked all night. He was a total slave and I swore to myself I was never going to do that.'

Apparently David Tomkies was a clever technician and inventor. In his spare time he made a model of a new kind of lace-making machine, all in wood and fretwork. Financial problems meant he had to sell the patent for £30 but that was felt to be a fair amount of money in those days.

Vincent lost his father at fifty-two, from cancer of the oesophagus, and started his first job at fifteen as a warehouse boy for Gray Nelson's where one of his tasks was to push railway trolleys of cloth and lace bales up the tracked streets of Castle Boulevard. There was a primitive hoist lift in the warehouse in which he and another boy pulled themselves up and down on ropes by their hands, carrying bales of netting. Then they had to trundle the bales down steps in wicker baskets on wheels, and through the streets of Nottingham to the wholesale depot.

'When we came back the baskets were light. We put them in the lift and always enjoyed the ride back up. We pulled at the ropes so hard we often banged into the roof, almost went through it!'

One day during the Armistice of 1918 one of the staff had been invalided out of the Army and everyone was happy. In high spirits Vincent grabbed one of the net bales for an impromptu game of football. He had just kicked one across the floor when the boss, Gray Nelson, walked in. 'He was wild because it was a wooden floor and scratched up the netting. He shouted "You're fired!" I went into his office a minute later and said "You can't sack me. Please sir, I can't go back and tell my father I've been sacked. He'll kill me!" He took me back but told me never to do it again.'

It was at this time that Vincent fell in love with my mother Adela, known to everyone as 'Bunty'. 'She worked in our office and at first I worshipped her from afar. The first time I saw her she was wearing a Viyella blouse, white with black stripes, which was popular in those days. I used to get angry as I had a real yen for this girl, but so had her married boss, Gray Nelson himself, and he used to keep her talking after work. One day I got so annoyed I kept talking on the phone next to his office. He came out to tell me not to use it outside office hours, and so let her go.

'For our first date Bunty bought a new hat. It was brown and had four big petals that hung down close to her head. I met her at the top of High Pavement and her petals were all blowing up in the wind. I always remember that. We went to the pictures that night, and started to get to know each other.'

While Vincent was courting Bunty, her father, my Grandpa Jack, hauled him in to help with the Sunday School teaching and insisted on his being baptized into the faith at the Baptist Chapel too. This went against the grain a bit for Vincent, who was not very religious, but he put up with it for the sake of winning Bunty. Jack even got his soon-to-be son-in-law to go prison visiting with him too.

Vincent left his job after the Great War, becoming friendly with another young man called George Sewell. They started, their own firm, Sewell and Tomkies, rented a one-room office and bought off-cut seconds of lace from the factories, which they sold from a stall in the open market. 'We parcelled these short bits of differently coloured lace on to little reels, tied them up with little bows of ribbons and sold them at tuppence each. They sold fantastically in the street markets. We made good profits and employed two girls at ten pennies an hour to wind the laces on to the reels.'

On the night before he was due to propose formally to Bunty and become engaged to her, Vincent went out with some male pals for a stag night. They went into a little bar behind the station and Vincent asked, 'What's *that* wine like?' The waitress replied, 'Oh, you'll like that, it's nice and fruity.' So they drank it – and probably a bit too much of it. Heading home, they came upon some new lamp posts in Long Road. It was now raining but the other lads dared Vincent to climb up one. Despite the wet, slippery surface he managed to reach the top. Showing off, he swung to and fro from the high crossbar with one hand, and then let go. He twisted his ankle badly on landing and felt great pain.

'I had to propose and get engaged in the morning but I couldn't sleep because of the pain. It was so bad I had to slide downstairs on my bum next day and get a taxi to the Kardomah Café where Bunty was waiting, but I made sure I had the ring with me. I can't recall how I proposed; all I can remember is the pain in my foot!'

When Vincent heard a new boss was hiring and firing at the prestigious clothing company William Hollins, he togged himself up, marched in, and won a job in the Costing Department. The boss handed him a shirt and told him to cost it. He got the price tag right to within one eighth of a penny. Later, he was handed one of their best shirts and asked if he could find a way to reduce the price. He took it home and after careful examination with a magnifying glass, he found that by 'opening up the stitch' – so that not so many stitches had to be made – the shirt was still sewn firmly but could be produced at lower cost, and this could be passed on in a lower price to the customer.

'Not long after that the big boss Sir Ernest Jardine called me in and said, "You're a clever little bugger. I'm going to put you out on the road, selling." We had no salesmen going out from head office in Castle Boulevard then, so I was the first. I climbed into our van with driver Ted Tarry and a pile of dance frocks and shirts. We set off for the Mansfield Co-op but on the way I went into a little shop on a whim. The owner was very excited about getting an account with William Hollins, and I got an order for six dozen shirts. I was so full of myself I went straight back and told Sir Ernest I'd got an order!'

After successfully selling dresses and shirts locally, Vincent, who was very handsome and well dressed – he believed in the old adage 'The apparel oft proclaims the man' – was the first salesman to be sent down to London. He booked into a temperance hotel in Oxford Street with a huge suitcase of Viyella dance dresses and ladies' underwear but was appalled when he tackled his first big store, Bourne and Hollingsworth, to find twenty other travellers queuing up before him, and it took three hours to see the buyer. He started going on trains to the suburbs with his heavy case, tramping the streets. His luck changed. He went into Bentalls in Kingston, saw the buyer quickly, and got an order for ten dozen dresses. He then had a very successful week, selling and getting regular orders set up. When he got back to Nottingham

Sir Ernest Jardine said, 'You deserve a putty medal!'

When Vincent and Bunty were first married they lived in a pokey little flat in Forest Fields but in July 1926 moved to a nice terraced house, 51 South Road, West Bridgeford, which was the only house in the street with two chimneys, one springing from a corner in the kitchen. It was in this house, at 9.30 in the morning of 25 May 1928, that I was born, and, as I have already related, according to my dad I was a runt.

2
From Sickly Child to Boisterous Boy

After two and a half years in West Bridgeford, and before I was even one year old, my father was doing so well as William Hollins's salesman of quality clothing in the Midlands that he was sent to the north-east – to the notorious 'travellers' graveyard'. Many a commercial traveller had come a cropper there as it was the era of the Great Depression, the year of the Wall Street crash in America and less than three years from the disastrous General Strike in Britain. But in his first week Vincent Tomkies, working mostly in the Newcastle, South and North Shields areas, took £3,000 in orders – as much as the average salesman took in a year. Years later I heard my father tell a colleague, 'I do not sell – I *allocate*!'

We moved into a small semi-detached cottage in Killingworth, Co. Durham, where when I reached the age of one my mother recorded my weight at 21.81b. She had also noted that I spoke my first words, 'Dad dad' at seven and a half months, and at nine months I came out with 'Oh dear, oh dear.'

After he persuaded his bosses to buy him one of the first little Morris-Cowley cars, my father's selling career began to take off in earnest. My sister Maureen was born in February 1930 at Killingworth but the only thing I can remember about that time – and it must be my earliest memory – was that I was afraid of 'the Whopple'. This was really the pointed bulbous end of the eiderdown on my bed which, when I was lying down and staring up at it in the half-dark, looked really menacing. The ceiling had speckled wallpaper, resembling mince, and sometimes my eyes made out the form of a giant toad and I was afraid it would come down and eat me. The railway line ran along the bottom of the garden, and when I was in my pram outside I recall being terrified of the steam train as it charged along belching plumes of steam, coming nearer and nearer, and I was sure this shrieking monster was coming for me, and yelled my head off.

In August 1930 we moved to a better house in Links Avenue, Whitley

Bay, because it was nearer my dad's work area and he liked to be near the sea. It was here that my mother Bunty died when I was four, in December 1932, giving birth to my younger sister Valerie. Bunty had suffered prolonged bleeding and then septicaemia had set in. My dad remembered the doctor and his assistant conversing in hushed tones in the bathroom and then being told there was nothing they could do as the septicaemia had gone too far. Dad had spent a lot on the new house and was so broke when Bunty died that at first he couldn't pay the doctor's bill. Bailiffs were sent in, and they sat in the hall all night. The following day Dad made them breakfast and coffee and gave them all the money be could find, a ten-bob note. They must have felt sorry for him for they said they accepted his promise to pay the bill as soon as he could and would stay no longer.

The strange and rather sad truth is that I cannot recall anything about my mother, or my relationship with her, yet old family album photos show I was constantly in her arms. For a long time I thought it must have been the shock of her death that blotted out childish memories of her, but many years later Dad told me it had not been too traumatic for me and Maureen. Apparently we both accepted that she was not coming back any more but was 'sleeping in heaven' and waiting for us there. Neither of us screamed or made a fuss. He thought we were probably still too young to really understand.

According to Dad and a few of her friends I met later in Nottingham, Bunty was not only religious like her father but very idealistic, indeed a little fey. She wrote poetry and lovely fairy stories, was very gentle by nature and always looked for the best in people. For a long time I thought that I must have inherited whatever little writing talent I had from my mother. But later I realized I had got as much again from my dad, for he wrote very good letters, and once when he was over seventy and I asked him to fill in some details about our early friendship with an extraordinary gamekeeper (of which more later), he sent me back a lengthy script full of detailed descriptions and anecdotes any professional writer would have envied. After his death in 1982 I found among his papers several scripts for charming children's pantos and his own Punch and Judy shows.

After my mother died William Hollins gave Dad two months off and he took the rest of the family down to stay with her sister, my Aunty Dee, in Brighton. Here Dad took on the role of mother as well as father, attending to all baby Valerie's needs, changing her nappies and giving her feeds at the correct times. When we returned to Whitley Bay in February 1933 we moved into a different house in Hobart Terrace, and I attended first a private kindergarten and later the local council school, which I recall was a lot rougher.

When Dad had to go back to work his mother Florrie, whom we called Granny Tomkies, or by her nickname, 'Mimi', came up from Nottingham to help him look after us, and she virtually became our mother. What a heroine she must have been, to take on three young children in middle age. She was kind and gentle and often sang us to sleep with lullabies.

I remember Dad taking me to my first film, Frank Buck's *Bring 'Em Back Alive*, in which I saw elephants, tigers and lions for the first time, marvelling that such awesome creatures existed in the same world as me. This was perhaps the very first seed sown for my future passion for wildlife. In our family albums there is a photo of me staring at a daisy. Later, Dad told me I picked the flower then spent a full two minutes turning it round and round in my fingers, enraptured by its beauty and intricate design. 'It was the longest time I'd ever known you to stay still.'

Dad also took me to see a Shirley Temple film, the title of which I cannot now recall, but one dramatic scene has stuck in my mind to this day. She was with her father in a bi-plane which was crashing with an awful roaring sound towards the ground. He opened the door and asked Shirley, 'How much do you love me?' She threw her arms around his neck, he said, 'Hang on tight!' and leaped out to parachute them both to safety. I thought she was lovely. I remember that in the council school playground, because I could not imitate Shirley herself, I imitated the plane, running around in loops and circles with my arms extended for the wings, making sounds like a plane engine and imagining Shirley was clinging round *my* neck. Dad took me to see two more of her films, which I think were called *The Little Colonel* and *Poor Little Rich Girl*. As I saw more of her singing and dancing, her lovely little face surrounded by ringlets, I fell madly in love with Shirley Temple! I even had dreams about her and remember wanting never to wake up.

By now I was deemed old enough to play with the boy next door sometimes on some nearby allotments. I was walking back home one day when I had my first experience of real pain. Two older boys walked up to me with oddly intent, leering looks on their faces, and the bigger of them said, 'Do ye want a fiette, mate?'

I didn't know what a 'fiette' was, not realizing it was Geordie for a fight, so I said I didn't know what a 'fiette' was but I didn't think so. The next thing I knew was hearing as much as feeling a bang, then sudden intense physical pain in my face.

Being hit on the nose produces a unique sort of pain, unlike that of being hit on any other part of the body, and I never forgot it. Ever since, whenever a street fight looked like looming (and I've been in over half a dozen), or during legal bouts in the boxing ring, my main concern was to keep my nose out of trouble. On this first occasion of first being actually punched by anyone, I was so dazed and shocked that the two lads ran off laughing, and disappeared round a far corner. Then I felt the blood streaming down my face and all I wanted to do was run home.

I remember the summers of the early Thirties as being mostly idyllic, especially when Dad drove us in his new car, a big Austin with chrome bumpers and FAU 782 on its number plate, to Beadnell Bay or Seaton Sluice, where there were exciting high sand dunes. Dad made huge, elaborate sandcastles, which Maureen and I ended wrecking with our little wooden spades when we tried to improve them. We both loved playing on the dunes, running to the top and rolling down again, in and out of the marram grasses, getting sand in our ears, eyes and hair until we were told to go and rinse the worst of it off in the sea.

Our Christmases were enjoyable too, us kids giggling as we lay in bed, always intending to stay awake long enough to see Santa Claus filling our huge long lisle stockings, but we never did. We opened our presents by the sparkling Christmas tree after a roast duck or goose lunch, and I recall spending hours cutting out cardboard shapes to make things like a carousel roundabout, holding the glued joints over the heat from the Aladdin paraffin stove until they were dry, and then making a cardboard hopper into which I poured sand which made the carousel go round as it flowed. There were hours spent with Meccano sets, toy cars and wooden boats that chugged along in the bath if you put a small lump of camphor at the back. When Maureen and I were both given little Hornby trains, my first act was to take mine to pieces, to see how it worked. With the debris of my engine lying around on the floor I would then ask to look at Maureen's, and promptly took hers to bits too, all without any objection from her.

Maureen was the quiet, calm one whereas, Dad told me later, I was always volatile, easily happy, easily depressed. I was thrilled when I got my first pair of roller skates and spent much of my spare time whizzing over the Whitley Bay pavements. I remember skating on the day King George V died. The streets were deadly quiet, with no one at all about, and I felt happy and in my element. Maybe the seeds of the eventual loner were there already.

By all accounts, I was a rather sickly child and caught all the childish ailments – asthma, mumps, measles. In March 1935 I fell seriously ill with scarlet fever; I recall that my temperature was far too high and Dad put hot flannels and sticky poultices on a great rash on my chest. Apparently they did not work and an ambulance came to take me to Tynemouth Hospital: I recall that the two men who carried me out to it were very kind and let me take my beloved Harold Lloyd mask with me. I was put into a large ward where, to my disgust, there was a very plain *girl* in the next bed!

As the days went by I felt increasingly unhappy, almost as if I'd been abandoned, for I didn't receive as many visits as the other patients. Dad of course had to be away all week on his exhausting salesman's rounds, and Grandma couldn't drive. But the hospital had special parcel days and Dad and Gran sent me toys and animal books as I was now learning to read properly. The book I remember most vividly was one of the new ones about Mickey Mouse. It was about eight inches square and three inches thick and it had the type on the left page and a drawing of what was happening on the right. I loved the book which I think was called *Mickey And The Gypsies* and in my mind I lived Mickey and Minnie's adventures. I had just got to a very exciting part where Minnie had been strapped to a lower mill wheel by an evil mill owner, and the topgrinding wheel was turning and coming closer. I put the book down on the bedsheets in order to prolong the denouement for a while.

Just then a golden-haired little girl wandered in from the next ward. She said hello with a shy, sweet smile and I thought things were looking up! Then she just picked up my Mickey Mouse book and toddled off back to her ward with it. I couldn't go after her as I'd been in bed so long that I found it difficult to walk, and when I complained to a nurse I was told I could not have my book back anyway as the little girl, who should not have wandered into my ward, was in a whooping cough ward and they didn't want those germs spreading to me. I was both furious and heartbroken at the same time.

I slowly got better but when I tried to walk for the first time I took one step and fell on the floor. My shame was accompanied by laughter from the others on the ward. Just as I was looking forward to going home again, I contracted chickenpox from somewhere within the hospital and was moved to another small ward. Things were better there as there was only one other young chap in it and we got on well; we swapped stories and he even let me read his copies of *Film Fun* comic, which I loved. Dad came on my seventh birthday with a clockwork toy tank and a big bouncy ball and I was allowed out of bed to play with them. After seven weeks the day came at last when I could walk well again and go out into the sunny grounds and talk to Dad and Gran Mimi through the railings. They annoyed me by saying I had become flat-footed and I resolved to be okay when the time came for me to leave.

My miserable, seemingly endless hospital stay was soon erased from my immediate memory when Dad took us down to a country farm belonging to Marjorie Nixon, an artist who had been my mother's best friend and had illustrated a book of charming fairy stories she wrote. I had never spent a happier few days. Marjorie's husband must have been the most tolerant farmer of all time for we almost wrecked his haystacks, making slide chutes from top to bottom and constantly sliding down them. Once, going down forwards, I nearly broke my neck on the barn's wooden floor. On an excursion by foot into the lovely countryside I found my first bird's nest, a blackbird's containing four blue eggs speckled with light brown. I marvelled at its new neatness and the work that must have gone into making it.

Ill health caught up with me again in September 1935 when I went down with severe tonsillitis and Dad decided I should have my tonsils out. I was carted off to Tynemouth hospital again where, on the operating table, I thought the rubbery pad pressed to my nose had a lovely smell, and did not feel at all frightened. As I was losing consciousness I could distinctly see two golden bells in the window through my half-closed eyes. I woke up in a ward with horrible chocolate-coloured walls and a terrible pain in my throat. I felt very hungry but even if the walls had been made of chocolate I could not have swallowed any. I was highly relieved when Dad came to collect me and didn't mind having to live on liquid foods for a few days.

One day in March 1936 Dad announced that we were all going to move south and live in a seaside town called Worthing. He had been promoted and would now be William Hollins's representative covering the Home Counties of Sussex, Kent and Hampshire, the choicest areas next to London but an enormous task for just one salesman. Before we set off on the long drive Dad left us three kids with Grannie Mimi in a playground while he had something done to his car. For some silly reason, probably because I was bored, I wrapped up a brand-new mackintosh he had bought me, tied its arms around the bundle and started kicking it over the dusty playground like a football. Dad arrived as I took my fifth kick, clipped me sharply around the ear and said I would receive appropriate punishment when we got to our new house in Worthing. I hated the dreary long drive – there were no motorways then – not only because we had to stop twice when I was sick, but because of my mounting fear of the punishment that awaited me.

Our new home was a three-bedroomed terrace house in Reigate Road, on the Goring side of west Worthing, with a nice little garden. As we carried things into the house in the dark I wondered if I was going to get the strap as Dad had now taken to using his trouser belt to give us painful whacks on our rears when we were naughty. Instead, he drew me aside and said I really had to start looking after my clothes, not kick things like new macs around, but as no doubt I had been worrying all the way down as to what punishment I would get he would take no more action on this occasion. What a relief!

I started going to Elm Grove Council School down near the railway line, and immediately ran into trouble as the other boys took the mickey out of my northern accent and I kept getting into fights. Sometimes a small gang of boys would chase me home at the end of school but as I ran everywhere and never walked, I was very fleet of foot and could outdistance them. Even so, this upset me enough for me to take little packets of pepper to school and if I was chased home by other boys, I would stop inside my gate and sling the pepper into their faces! I never seemed to anticipate that I could be in big trouble the following day when I faced the same boys at school. I recall how once a group of boys held me prisoner, pinioning my arms so that a boy called Randall could pummel me at will. Two days later I got my revenge when I saw him standing alone near the wall of the toilets. I sneaked up silently behind him and dropped to my hands and knees, then put my head an inch from his bum and jerked his ankles backwards with both hands. Apart from the sudden shock, he received minor injuries to his hands and face and left me strictly alone from then onwards.

I enjoyed the evenings most of all at this time. When Dad was away on his travels Mimi entertained us with little stories and songs before we went to bed. She was very sentimental, a trait I have inherited. One evening she told us a tragic little story about a sailor who is shot in a sea battle while his ship is sailing home. As he is dying he gives his shipmates a message. She broke into his little song in her gentle, quavering voice:

> 'Just break the news to Mother
> And say how much I love her
> And tell her not wait for me
> For I'm not coming home.
> Just say there is no other
> Can take the place of Mother.
> Just kiss her dear sweet lips for me
> For I'm not coming home.'

It seemed terribly sad to me and I bawled my eyes out!

In our last years in Whitley Bay, after my mother died, Dad had employed a pretty young secretary called Bettie Mathieu, the daughter of a Newcastle mother and a Belgian father. I can't recall ever meeting her as Dad probably never brought her home, or only did when we kids were in bed. One day in March 1937 he broke the news that he was getting married again and had to go back to Whitley Bay for the wedding on 20 March so that Bettie could have all her family around her. We kids went to stay with Aunty Dee in

Brighton for two weeks while he and his new wife were on their honeymoon.

I did not mind this at all. Aunty Dee was good fun and so was her bank manager husband Tom Bowis, soon known to us as 'Uncle Tom'. He was a first-class amateur artist and had a fascinating old-world studio among the trees in the orchard in their large walled garden. He let me sketch for hours on end, giving me useful tips and praising my drawing of three stags. We ran about the garden, ate all the fruit we wanted, and were taken to the beach where we investigated fascinating rock pools. And our cousins, the Bowis sons Peter and Derek, took us flying kites and model balsa-wood aeroplanes up on the South Downs.

When Dad and Bettie returned from honeymoon to take us home I didn't want to leave. I couldn't help crying but tried to cover this up by saying I had a pain in my stomach. Although they consoled me I saw them look at each other and I knew they knew that I had nothing of the sort. One consolation was that they soon bought a dog, a playful cocker spaniel called Robin, and I had fun taking him for walks. I was sorry, however, when Dad and Bettie agreed that Granny Mimi had done a more than good job and could now return to her old life and friends in Nottingham. When she waved goodbye, sitting on her seat in the train, I saw tears in her eyes, matching those that welled up in mine.

On Sundays now Dad gave us money for the collection box and despatched us to a nearby church. I had a fine treble voice and greeted with a mixture of fear and pride being selected as an occasional soloist chorister. We were not long in tumbling to the possibility that Dad and Bettie didn't send us off to church for ultra-religious reasons. It gave them a nice little break on a Sunday to visit the pub. We then began playing truant from church and spending the collection money at Jenkins's sweet shop opposite the school on things like Tiger nuts, a pomegranate (a real treat) and little board games where if you pushed a pencil into the right colour you got some sweets.

By now I had settled down at school and made a few friends. I formed my own little gang, consisting of my two sisters, boys called Denzil, Allan and Maurice, and one of their sisters whose name was Myrtle. I made them all special badges out of coloured cardboard and we went into nearby woods and made little camps from materials purloined from the new building sites on the outskirts of the town, using corrugated iron sheets for the walls and roofs. I pinched matches from the kitchen and cadged old newspapers from Bettie, saying I wanted them to swat butterflies, but really they were for burning, so that we could have fires and boil up nettle soup, which we never drank. We played naughty little games like Nurses and Doctors, and 'No, you show me your's first', and used scaffold poles as battering rams to knock down walls of half-demolished old buildings.

We had a lot of fun with a large wooden trolley, I found an old pram on a rubbish dump and managed to get the wheels off. Dad said he would help me make the trolley provided I made a detailed drawing of how it should be. I did so and we ended up with a three by two-foot platform on wheels, with a swivelling crosspiece on an extension board for the front ones, so they could be steered by a rein like a horse. The brake on this little monster was just a hardwood teak stake, hinged to the right side of the trolley. When you hauled the top of the stake up. the bottom would scrape along the ground in an attempt to slow it down, which was almost totally ineffective. One of us would get on the trolley to steer it, while the other would hare along as fast as he or she could, pushing the trolley, then leap on for the free-wheeling ride. We charged up and down George V Avenue in Goring as in those days it ended in interesting wasteland. When we hurtled down either side of the railway bridge in Shaftsbury Avenue it was amazing how fast elderly, rickety old pensioners could leap out of the way when they saw this contraption with two yelling boys coming at them.

One Sunday we discovered a new four-storey block of flats being built near the sea in a place which, I think, was called Courtney Close. All round the base were long planks resting on brick pedestals, presumably so the builders would not wreck the ground with their boots and debris. We climbed up to the fourth floor by ladders and when I found two bricks cemented together and saw the planks far below I had an idea. I reckoned if I dropped the bricks in the middle of a plank they would probably bounce interestingly. Telling the rest of my gang to watch, I let the double-brick bomb go – just as an old age pensioner couple came doddering round the corner.

Down went my missile, which hit the middle of the plank and bounced up nearly two storeys as the couple's heads turned as one, staring in amazement at the vibrating plank, although the brick missile was now above them and out of their sight. Then down it went again and landed in the mud a mere yard behind them. There was a stunned silence, then the old man let out a yell and peered upwards as we all cowered back by the inner wall where he couldn't see us. I hissed to the rest of the gang not to move and in the end he must have assumed the bricks had fallen by accident, and the couple walked on.

One weekend we invaded the orchard of an empty house and scrumped bags of apples, pears and plums, until a large policeman came through the same hole in the fence we had used and insisted on taking down our addresses so he could tell our parents. We would almost certainly get the strap for these misdemeanours and for days awaited the inevitable call into his study by my dad, but nothing happened. Obviously the copper, who had chuckled as he left us, had decided to let us off.

We all liked Bettie, with her beauty and vivacity, plus the fact that at only twenty-one she was a good cook. But she didn't stand much nonsense from us kids and was far more of a disciplinarian than Granny Mimi had been. Apparently (my Dad told me this years later) in the early part of their relationship I would yell my head off on weekend nights until Dad had to stop writing up his sales orders and come up to sing me a song or tell me a story. Eventually Bettie said, 'If you go on doing that he will expect it every night and you'll never be able to stop.' So one night Dad just let me yell myself to sleep, while making sure I was all right from time to time. I had the usual kids' playthings and became the school's expert at Whip and Top. I lost my first little tricycle when I left it outside Worthing Library – when we came out we discovered someone had stolen it. I enjoyed a little scooter that cost Dad 2s 6d, and went everywhere on it, but after a while Dad complained that I was always wearing one sandal out too fast. A little red bicycle followed and when I went out on the quietest streets I suddenly felt in my element, making it go as fast as I could, the wind whistling past my ears, never dreaming of course that one day I would be contemplating turning professional as a racing cyclist.

Towards the end of 1938, despite the threat of war, Dad had been doing so well that he bought us a really posh detached house with impressive swooping wings on each side in the sought-after Offington Avenue area in the Broadwater part of Worthing. There were large rear and front gardens with a few trees and we all felt much freer. We were very close to Broadwater Green, which had a fine large 'wishing' oak in its nearest corner. I loved running round the Green and when I got a football for Christmas I booted it about, pretending I was Stanley Mathews. I must admit this early interest in football was extremely shortlived. When I had to sit the Worthing High School entrance exam, I walked to the school, making a fervent wish at the wishing tree on the way, and was as surprised as Dad when I passed it with flying colours.

3
Revelations

At the High School I had the usual problems most new boys have to solve, as I adjusted to a new set of boys and masters, and while it soon became clear I was no good at football as a team member, I thought I had found a new string to my bow, as it were. I always ran to and from school and in fact was now running almost everywhere, and in gym classes and sports races I was doing quite well. When the first Sports Day loomed I was in Form 3, and entered the half-mile trials for the Juniors.

We lined up, the master shouted, 'Ready, steady – go!' and off we went, round the slightly wonky whitewashed line that marked out the two-lap 880 yards race. I shot out in front, felt really great all the way round, and stayed there, to win! It was my first important result and I was elated and ran home to tell my parents. Naturally, I thought I would be selected to represent my form.

Two days later the sports master posted up the list. To my intense dismay, the three boys listed were among those I had beaten. I had won but was not even mentioned. I went straight to see the master, a Mr Foinett. I pointed out I had won the trial and asked why I was not being selected.

Mr Foinett gave me a half-smirk, half-smile. 'Because, Tomkies, you have Duck's Disease!'

'Duck's Disease?' I repeated in surprise. 'What is Duck's Disease, sir?'

'You have a too-long back, and short little legs!'

I was so shocked by this that apart from stuttering out, 'But I won!' I could not think of any further protest. This was the first injustice that really registered in my young life. As soon as I got home I ran up to my bedroom, took off my clothes and surveyed myself in the full-length mirror. Mr Foinett did have a point, I thought. My back *was* long in proportion to my legs. I also suffered from having very narrow shoulders and a long neck; so much so that some boys at the school had nicknamed me 'Swanee'. Standing there, relaxed with nothing flexed, even I could see my upper half had the shape of a milk bottle. This also explained why one or two of the bigger boys, on walking towards me, would suddenly give a laugh, leap forward, throw one arm round my neck, and try to bring my head down to the level of their hips to attain the 'head in chancery' lock.

If I was having trouble with the boys at school, I was also having problems at home. My dad had become more of a strict disciplinarian and a perfectionist. An infringement of good manners at the lunch or dinner table could result in a hand slap or a clip round the ear. More important infringements resulted in his taking me up into my bedroom, where I had to lie over the bed and get strapped on my bottom with one of his leather belts. Dad was constantly exhorting me to do better at school, remembering how I had failed the 9-plus exam, which I had not realized was on. I slaved and swotted and began coming second or third, and once even first, in my classes, trying to please him yet dreading my school reports at the end of every term.

He gave me little jobs to do about the house, which was natural enough, but he insisted on very high standards. Once, when I'd failed to repair something in the garage, he said, 'Michael, if a job is worth doing, it's worth doing properly.' And I had muttered under my breath, 'What if it's not worth doing in the first place?' He'd heard this and immediately ordered me upstairs with 'How dare you answer back? I will teach you!' As the strap kept stinging my backside, I suddenly felt enraged at how this punishment did not fit my crime, and rose up sideways, dying to hit him in the face.

'Get you down!' he shouted and I sank back to take a few more blows. Dusk was falling and my father was going out to a pub with Bettie. As I lay there, hearing them leave, I had never felt so low. I decided I would leave home. I climbed out of the window, as my father had told our maid, Megan, to keep me locked in for one hour, on to the garage roof, and jumped to the ground. But as I walked the now rainy streets of Broadwater, I realized I had no money and no idea where to go anyway. I sneaked back, confessed all to Megan, who promised not to tell my dad, and I went up to bed, where I lay awake a long time.

Another problem at this time was that I had developed what was known as a 'septic system', and nasty little boils kept appearing on my scalp. They itched, I scratched, which made them worse, and they did not help my popularity at school either.

I had also somehow developed an odd facial tic, which involved suddenly pulling a long face, then reverting back to normal, which gave some of the other boys an additional excuse for imitating or tormenting me. My father hated this latest manifestation of my nervous state and if he caught me pulling the face at the meal table, I got a sharp slap on my cheek. Obsessively, I tried to foil him by just pulling a quick one when I thought he wasn't looking.

But the real crisis came during the onset of puberty. Like most boys of around eleven in those days we were kept in the dark about adult sexual relations and how babies came into the world. Amid sniggers, we lads exchanged rumours, theories, stories we heard, and finally I decided I knew what happened: men put their willies into their wives' fannies, wiggled them about until both had a nice feeling, then about a year later a baby came out! And my understanding was that this act was called a penis.

My elder sister Maureen and I were very close and I soon imparted some of this fascinating information to her. Wanting to know more, she started asking questions of Megan, who, worried I had been telling Maureen things she should not be hearing, told Dad. One night he called me into his study, where he was writing out his eternal tiny orders for two vests or three pairs of socks to this shop or that, and said he wanted a serious talk. He then told me the basic facts of life emphasising that marriage and love were essential ingredients.

He then said he had a more delicate and personal subject to discuss and wanted me to answer truthfully. He explained what male masturbation was, how it was done and asked if I had ever done it. The question shocked me as I certainly had not, and I told my father so. He seemed relieved and said I must never do anything like it, as it was wicked self-abuse. He said that those who practised it became walking wrecks before middle age, got the trembles, could not function like normal people and died young. It was in fact an awful disease but one would not suffer from it if one lived a decent life and exercised willpower.

That night as I lay in bed dozing, I woke with a sudden feeling of terror. Not only might I have lied to my father but perhaps the dreadful fate he described did lie ahead for me. From about the age of six I had accidentally discovered that if I lay on my stomach across my pillow and rocked gently to and fro, I could induce an enjoyably climactic sensation in my nether regions. Was this the 'nice feeling' my father had described? I was now scared and unsure whether I might have been performing for years the 'wicked' act my dad had described, yet I dare not approach him about it in case he thought I had earlier lied on purpose.

This fear, almost terror at times, began to wear on my mind and coupled with Dad's constant exhortations to work harder and get better exam results, the humiliating scabs on my head and my facial tic which brought on bullying by some of the bigger boys, plus not being allowed to shine at the one sport I was good at, led to yet another strange obsession. Every time I felt the need to urinate I was convinced my bladder would burst if I did not immediately relieve myself! So I was constantly sticking up my hand in class and asking to be 'excused'. This led to further derision from my classmates and one teacher even rang my father about it. I was now feeling I was born to be an outsider. All this eventually brought me to a nervous breakdown.

One night I woke up, crying for no apparent reason and shivering all over, and I staggered downstairs to Megan, who immediately called my parents back from where they were visiting friends. I was put back to bed with a cup of cocoa, told I could have the light on all night (for I had now become afraid of the dark again as when a young child) and Dad at last showed some concern.

The following day he took me to the doctor, who could find nothing physically wrong and recommended my father take me to a psychiatrist, which he did, having to drive me to London. I answered all the psychiatrist's questions and he later informed my dad that although he could find nothing mentally wrong I was a very sensitive child – 'highly strung' was the phrase he used – going through the usual anxieties of puberty more intensely than most kids, but would eventually 'grow out of it.'

Growing out of it took a long time but shortly after this things began to improve at school. The following term a new master, Mr Scudamore, took over our form and one day he called me over after class and said he liked my divinity essays and that I had a good young mind. He liked the fact that I asked as many pertinent questions as I answered. Next to biology religious studies was my best subject, although even at eleven and a half I could not accept some of the religious tenets. I liked Mr Scudamore for more than this, however. He was a bit of an iconoclast himself and some of the other teachers didn't like him. Every morning at Assembly the school sang patriotic songs like 'Rule Britannia'. On his first morning we all piled back into the classroom, and he banged his books down on the podium.

'Rule Britannia – Britannia rules the waves,' he repeated loudly. 'Pah. Go out in a rowboat and you're sea sick!' He did not like all the jingoistic patriotism that filled British education in those days, and his methods of teaching were eccentric and, as far as I was concerned, most effective. In an unobtrusive way, he took me under his wing. He asked me what I liked to do when I was not at school, so I told him that I liked running around Broadwater Green, cycling on my small-wheeled bike, roller-skating (my parents had bought some skates for Christmas and the Broadwater area of Worthing had huge flat paving stones, providing perfect skating for a small boy), and that

I had a catapult with which I did target shooting in our long garden.

On hearing this, Mr Scudamore invited me to his home for tea the following Saturday morning and gave me a pleasant surprise. He presented me with a superb longbow and some arrows, and taught me how to use them.

'Practise in your garden a few times,' he said. 'Then you can try taking them on to the Downs and see if you can pot a rabbit – but leave the birds well alone! And visit me any Saturday morning and let me know how you're doing.'

I did just what he said, and one sunny early morning I hiked up a winding path to the Downs behind our home. It was then that I had an experience that was eventually to transform the course of my life.

I did not pot any rabbits for the moment they caught sight of me they shot off to their various burrows, white tails bobbing the alarm to others. I set up a few targets at forty yards, missed more than I hit and soon tired of trying. There was a large buddleia bush in full flower at the base of the next steep slope, and I felt sure that if I waited partly hidden beside it and kept dead quiet, the rabbits would come back and I could shoot one. I saw myself arriving home, juicy rabbit held aloft, the mighty hunter!

I had waited about half an hour, almost a lifetime it seemed to a young boy, but no rabbits returned. I heard a slight swish by my ear, saw a brief flash of colour and suddenly there was an upright black triangle perched on the nearest long purple flower. I saw a long proboscis appear and probe into a floret for nectar, then the butterfly, for such it was, slowly opened its wings. I was dazzled, enthralled and hypnotized by the glorious colours – bright reds, blues, whites, blacks, yellows, shimmering purples – and on each of the four wings was a huge multi-hued 'eye'. I knew butterflies and moths came from caterpillars but as this magical creature pirouetted in a full circle in the bright sunlight, I marvelled that such beauty could evolve from what had been a heedless, insatiable grub. Ugliness transformed into glory. How? Why? At that moment I desperately wanted to own it, to catch it and take it home, so I could look at and admire it for ever. There was a slight brushing sound as its wings beat down on the flower and it was gone, zigzagging powerfully away and quickly out of my sight.

I lay there in the long grass, feeling I had been trapped in eternity, or at least been given a glimpse of it. Above me the blue, boundless arch of heaven reached to every horizon. I heard the ascending song of a skylark, the humming of bees' wings, the sighing of the grasses, and felt a strange peace and a rare happiness. I am sure it was this tiny experience that first inspired my love of nature. On my return home, I found we had no books on butterflies, so I hiked down to Worthing Library and soon identified my marvel – a Peacock butterfly, which I was surprised to read were 'fairly common', for I had never previously seen one. As I looked at the colour pictures a resolve was born: I would not only study butterflies and moths, I would – and I look back on this decision with some horror from my dotage – *collect* them. Unconsciously, though, I now had an escape hatch from school lessons, bullying boys and my psychotic fears. I must say Dad and Bettie came up trumps at this time: once they realized how strong my interest was they bought me *A Pocket Book of British Butterflies and Moths* by Charles A. Hall. It became my boyhood bible. I bought a butterfly net and a 'killing box', which was one of Dad's old cigar boxes – black with green dolphins on its lid – into which I fastened a compartment for the ammonia pad that killed the insects.

At weekends and in my spare time from school I ran and hiked all over the nearby Downs, soon getting familiar with and collecting the Meadow Brown, Gatekeeper, Wall Brown, Common Blue, Small Copper and the like, but the fast-flying Peacock eluded me all that summer.

Mr Scudamore encouraged my new interest, which also seemed to improve my attitude to life and helped me make a few friends. I remember Sturton, who lived in a very big house in Salvington. He had one of the first big tape recorders and we spent hours in his garage recording our own voices, even singing, and listening in wonder as we played it all back. We even recorded a few swear words, then made sure all doors and windows were shut when Sturton played them back!

I loved the *Dandy* comic, which my parents bought for me each week, and my favourite hero in it was Smasher John. Another friend, Mike Rawley, son of a fishing pal of Dad's, had one of the new epidiascopes, which seemed to me a wonderful machine. You laid a small picture of anything on its platform, pressed a button, and it could reproduce the picture five times the size. Smasher John was my first production and was stuck on my bedroom wall. The others were pages of butterflies.

All this chasing about the Downs was making me very fit, and I enjoyed accepting a challenge from other boys my own age to a sprint race. I always won the bets, thus collecting a few new marbles, a model car, a copy of the *Beano* comic, sweets and the like. I was no good at rugger, however, once I got the ball I had to run for a try and would never pass it. My idol at this time was Sydney Wooderson, a frail-looking, bespectacled 'bank clerk' type in appearance, but who had just smashed the world mile record in 4 minutes 3 seconds. The papers and radio (no TV in those days) extolled his exploits and when I heard he was to give an exhibition run in Homefield Park, I begged to go along as I wanted his autograph. My dad took me along by himself because my stepmother Bettie was in hospital, about to give birth. I watched my hero hare round for two laps, then he accidentally spiked himself and had to leave the track.

'Now's your chance,' said Dad. 'Go and ask for his autograph.'

I stood rooted to the spot. I was far too shy and didn't dare do it, which I regret to this day.

Dad took us to a public phone and when he came out he had a smile like a pumpkin's at Halloween. 'You have a baby brother,' he said. I just said, 'Oh good,' but I can't recall feeling any emotion at all.

I was now quite good at woodwork and carved several ornate daggers, a sword and even a big beetle, which ran along the floor. Its 'motor' was made from an elastic band, the tip of a candle and a matchstick. One end of the band was fixed to the side of a hole in the beetle. The other was passed through a central hole in the candle, and the matchstick passed through its loop. The rubber band was then wound tight to a notch in the candle, and when you put it on the floor it moved forward until the band ran out of tension, slowed down by the candle rubbing against the beetle's side. We boys made 'tanks' by this method, using cotton reels, into the rounded edges of which we carved little notches. By exchanging marbles and some precious 'alleys' (big marbles with spiralling colours in them) I obtained a huge bobbin of a silk reel, which would climb obstacles more than an inch high. It won all the contests but I was penalized because my 'tank' was bigger than the others.

We were also encouraged to take up fretwork and when, after several weeks of woodwork lessons, I made a three-tier letter wrack, I was enormously proud when Dad smilingly congratulated me and actually used it.

My weekly treat was to run over the Green to the local Odeon cinema. I loved the cowboy stories and actually managed to carve a wooden revolver that worked – well, in that it fired little percussion caps. In one of these movies Gene Autry sang 'A Four-legged Friend' as (I think) his horse was dying, reducing me to tears. Like my grandma, I was very sentimental – and still am!

Life at school had now improved greatly. A big fellow called Bissett, one of those who used to throw an arm round my long neck and attempt to get my head 'in chancery', tried it again. I saw him coming, took a step back, and hit him a hard straight right just below the left side of his nose. Astonished, he stepped back and we had another short skirmish, but he didn't get the best of it and suddenly muttered, 'All right,' and stopped. I smiled and held out my hand. To my surprise he took it, and after that we became quite friendly, often walking home together over the Green. As a result the other big boys left me alone.

A far greater battle was now taking place, however: the Second World War had started. I felt it would all be far away and so felt little fear – until we learnt the Germans would soon be sending waves of bombers over, to attack not only London but ports along the south coast as far as Devon. I think I was more scared than the rest of the family for when we decided, like many panicky urbanites, to install an Anderson air raid shelter, I dug most of the hole for it. I went at the hard ground in a series of frenzied attacks with a pickaxe, hating all the big chalk-covered flints that had to be removed by hand. In due time the shelter was lowered into the trench and covered with the requisite earth and debris. I'll never forget our first nights there with the siren wailing: we all scurried into the cramped shelter, biting on pencil ends or hard rubbers so that our teeth, chattering through fear, would not sever our tongues. The first night was the worst, and I shivered with terror as the booming roar of the German engines throbbed through the air. I thought our lives would end with one big bang.

In fact only once did a bomb land nearby while we were in Worthing. Dad and I were walking past the public shelter in Broadwater High Street when we heard the whistling sound of a bomb heading earthwards. 'Down!' yelled Dad, and I followed his example and threw myself flat into the deep gutter. The bomb didn't go bang or boom as I had expected but had more of a 'bink' sound, and I was conscious of the rush of air and bits of tarmac debris slashing past above me. My fear was quickly replaced by a feeling of annoyance when Dad upbraided me for having thrown myself into a puddle, saying I should have taken better care of my clothes!

Oddly, it was during my second French lesson that the school heard of France's capitulation. Our parents decided in July 1940 that in view of the ugly crisis, the whole family should take a last holiday in the country, before it became impossible to do so. We were going to stay for a month in an isolated cottage called Jessops about a mile outside a small village called Ashurst. One sunny day we all set off on our pushbikes, with my young brother Richard being driven by Dad in his car. I was thrilled at the prospect of some real butterfly collecting but little realized I was about to enter what for me was truly paradise.

Jessops Cottage stood alone, amid a small cluster of trees, at the end of a barely discernible footpath which wound over two large fields from a relatively unused country lane. The silence was idyllic. There was no electricity, only oil lamps, and for water we had to trek a hundred yards to a brook and fill buckets which we lugged back to pour into a large zinc tub in the kitchen.

Apart from fetching our milk every morning from Kingsbarn Farm, and picking up 'eggs from hens' nests on the way, I was free to do as I liked. With my butterfly net I wandered for miles over the hot, lonely fields where grasshoppers leaped and fiddled in the summer hay, and along tranquil rides in the woodlands where I saw my first magnificent Emperor butterfly sunning the glossy sheen of its wings on an old oak stump. I heard the strident laughing call of the green woodpecker, then glimpsed the flash of its red, green and yellow plumage as it wove between pine trees. From the marshes came the plaintive love call of the lapwing, and I even saw one herding her young chicks through green tussocks. Some days I felt so happy I burst into song as I walked along, singing my favourite 'Over the Rainbow' song, feeling the same sense of wonder Judy Garland had conveyed so superbly in the marvellous film *The Wizard of Oz* which I had recently been taken to see. Indeed, I felt I too was now in a magical land. Alone, I was transported into a creation more miraculous than I had ever known could exist. Every night when I returned in the twilight, little pipistrelle bats flew on skinny wings around the eaves of our isolated cottage. I had never been happier in my life.

My father, who was finding it harder to carry on his travelling-salesman work throughout Sussex, Kent and Hampshire without a phone, still managed to take the odd day off. All his life he had been a keen and excellent rod fisherman and to my delight, he began to take me fishing with him. He bought me a rod for my birthday and in the two lakes nearby taught me how to thread a worm on the hook, to make the baits from bread, to weight the lines so that the bait was at the right height from the float, and how and when to strike when the fish moved the float. Most of the fish, like roach, dace and perch, were always caught on the hard outer lip and were unhurt. He kept them in a special 'keep net' and let them all go before we left. But eels were another matter. Some, in Peppers Lake, were two feet long and put up such a long, hard fight, that when you finally landed them the hook would be way back inches down their gullets. Dad had a special 'disgorger', which he used to push down, dislodge the hook and draw it out, but I flinched on the occasions when I had to do it myself. We sometimes killed and ate the eels, as Bettie had special recipes for them. Dad killed them with a blow on the head with a special metal tool he called a 'priest'. When I noticed that even an hour or so later the eels would still be moving, my dad said cryptically, 'Eels never die before sundown, no matter what you do to them.'

One fine day I wandered with my net down to a large pond I had discovered in a deep dell beyond a small coppice, which screened it from view. I stood partly hidden by tall reeds, hoping to see again the bright yellow Brimstone butterfly I had almost caught in the area the day before: I had nearly wept with frustration when during a long chase I had missed it with every swipe.

The still air hummed with the whine of innumerable insects' wings. Suddenly there was something hovering before me like a fairy helicopter, its long gauzy wings shimmering in the sunlight over the pond. Two huge bulging eyes, speckled with countless lenses, blazed metallically into mine, a mere two yards away. Stifling an icy tremor before that frightening primeval stare, I swung my butterfly net – hopelessly. With contemptuous ease, the creature seemed to reverse the plane of its wings and shot backwards in a way no other insect could match.

Forming its six black legs and open jaws into a deadly scoop, it dashed through a cloud of gnats, engulfing a dozen in a single sweep. As it munched them with apparent boredom, it suddenly spied a bluebottle droning overhead. Dropping the gnats, it looped up with a brittle rattle of wings and struck the more worthy prey from the sky.

This was the first dragonfly I had seen. It looked like a glorious hawk of the air, the dashing Red Baron of the insect world, which is how I think of it still, sixty years later. As I watched it swooping relentlessly above the reeds I longed to possess this incredible creature of darting fire. Over the next few days I spent many hours by that pond, my net held at various angles to give me the fastest possible sweeps, but it always dodged me, sometimes returning to the same spot as if to tantalize me with its skills. Then it happened. Snap! And it was in the net. I swiftly put a cloth round the handmade 'globe' that contained it, so the brittle wings would not be damaged by struggling, and ran home.

On my best bobbin 'tank' I still had plenty of fine silk line After some intricate work. I managed to tie the end round the dragonfly's thick, hard thorax, between the two sets of wings, making sure none of the legs were entangled. I wanted to fly it, to control it, as one would a kite. But after I took it outside and launched it into the air, it just fluttered slowly down to the ground. Even on that lightest of lines it could never fly truly free. So I let it go, content to admire it from afar. I really had no right to entrap our most extraordinary insect, a species which was flying 150 million years ago.

My country idyll came to a rather abrupt, if temporary, end. One afternoon we kids were all picnicking with Megan and were just horsing around in general. I was in unusually high spirits. We were playing a chase game when I spied a small branch with lots of twigs and leaves at one end, which meant it might just fly through the air like a slow arrow. I picked it up and hurled it playfully, shouting, 'Look out!' To my horror it went far further than I had intended and hit poor Maureen on the elbow. Megan was angry and told me to wait where I was while she left the others to tell Dad what I had done.

He had been fishing all day and hadn't caught a thing, and he was in a bad mood. I waited in apprehension, which increased greatly when I saw how he was glaring at me. He paused to break off a thick stick from the hedgerow and beat me with it until I was on the ground and in so much pain I couldn't get up for a few minutes. It was the worst whacking I had ever had. When he ordered me to go to my room it was as much as I could do to stagger the 200 yards back to the cottage. I lay on my bed sobbing quietly, not from pain but more because it seemed my month of bliss had come to an end. About an hour later I heard a knock on the door, and my father's quiet voice.

'Can I come in, Michael? Are you all right?'

He had never asked to come into my room before, but I said yes.

He came in and sat down on the bed beside me. 'I have come to apologize, Michael. I really shouldn't have hit you like that, so hard.' I saw, amazed yet strangely comforted, that he had tears in his eyes. He put his hand to my forehead, stroking back a strand of my hair, looking straight into my eyes, and continued, 'I really don't know what came over me. I just lost my temper. Things aren't going well at work and I'm having terrible problems with the Army over our house. We might lose it. Try to understand – and please try and forgive me?'

He had never spoken to me like that before, nor touched me in any loving way, and before he had finished speaking I had almost forgiven him. The bruises did not last more than a few days and the glories of wild nature around me soon restored my good spirits. I now had over thirty species of butterfly, all neatly pinned out in a special exhibition cabinet Dad had bought me as a 'make-up' present.

The only other traumatic incident that summer was when I was chased by a bull. On my walks to shop in the village or collect free hens' eggs, I often saw a black and white Friesian bull standing with his cows in the field and he seemed to look up only with mild interest as I passed. On this occasion I had gone well past him when I heard a thudding sound. I looked around to see him heading for me, but only at a trot. I turned back and started to flee and then he broke into a gallop. Fifty yards ahead were three trees, in a line before the big iron gate and I'll never forget my desperate fear as I tried to run in a zigzag between the trees trying to keep the bull on the other side of each tree as I ran. Luckily I could scale the gate very quickly and with the bull only a few yards behind I got my left foot on the first strut of the gate, struck the top with my midriff and grabbed it with my left hand, while grabbing a strut low down on the other side with my right hand and swinging my legs over to the ground. The bull saw the gate and tried to pull up but still hit it with a resounding clang, and then gave it another upward clanging gore for good measure. I was trembling all over, and even today will not go into a field that contains a bull.

Our holiday came to an end a few days later and while my father was doing his work and negotiating with the damned Army over our lovely home in Worthing, Bettie and us kids went to stay with friends in Ashurst. Lil and Nell Cartersers had a lovely big rambling old house called Blocques, with a fine orchard full of fruit which we were allowed to pick and eat to our hearts' content. They also had a piano, and provided I kept solely to the easy black notes I soon found I could tinkle out simple tunes – mostly hymns, the tunes of which I still loved despite my young doubts about religion.

When cycling along a lane one morning I found a young swallow on the road which couldn't fly. I brought it back to the house, fed it for two days on flies and some fine mince, and was rewarded when it recovered enough strength to fly into the air from my hand and away over the trees.

After ten days at Blocques, Dad arrived from Worthing grim-faced. We all expected he would be taking us home but he had a letter in his hand. It was from the Military confirming that they had taken the house over for the duration of the war and we could do nothing further about it. They were offering two alternative places of accommodation, both in the town, and none of us liked the sound of either of them. By now I totally hated the idea of returning to any kind of town life and Dad had rather taken to life in the country. When a few days later he announced he had found a small country cottage near Henfield, a neighbouring village, which we could rent, I heaved a huge sigh of relief.

The cottage was on an estate at Tracadie, owned by Lady Montague, the daughter of Lord Beaverbook, and when we drove along the drive past the big house and I saw the rows of sweet chestnut trees I felt it was a swell sort of place. Our cottage, however, was initially a disappointment. It was semi-detached, and next door lived the estate's head worker, who was pig, cowman and odd-job man rolled into one, and his two big tough-looking sons. Behind us were the pigsties and at first the stench seemed overpowering. But we were at war, and meat production was a very high priority, so we gradually got used to it.

My first excursion into the wood-surrounded field immediately opposite soon cheered me up. There were buddleia bushes amid the oblong of trees, and butterflies everywhere. Then I saw it – brilliant flash of pink, yellow, black, rainbow wings and a white rump weaving through the still shadows of the pines. This was my first glimpse of the wary, elusive jay, the most brightly coloured of the crow family. Here was a beauty worth studying – if I could get near enough.

One Friday Dad drove home from his calls in Hampshire and said that if it was fine next day, he would take me fishing on Peppers Lake – for the whole day. I was so excited I could hardly sleep. Little did either of us realize what a momentous meeting was about to take place.

4
Gamekeeper Extraordinary

'Had any luck?' The words rang out starkly on the still summer air. My father and I turned from our fishing on the lakeside and saw an odd-looking man standing on the path above. He was short but stocky and wore long plus-fours tucked into brown gaiters above his muddy boots. On his head was a funny brown floppy cap which looked as if someone had crowned him with a giant mushroom. His look was friendly but his right eye had a slight cast, looking upwards as if keeping a constant look-out for a pigeon or pheasant flying overhead.

As he and Dad got talking, I turned back to my rod with slight irritation. This was supposed to be my whole Saturday fishing with him and I resented the sudden interruption. As they chatted away some yards from me I caught odd phrases like, 'How about a drink ... I'll tell you all about the place... there's a good one up the road...'

When Dad said he was going 'down the road awhile' with the stranger whose name I now learned was Jim Adkins, I lifted my rod with a faint sigh. I'd never understand grown-ups! Three hours later, after I'd fought a losing battle with a giant eel in misty rain, my dad was back. He had a dazed look on his face and from his hand dangled two dead pheasants. 'I still can't believe it,' he said. 'He has only one good eye but he's the best shot I've ever seen.'

It was some time before I heard the full story. With the immediate mutual liking that comes when true friends meet for the first time, they had dropped into the village pub. After a couple of beers in convivial company they were standing outside in the rain when Jim said 'Do you want a brace of pheasants to take home?'

My father blinked. It was wartime. The meat ration was just 4 oz a week. 'Good heavens, you don't *mean* it, do you?' he said. With that they called at Jim's cottage, picked up two guns and within minutes were in a nearby wood. After a mere 100 yards through soaking-wet undergrowth, Jim stopped, looked, then said, 'Felore Sally,' using his own invented word to make his gun dog work. 'Felore!' But she needed no telling. Slowly she crept for thirty yards, froze and looked back. Another 'Felore' and up into the air went two pheasants at a fast lick. Before Dad could take his gun off 'safe' there was a left and a right and down they came. Sally retrieved the pheasants and brought them to her master's feet. It was over in seconds.

This was how Jim Adkins, gamekeeper extraordinary, came into our lives. He not only became one of the best friends my father and I ever had but a kind of Mr Bountiful. In those years of stringent war rationing, feeding a wife and four children wasn't easy, especially as it took some time for Dad to establish a vegetable garden. But Jim could always be relied on for a sack of spuds or onions, the odd brace of rabbits, pheasants, or even a goose or turkey, which he bartered with friendly farmers. He even set aside part of his large garden for us, planting and tending the vegetables himself.

For me, a young boy still new to the countryside, the meeting with Jim Adkins was the start of many wonderful years. Not only did he teach me to shoot, he showed me how to net rabbits by using ferrets to bolt them from their 'bury' (they were over-prolific then and needed to be kept down), to track deer, wait at dusk for flocks of crop-eating woodpigeons to come to roost, keep watch in the right places for foxes and spot a sitting woodcock. He was my first nature teacher. For the next quarter-century, wherever I was in the world, Jim's quiet country cottage with its mossy roof, red roses and old mud scraper outside the door, became a beloved refuge.

I learned a great deal during my first full day with Jim. At my age I wanted to take possession of any young or sick wild creatures, to look after them myself, but Jim taught me better. One spring morning we were walking through Calcot Wood, surrounded by waving bluebells and wild narcissus. It was dark but quiet and peaceful in there; the shadows seemed old and permanent, the silence broken only by the ripple of a brook, ribboning its way like a suckling animal to its parent, the sea. Suddenly a baby thrush tumbled from a bush before us, fluttering feebly on wings as yet unable to fly. Immediately I ran and caught it.

'Let it go, Michael,' said Jim quietly.

'But it's alone. Its parents have left it.'

'How do you know?' said Jim. 'Come with me.' We retired into a thicket and waited. Within ten minutes the mother thrush appeared with a beakful of grubs and worms, found her youngster and crammed the food into its wide-open beak.

'Never take a young bird or animal until you're absolutely sure it's been abandoned,' said Jim. A lesson I never forgot.

As we walked on over a floor of wood anemones beneath oak trees, the chirping chirr of a squirrel sounded from a trunk above us, and then from a field outside the wood came a sharp harsh cry, 'Kah-a-a-a.' We pulled in behind a tree and waited.

'That's a fox,' said Jim. 'A vixen out hunting. She's probably with her cubs, teaching 'em how to catch mice. Wouldn't I like to have a dog that could work a field like a fox! They're more like a cat than a dog, y'know, work real close, so low and flat to the ground. If there's a mouse in that field, she'll have it.'

We stayed there a fair while hoping the fox might come into our view through the trees, when suddenly a doe rabbit came loping up the woodland ride towards us. Jim grabbed my arm to keep me back. 'Stay still,' he murmured,. 'there's a stoat about.' How he knew that I didn't know, but the rabbit loped a few paces, stopped, loped on, stopped again. Suddenly the long chestnut-brown, white-bellied form of a stoat streaked out from below a bush and went for the rabbit's throat. Instantly she stood on her hind legs and lashed out with both her forepaws in a furious flurry of blows, like a boxer. But the stoat was too fast; it dodged back twice, then shot in again on its quarry's throat. As the rabbit squealed Jim rushed out, the stoat ran off, and he easily caught the limping doe. As she was mortally wounded he mercifully ended her misery with a quick blow from the side of his hand on the back of her neck. Then he put the doe into his bag, saying she was in fine condition, and reasoning the stoat could easily catch another.

'Don't often see that,' he said as we walked on. 'Only seen it twice before in my life. Little devils, stoats are. Once they're after a rabbit they'll keep to the same one, even if she runs through a dozen others. And now you know even a cornered rabbit will fight!'

Every day with Jim I learned some new country lore, and seen through his one eye, the countryside became an even more enchanted place. However, I was lucky if I spent just one day, or an afternoon, with Jim and my dad or Jim alone. Most of my daytime hours were spent at school, and as I could no longer get to Worthing High School, I was sent to the local council school on Henfield Common. To get there meant a mile-long cycle ride, the start of which was really tricky. There was a short cut down a steep muddy path and across a wooden bridge, then up the next slope to get back on the road. The bridge consisted of two thick wooden planks, which, I forgot to note on my first ride, had a two-inch gap between them in the middle. My front wheel hit into this gap and I did a header over the handlebars, grazing both knees in the process. From then on I only rode over the bridge if it was dry. In the wet, I wheeled the bike over.

I didn't look forward to going to this school because when Len, the younger of the two lads next door, was showing me their prize saddleback pigs out back, he told me that 'christening' new boys meant them being thrown into the holly hedge three times. This never happened to me but I did fall foul of the toughest lad in the school, Nobby, after we had an argument and one of the masters told us to settle it. I got my first real pasting but luckily Nobby left the school at the end of my first term. Another tough boy, Ken, was also a bit of a bully, but when he picked on me in the bike shed I got the best of it, and was left strictly alone after that. I found lessons easy at the school, even earning some fulsome praise for one of my essays from Mr Foster, the biology master.

Most of my spare time was spent in the wild garden or what I called the Ashgrove. I had started a birds' egg collection (quite legal in those days) but I only took one egg from any nest and none at all if there were only two. I soon had all the common birds' eggs, and I was over the moon when I found a nest with five eggs belonging to the colourful jay. I planned to keep a close watch but the other four eggs disappeared a week after I'd found them. I longed to catch a jay alive, to keep it and look at it up close for just an hour or two, then let it go again. I set cunning little horse-hair nooses under the trees and scattered grains but had no luck whatsoever.

One minor triumph in the Ashgrove was being lucky enough to see a green woodpecker poke its green head with its bright red helmet out of a high hole in a dead tree and fly off. Sure it had eggs in a nest, I skinned my knees in vain efforts to climb the tree as there were no branches. I even toyed briefly with the idea of cutting the tree down! But I wasn't that desperate for a woodpecker's egg.

At school now, coming up to my thirteenth birthday, I was proving quite good at running and usually won minor sprint races over the Common. When the annual cross-country run, right round the Common, was looming, I felt pretty sure I would win it. I didn't bother to do any training but the night before the race I started worrying about it and couldn't sleep. Nevertheless, as we all lined up, I was laughing and bouncing about on my feet when the Bowman twins, both good runners, started protesting that I should have a handicap and the sports master set me back some thirty yards with the more senior boys. I was ready for it, though, and planned to start easily, at no more than a fast jog and pick off the other boys as they grew tired.

To my amazement, everyone shot off like rockets. I tried and tried, but couldn't catch up with the front lot where the Bowmans were running. Then towards the end of the race the group I had set off with all went past me. I stumbled on – and came last! It seemed a terrible humiliation at the time, especially as the Bowman twins won. And I had set my heart on winning the prize.

On my next visit to Jim we were walking past some laurel bushes near Whyton Wick Wood when Jim stopped, pulled the branches aside and pointed to a goldfinch's nest. Inside it were five pale blue eggs spotted with reddish-brown.

'Most unusual to build in a laurel,' he said. 'But it's been a wet spring. Maybe she built it there deliberately, knowin' the broad leaves would give good shelter. Birds often work out things like that.'

Later we were walking along the edge of Stoney Copse when we found some broad pathways which seemed to lead into the wood then suddenly petered out. 'That's strange,' I said. 'Who'd make paths like this that lead nowhere?'

'Not who,' said Jim, 'but *what*! Look.' He pointed to where one of the paths went under a fallen branch, and to where another penetrated straight through a bramble patch. 'No man could make paths in places like that. They're badger trails. They've had a sett here for forty years or more, And when one family goes, another takes its place.'

He showed me the badger sett, the huge entrance hole surrounded by almost a ton of soil and sand the animals had dug out, and the exit hole some twenty-five yards away. Then he pointed to two round holes, one empty and one half full of blackish droppings.

'Badgers are very clean,' he told me. 'And those are their outside toilets.' He peered at the ground by the entrance. 'I don't think they're in there right now, or we could stay and watch them. I've often seen them playing around here. When they're young they're as frisky as lambs and I've seen 'em dance about with their paws on each other's shoulders!' Clever too, almost like foxes. If a badger smells anything suspicious he *rolls* out of his home. It's no good settin' traps for 'em there – all you catch is a handful of hair!'

Although in his early years he had gone along with the notion that badgers, like foxes, were vermin, and had killed many of them, he now welcomed them on his land. 'They do more good than harm. I've known 'em destroy wasps nests, eat crates of 'em. They kill mice and voles, eat beetles and things no use to us like berries, wild bulbs and roots. But they never raid my pheasant chicks or hen houses.'

On our way home Jim suddenly stepped into a thick hedge, whipped out his big penknife and began to hack away. Presently he emerged with the rough form of a catapult. 'It's a perfect strod,' he said, holding it towards me. 'That catapult of your's really ain't no good, Michael. I'll show you how to make the best catapult in the world!'

Back at his cottage, he did. My crude effort consisted of two rubber bands out of an old inner tube, the end of each passing through a hole at the top of both prongs and tied in a knot so it couldn't be pulled back through. The propelling pouch was an oblong of leather into which I cut holes at each end. Each band was passed through the holes, doubled back and tied to itself. Often, when I fired, the stone hit the strod, or sometimes my thumb!

Jim set to work like a master craftsman. He cut little flat faces on the front and back of the top prongs, then bound four strips of leather to them with fishing line. He then produced two eight-inch lengths of stout quarter-inch-thick elastic, the kind used for excluding draughts on doors. The front end of each length was bound between the leather strips, making the smoothest of fastenings, and the rear end was bound between an extra lug cut into the leather pouch. Handing it to me, he said, 'Now that is a catapult. You'll not miss much with that!'

He was right. On every shot the stone, or ball-bearing for serious target shooting, had a more true, unhindered passage, and the powerful elastic more than doubled the range of my crude strod. After a few weeks of practice I could have fed myself with this almost silent killer, for I could nail a rabbit at twenty-five yards, if I could get that close.

One Saturday afternoon I was prowling through the Ashgrove when I heard the *cackalump*, *cackalump* of a cantering horse in the field by the wood. To my delight, astride the horse was a girl I had seen twice but never spoken to. She was Jeanne Montague, daughter of Lady Montague and granddaughter of Lord Beaverbrook. She was about my age and very pretty. Hidden amid all the foliage, I watched as she cantered almost all the way round the edge of the wood, then brought the horse to a halt and turned it round, to go back the way they had come.

I don't know what devil possessed me but as I looked at the huge swelling muscles of the horse's powerful hindquarters, they seemed such a perfect target! I quickly realized I couldn't fire a stone or ball-bearing but there were acorns all over the ground. I swiftly fitted one into the pouch and let fly. The horse whinnied loudly, reared up and almost threw Jeanne to the ground but to my intense relief she maintained control and soon they were cantering away again, The next time I was in the wild garden she rode by again, and as I was now in the open she drew up and we had a short chat after she'd asked me if I liked the place. I told her yes, very much, hoping she wouldn't notice the 'cattie' stuck in my pocket! There were some huge sweet chestnut trees lining the drive at Tracadie, so I took the chance to ask her if I could pick some, just windfalls. She said I could any time I wished.

A few days later I was collecting chestnuts when she came by, on foot this time, and invited me into the big house for tea. I can't say anything momentous occurred except by then I had a juvenile crush on her. We talked about birds and looked around the garden, and I was conscious of some disapproving looks from her mother, who eventually came over and took her daughter into the house.

'Do come for tea again sometime, young man,' she said holding the gate open for me to leave, but I knew she didn't mean it.

I never saw Jeanne again because a week later Dad announced we were moving house, this time to a bungalow called Hazeldene a few miles away in Shermanbury, near Partridge Green, and at the end of the summer I was sent to boarding school. Nevertheless, I was pleased that my mischievous catapult shot had not deprived society of a very pretty member of the aristocracy, as it quite nearly had.

As soon as I saw the long garden at the new bungalow, and the jays which were flashing their rainbow colours among the many nut-laden hazel trees, I felt both relieved and happy. Across the road there was a path beside cornfields to a wonderful pine wood and beyond that I could wander down to The Brooks where the Adur river wended its way through small wetlands known locally as 'The Floods'. On my very first walk I saw many lapwings, some diving crazily about the sky with calls of 'Peeoo wit wit wit, peeoo wit.' There were wild mallards in boggy areas, a lone barnacle goose rose from beside a ramshackle wooden bridge, and I saw my first snipe. It rocketed away from my feet, twisting madly from side to side as it shot towards the horizon.

Some evenings Dad took me fishing on Shermanbury Lake, my bird's eggs and butterfly collections were increasing nicely, and I started making little paintings with a primitive box of Reeves watercolours. But the highlight of any week was when I went shooting with Dad and Jim Adkins. Although his job demanded that he control vermin by any means, Jim always insisted on rigid sportsmanship and taught us to be ultra-careful with guns. Before climbing a stile, Jim would break his gun and remove the shells, put them in on the other side and check the safety catch. He held his guns on 'safe' even when empty and on the way home he checked two or three times that the shells were out. He taught us how and when to shoot. 'Don't pull the trigger, you *press* it, and you don't press it until you are sure you can kill outright and not just injure.' He lost no time reprimanding lazy guns if they just fired into the middle of a covey of flying birds, hoping to hit something.

'That's not good sportsmanship,' he said. 'A good gun picks an outside bird, just one in particular. I like to see a bird killed right. I hate to see 'em come down with a broken wing or one eye out. And you should never go shooting without a good dog. Too many get lost that way. Amateurs go out and just wound birds. The poor things lie undiscovered for days, their lives ebbing away slowly – wasted.' But if he taught me how to shoot and helped my father become a better shot, it was no one-way transaction. Dad was a fine angler and taught Jim something of the fishing art. And once Jim fell for the sport he obtained sole rights to two and a half miles of the Adur river for Henfield British Legion Club of which my father was fishing secretary. I loved fishing for roach, dace, perch and bream with Dad but when he taught me how to fish for the mighty pike, the freshwater 'shark' of our rivers and lakes, I knew I had found my metier.

There were two main methods. Live baiting consisted of fixing a live roach or dace on to two treble hooks then fixing a big cork float two or three feet above it, with two small pilot floats after that. Usually the pike struck the bait fish a powerful blow with its head, presumably to stun it, then left it to turn round and come at it a second time. It was then that the fisherman had to make his own strike. The big float would disappear under water and the two pilot floats following it showed him which way to jerk his rod and drive the hooks home. The excitement of hooking, fighting and landing the ferocious pike overcame any slight boyhood scruples I may have had about the cruelty inflicted on the bait fish. And every other pike fisherman in those days was doing it. The other method was spinning. I liked spinning the most because it involved far more skill. You tied a special silvery 'spoon' or coloured swimming plug to the end of your line, then set a small lead weight about two feet in front of it. You had to cast out as far as you could, ideally along and just outside long banks of reeds, then wind it back in a series of jerks and lifts so that the bait, held under the surface by the lead weight, looked to the pike as though it was swimming. Usually I let the smaller pike go, but when I caught an 8½-pounder, the biggest I ever caught, I took it home so Bettie could try out an old pike recipe she had never used. It was a free and delicious meal!

Jim and I were pike fishing at a pool called Snatcher's Hole one evening when we heard squealing from the rushes below a tree on the far side. Jim was sure it was a rabbit being attacked by a stoat but suddenly there was a plop and a huge otter came swimming past as we stayed motionless, its whiskered mouth dragging a rabbit by its back leg. The rabbit was still kicking as the two went past, then the otter dived with its prey, and surfaced in the reeds where we couldn't see it.

'Well I'm blowed!' said Jim. 'I've never seen that before. It must've been tryin to drown it.' He removed his huge green cap and scratched his greying hair, puzzling it out. 'I know an otter will take an odd rabbit but mostly it lives on fish with a few frogs and mice. Maybe, it being winter, the fish are all deep down in the mud. The otter couldn't find 'em easily, came across this rabbit, managed to grab it, then took it back to its native element, the river.

'Can't think what else it *could* be. It was too big to kill easy on land, so it got it down to the river. We'll never know for certain if it was tryin' to actually drown it.' Jim had known otters to breed in rabbit burrows near a river, had even seen them carry their young to the water and teach them to swim.

Most of my days with Jim were spent rabbiting as there were far too many and they had to be kept down, especially in wartime, as they did so much damage to crops. We hiked out to the various burys with guns, armfuls of nets and a box of ferrets. The nets were spread over the holes, a ferret put down, and as it hunted through the tunnels the rabbits bolted out and into the nets. If I had faint scruples about using live fish as bait for pike I had to forget any when it came to rabbits. When the animals hit the nets, rather than waste a costly shotgun cartridge, Jim just grabbed their back legs with one hand, grabbed the head with the other, stretched them across his thigh and with a pushing-down jerk broke their necks, severing their spinal cords at the same time. I too learned to do this, imitating the way Jim immediately dropped them, ignoring their last two or three spasmodic death kicks as he went to seize another. If a rabbit dodged past a net, he could grab his propped-up gun and nail it within thirty yards. To make the rabbits easier to carry, Jim cut a slit between the hamstring and bone of the rear leg, threaded the other leg through, cut its hock tendon, gave a pull, and this formed a perfect carrying 'handle'. Often we staggered home each with twenty to thirty rabbits dangling from the very nets which had caught them slung across our shoulders. Rabbits were a great source of good meat during the war. Jim killed 14,000 on a Falmer estate one year and there were still plenty left.

Although he was small, Jim was exceptionally strong. He always carried a sharp spade that he called a 'grafter'. And how he could graft with it! If a ferret got holed up behind a rabbit and we didn't know where it was, Jim would put in his 'liner' – a specially trained ferret which had a stout line attached to its collar. Once the liner had found the missing ferret and its prey, off would come Jim's jacket and he'd graft up the bury in seconds, following the line and tearing through root tangles as if they weren't there.

It is said that no man can out dig a badger, for while he's spading away up top, old Brock is digging himself in even faster three feet down. But once, when badgers were considered vermin, Jim actually outdug one. He got his spade carefully under its powerful body and lifted the animal out. It promptly charged straight at him and escaped through his legs. Jim just laughed, respecting his doughty opponent, and didn't try a shot.

Once, when Jim was rearing 3,000 young pheasants, his underkeeper, who had taken over 1,000 of them, came running to his home, asking him to bring his gun as there were weasels in the run. Jim calmly handed the man the pheasants' food and they went back to the run in the wood. 'Put the food down, then go and have your dinner,' he told the man. 'I'll see to 'em.' Jim had shot the two weasels before the man had crossed the field. I had seen many times what a superb shot he was, despite only having one good eye. He could keep up with the best in the artificial sport of clay-pigeon shooting and was a mean player of darts and billiards too.

It was years before I heard the full story behind the loss of Jim's right eye, before he felt he knew me well enough to tell it. Born in 1892, when five Woodbines cost a penny, beer was tuppence a pint and a loaf of bread tuppence three-farthings, Jim was riding horses so well at the age of five that his family thought he would become a jockey. By eleven years old, Jim had felt the call of the wild woods, but his father, who ran a pub, a bakehouse and a coal business in Wardington, near Banbury, Oxfordshire, didn't want him to be a keeper. Instead he apprenticed him to a butcher. But Jim spent all his spare time with local keepers and they taught him how to use a gun. In 1914, while on a visit to relations in Smethwick, Jim and his older brother Harold decided to join Lord Kitchener's Army and get into the Great War, and ran away to recruit.

On the train down, they wrote a message on a piece of paper 'We've joined the Army. We're off to Winchester,' wrapped it in an old cap and hurled it out of the train as they passed their home station. It bounced along the platform and was picked up and taken to their mother, who read the message and broke the news to their father.

Sent out to the front line in France in the Rifle Brigade, Private Jimmy Adkins (later Sergeant) went through the battles of Messims and Festibert as a grenadier, throwing the old Newton pippins, and then as an advance base sniper. He was wounded during the battle of Ypres on Saturday, 25 September, a day indelibly imprinted on his memory. A machine-gun bullet went into his right wrist and out at the elbow, while at the same time shrapnel from a shell hit him in the throat and shoulder, and sent a splinter into his right eye. His right arm dangling, almost blinded, he managed to run two miles to the nearest field dressing station, then somersaulted into the trench and blacked out. He came to in the 1st Canadian General Hospital at Etapes.

Sent back to Dover in the first hospital ship, he found himself brought up from the bowels of the vessel and lined up with other soldiers on stretchers as King George V and Queen Mary passed along the lines, offering condolences to the men. When he came out of hospital, the Army offered to promote him to Sergeant Major if he would return to France, well behind the lines, and teach men to ride horses. But Jim, now unfit for active duty, wanted to return to his wild woods and said no. A few days later he was back in civvies, with a 55 per cent war pension.

Losing his eye meant he had to learn to shoot all over again but he soon became an expert left-hand shot. Working as under-keeper on various Sussex estates, his one eye became legendary. Jim could spot people moving about on Chantonbury Ring from eight miles away when others could see nothing. Sometimes he could spot sitting woodcocks, an almost impossible feat, even before his gun dog had their scent.

For five years he worked for the famous John Christie at Glyndebourne. An accomplished pianist from his youth, Jim longed to have a go at the great organ in the Organ Room. One afternoon, when he thought no one was about, he crept in and played to his heart's content for fifteen minutes. During a pause, a voice rang out 'Jolly good, young man!' It was Mr Christie.

Jim then worked on Falmer and Wiston estates, yearning to be his own boss, so when the tea and wool magnate Andrew Harvey offered him the head keeper post on his 4,000 acre estate at Lock, near Partridge Green, he leaped at the chance.

Jim became a keeper in the old days shortly after the turn of the twentieth century, and in his first years went along with the restrictive ideas prevalent in his profession. His job was rigidly defined – to rear game, mostly pheasants in their thousands, and keep them safe, along with deer, partridges, hares and even rabbits, not only from poachers but from all harmful vermin. In those days many animals were on the vermin list – foxes, badgers, stoats, weasels, hawks, jays, magpies, rooks, crows, even owls. Long before the days of deep litter bins and artificial incubators, Jim, like all keepers, worked from dawn to dusk in all weathers, hatching, rearing, feeding and tending his chicks from mid-March to November.

He did all this as well as all his shooting duties, keeping vermin down, and odd manual jobs like clearing ditches, cutting back foliage along the woodland rides and so forth. After such hard work it was small wonder Jim regarded his pheasant chicks as rather like children, and had little mercy on determined predators that raided them. In his early years, like most keepers, he had his gibbet lines of dead crows, magpies, stoats and so on, but later he ceased the practice.

'Mostly we strung 'em up so our employers would know we were really killing the vermin,' he told me. 'But I had another reason too. Flies bred in the bodies and all the maggots dropped out, so the creatures that were killing my chicks were now helping to feed 'em!'

I witnessed a practical example of how Jim combined gamekeeping with conservation. His sharp eye had seen a woodcock on its nest with three eggs. Telling me to tread softly, he took me to it, moving stealthily. I thought he would shoot the woodcock for it was a renowned delicacy.

'Only a scoundrel would shoot a bird that's as beautiful as a woodcock in flight,' he said. 'Besides, they're not common. You've got to look after what's rare because it's precious.' Marking where the nest was, he telephoned a friend who was a good amateur photographer. They got fine pictures of the bird, the nest and eggs and later of the chicks actually hatching out.

I had not been long at Hazeldene when much of my holidays was taken up with looking after wild creatures. I had a young tawny owl which I reared until it was old and strong enough to fly free, a young crow I found tumbled from its nest, and a female sparrowhawk which I found flapping and struggling in a hedgerow after being hit by a car. She was beautiful, with fierce yellow eyes and sharp talons, but I could not get her to eat. The following morning, obviously injured far worse than I'd thought, she was dead.

But the crow was quite a character. I called him Clark and as he gained strength he also seemed to gain a wicked sense of humour. He delighted in tormenting our cat, Ginger, a big but good-natured marmalade tom. Two or three times a week, while Ginger snoozed in the sunlight in the greenhouse, Clark would tweak his tail with his beak. Then, as the furious cat swiped unavailingly at his rapidly rising form, Clark flew to the safety of the greenhouse roof and strutted about with hoarse, guffaw-like sounds, as if enormously pleased with his joke.

At times I almost regretted befriending Clark. Because he always led me such an exasperating dance when he accompanied me on walks through the pine woods, I decided on one occasion to leave him behind. Although he squawked his grievance as I shut the gate in the garden's high lattice fence, he could not follow me. When I returned I found he had had his fun just the same – at my expense, or rather Dad's expense. He had plucked every tulip in the garden, then arranged his handiwork in neat rows along the edge of the lawn. Although his sober black plumage gave him an air of respectability, like an undertaker perhaps, Clark was eighteen and a half inches of mischief. When he finally went wild of his own accord, I really missed him.

At the start of the summer holidays, with time on my hands, I was browsing through our big bookcase when I came across a book called *Animal Heroes* by Ernest Thompson Seton. I had a few nature reference books but never bothered with fiction; now, however, I was reading some of the finest animal stories ever written... 'Badlands Billy', (the wolf), ... 'The Boy and the Lynx'...'Little Warhorse', (the jackrabbit), 'The Legend of the White Reindeer'. 'Arneaux', the story of a heroic homing pigeon. It was the sheer power of the descriptive writing which so impressed me. The author could convey the very hearts, minds and spirits of his creatures without being anthropomorphic. I loved most the story of Arneaux. After being imprisoned in a strange loft for two years, refusing to breed with the females the thief fancier introduces, Arneaux finally escapes and begins the long flight back to his faithful mate in his home loft. Some passages:

> *Out from the crest of the Catskills there launched a Falcon. Swiftest of the race of rapine, proud of his strength, proud of his wings, he rejoiced in a worthy prey. Many and many a pigeon had been borne to his nest, and riding the wind he came, swooping, reserving his strength, awaiting the proper time. Oh, how well he knew the very moment! Down, down like a flashing javelin...*

Arneaux is too fast for him... He carries on down the Hudson valley.

> *Home! home! home! and the towers of a city are coming into view. Home! home! past the great spider bridge of Poughkeepsie, skimming, skirting the river banks. Low now by the bank as the wind arose. Low, alas! too low! What fiend was it tempted a gunner in June to lurk on that hill by the margin? What devil directed, his gaze to the twinkling of white that came from the blue to the northward? Oh, Arneaux, Arneaux, skimming low, forget not the gunner of old! Too low, too low you are clearing that hills. Too low – too late! Flash – bang! and the death-hail has reached him; reached, maimed, but not downed him. Out of the flashing pinions broken feathers printed with records went fluttering earthward... A dark stain appeared on his bosom, but Arneaux kept on. Home, home, homeward bound.*

Arneaux comes in sight of his own city loft but has to go under a peregrine's eyrie.

> *...under the pirates' castle where the great grim Peregrines sat; peering like black-masked highwaymen they marked the oncoming Pigeon. Arneaux knew them of old. Many a message was lying undelivered in that nest, many a record-bearing plume had fluttered away from its fastness. But Arneaux had faced them before, and now he came as before – on, onward, swift, but not as he had been; the deadly gun had sapped his force, had lowered his speed. On, on; and the Peregrines, biding their time, went forth like two bow-bolts; strong and lightning-swift they went against one weak and wearied...*

The end is tragic, merciless – and brilliant. I wept then and even today, sixty years on, I cannot read it without a tear; it remains my favourite wild life story. Seton became a great inspiration, and I began writing notes about the birds I'd watched, to go with the paintings I'd made of them. Now I longed to have a pigeon of my own.

Two days later I was wandering through the sun-dappled pinewood when there was a great crashing in the foliage above me. No bird crashes through twigs and leaves more strongly or loudly than the chunky, powerful woodpigeon, and I looked up. Sure enough, only about twenty feet up, in a trident of branches, there was a small nest of sticks. I climbed up and found two squabs in the nest, almost fully fledged. One shrank as my head appeared but the nearest one seemed to stare back at me boldly. Without thinking, I picked it up and carefully climbed back down. Then I half ran, holding him gently in both hands, to the bungalow, where I installed him on hay in a spare rabbit hutch in the little hazel wood.

I dashed across the road and picked many ripe heads of wheat and some oats but when I held them out, Pergy, for so I named him, would not eat. He looked down briefly but didn't seem to recognize the grains as food. I consulted my books and learned that young pigeons are fed by their mothers by regurgitation, on partly digested food. So I warmed up some milk, crushed the wheat and oat grains with a hammer and made a mushy pulpy mash. I hammered a teaspoon until its cup was narrow and with this, opening his beak with my left hand, I got a small spoonful down Pergy's throat. To my delight he swallowed it all quite readily and before long I had his crop fairly full. I sat beside his hutch for over an hour, talking gently to him and sometimes stroking his thick blue-grey plumage with one finger. I just hoped, after shutting his little gate at dusk and leaving for my own supper and bed, that he wouldn't die overnight.

Far from it. When I appeared next morning, with new food mash and the spoon, he began shuffling his wings and making soft cheeping 'pee-ee-ee' calls, clearly the kind of soliciting calls he had made to his parents. After another good feeding session, I pushed the inner edge of my right hand softly against his chest and he promptly climbed aboard. As I walked round the garden and among the hazel trees, he moved his head backwards and forwards, taking in all the surroundings but making no effort to fly. I spent most of the day with him, touched by how easily he seemed to have accepted me. The plumage on his neck had the sweetest smell, like peeled chestnuts.

Within a week he was picking up his own food and I varied his wheat and oats diet with lentils, wholemeal bread morsels, currants and sultanas, mashed peanuts. At first he ignored the small container of milk I tied to the wire netting of his hutch but when I went out after lunch, I caught him drinking from it. To my surprise he did not put it in his beak then tilt it upwards so the fluid went down his throat, as most birds do. Instead, he pushed his beak in deeply and sucked the milk down, drinking deeply, like a horse!

At first I encouraged him to fly, and strengthened his wing muscles by lifting him high, then pulling my hand away. As he flew more strongly, I was afraid he would fly out of the rear garden, over the roof and into the road. So I took fairly long walks and exercised him near the wood where be had been born. I recall these days, constantly sunny, as being among the happiest of my young life. He was not just my pet but my pal, my only companion in fact.

Wanting to find out if he had any homing instinct, like that of a racing pigeon, I began putting him in a large shoe box on the handlebars of my bike and cycling a distance away, then letting him go. My heart was in my mouth the first time I did this because I had no way of knowing if he would just fly off into the wild. He flew up, went round in a full circle, then set off in the direction of the bungalow. When I arrived home, panting, there he was, perched on the roof of his hutch.

I now cycled with him two or three times a week. The longest distance was five miles and I always tried to beat him home – and never did! Always he would be back on his hutch, or very near it, 'pee-ee-ee'ing away and shuffling his wings when be saw me coming. I really began to love him.

When I read in one book that pigeons need a little grit in their diet to help their gizzards grind up harder grains and so help the digestive system, I felt a bit guilty as I had never made any available for him. I went into the road and scooped up some small gravelly grit. I went back to Pergy, held his beak open and put some down his throat. As the tiny bits left my fingers I thought I saw a small flash in the sunlight. I put him back in his hutch and went indoors to finish a butterfly painting. I was trying to capture the radiant colours of the Purple Emperor in sunshine and it took me three hours to finish.

About four o'clock I walked through the hazel bushes to Pergy's hutch. He looked oddly weak, standing but shaking slightly. I gathered him up and took him to a clear area, then, as always, gently tossed him into the air. Instead of the usual powerful wingbeats and sudden speed, he just fluttered weakly to the ground. When I picked him up he suddenly started choking. Then I saw it – blood. He was bringing up bright red blood and too much of it. He gave a last shiver, his body jerked, and he died in my hands. My loud wail, a mixture of grief, fear and rage, must have been heard throughout the neighbourhood. I could not believe it, did not want to believe it. I wept copious tears on to his ruffled plumage, kept trying to revive him, all the while knowing it was futile. My Pergy, my beloved little Arneaux, was gone for ever.

I had never experienced real grief in my young life. I stamped my feet in impotent rage, was sick, had a constant pain in my guts. And the worst thing of all was my realization that the little flash I had seen when feeding him grit must have been from a small shard of glass and that therefore *I* had killed him. By sheer stupidity and lack of attention to detail, I had killed the creature I loved most. I put his warm body reverently back on the hay in his hutch and next morning, after a near sleepless night, went out hoping and praying that I might have dreamt it. But no, his eyes were shut and his body was cold and stiff. I blubbered as I buried him in a sunny spot and made a little wooden cross with his name on it which I pushed it into the earth at the head of his grave.

My parents did their best to comfort me – Dad took me on a special pike fishing trip – but I was inconsolable for many days. Now, however, a new era in my life was about to begin, one that presented many problems.

It was called boarding school.

5
Boarding-school Trials

In September 1941, after I had passed an interview with the headmaster, my father drove me to Steyning Grammar School, as a boarder. I hated being torn away from my wild woods and fields but hoped I could obey Dad's exhortations to make the best of it. By now I had been to so many different schools in various parts of the country that it seemed I had to spend most of my time trying to adjust to different sets of boys and masters. I was always the stranger from another place or area, and at this school I felt more of an outsider than ever. To start with, the village school years had set my education back, and when I was put into Form Four, the correct one for my age, I could not do the work, and had to be relegated back to Form Three.

I was put into a small dormitory with a prefect and half a dozen other boys. Most of my new companions were from upper-class families, had double barrelled names, spoke with toffee-nosed accents, and were in higher forms than mine. I felt like a wild beast among more sophisticated but clannish and spiteful brethren, as though I was from 'the wrong side of the tracks' (just the opposite of what had happened at the council school).

For some reason I had developed an obsessive nervous sniffing habit. On the second night I had just given two loud sniffs after lights out and was settling down to sleep, when I felt a tremendous thump on my head and shoulders. One of the other boys had whacked me with his pillow. I just caught sight of him climbing back into bed but when I got up to avenge the blow the prefect ordered me back into my bed. This seemed to give some of the other boys licence to do the same, and for several nights I could not go to sleep until I had endured a pillow battering from as many as four boys at once. There was little I could do against older, bigger chaps but if in the near darkness I could recognize a lad of around my own age, I would seek him out, when he was on his own the following day, and redress the balance. Consequently I got into a lot of fights, just as I did with boys who imitated my facial tic, of which I still had remnants. I didn't like fighting but I had a strange sense of personal honour, and hated my peers taking any liberties. I recall I had fights with five different boys that first term, of which I lost one – against a powerful farm lad called Paul, who held me up so hard against a wall in the sports field I just felt helpless. I acknowledged his superior strength and knew if I tried to hit back he could punch a hole in my ribs, or worse. Even many of the boys in Senior School were afraid of him although he was never aggressive unless provoked. We finally became quite good friends, although I was very much the acolyte, glad to run errands for him, a strange new feeling for me.

Lessons? I loved woodwork and art, and longed for Wednesdays to come around as we had double periods of both. Some of the lads lusted after the young brunette art mistress, Miss Sage, and the bravest of us would sometimes drop items deliberately under our desks, so that we had an excuse to bend right down and try to look up her skirt! But after my home drawings and paintings of birds and butterflies, I did take art seriously and was always in the top three in the marks. Once our school entered a county school competition for the best art poster, with Savings as the subject. I drew and painted a complicated coloured picture of a Dick Turpin-type highwayman holding up a stage coach and demanding from the passengers: Your Money – *For* Your Life. It won the competition!

In woodwork, I made the usual items and was taught to use the lathe, on which I turned breadboards, ashtrays and a salad bowl. Then I was shown a box of brand new carving tools and had the inspiration which was to take up an entire year of woodwork lessons – to carve my favourite bird, a sparrowhawk.

My good luck so far was to have been put into Holland House, whose master was Sebastian Bayliss–Smith, an enlightened teacher with a fine sense of humour. I knew from the start that he was a keen ornithologist and birdwatcher as at my first interview I had seen some fine photos of birds and mammals he had taken himself, in his quarters. I had not dared to tell him of my passion for nature for fear the other boys would think I was trying to creep. But now I had a good reason. I knocked on his door and timidly asked him if I could borrow his photo of a sparrowhawk as I wanted to carve one. He readily agreed and said that as he never locked his door during the day I could pick it up before every woodwork lesson. In fact, I never did use that photo for only three days later he called me into his study and handed me a beautiful stuffed male sparrowhawk he had managed to borrow from a friend. I had to protect it with my life and make sure it was kept in a locked cupboard in the woodwork shop. It was clear he had driven several miles to fetch it and I felt almost overcome with gratitude as I stammered out my thanks.

I had been told that walnut was the best wood for carving but it was wartime and even wood was rationed. Eventually the woodwork master located a small chunk of walnut which measured 15 × 4 × 4 inches. It was big enough for me to carve out a life-size sparrowhawk, provided I made no mistakes. I had no experience of using the varied and intricate carving tools but what I had to do seemed obvious – cut away everything that didn't look like a sparrowhawk! I set it in a vice, held the stuffed hawk in the opposite vice, and carefully sawed out the rough squared shape I wanted. Then I set to work.

Carving that hawk was my weekly release, my main target, my task of love, and lasted for a whole year of woodwork lessons. I etched in bas-relief every single feather, the beak, the sere, the eyes, the tufted legs, the toes, the talons. When some of the other boys paid me compliments on my work I realized I had found something else, apart from art and biology, that I was good at. It certainly helped increase my confidence. As I worked it was as if I was in some way recapturing the spirit, the essence of the wild woods and fields from which I was now separated. Even today, over sixty years later, that wooden hawk is my most treasured possession, and has been across the Atlantic fourteen times.

It was about this time that I found another way of keeping in touch with my country life. Ever since moving out of town, my family had kept rabbits and hens, and I had the idea of starting a Rabbit and Poultry Club on the narrow strip of land at the back of the school's gymnasium. I drew up rough plans and took them to Mr Smith who said he would let me know the following day. His final decision was that I could start a Rabbit Club, but no chickens! Rabbits were quiet but hens and cockerels were noisy and might disrupt morning Assembly and classes held in the gym. I could see his point.

As I knew more about keeping rabbits than anyone else, I could run the Club more or less how I liked. Membership was limited to four boys, as there was only enough room for half a dozen hutches, and they were either pals or lads I knew I could control. I brought my own lovely Silver Fox doe in from home and we got started. Eventually we were breeding rabbits and selling the youngsters at the Steyning Ministry of Food market down by the station, thus paying our own way in food, hay and other items we needed.

There was one big bonus to the Rabbit Club that none of us boys had thought of. As it was wartime the school was under pressure to open the gym for outside organizations to use in the evenings, a sort of communal service. And one of these was the local Girls' Club. We became expert peeping toms, using ingenious camouflage techniques so that we could see without being seen. Those showers would never seem the same!

The fact that I hated football and cricket, and was therefore no good at either (in fact all team and ball sports bored me) did not help my popularity. But I partly made up for this by being a good runner. After the humiliation at the Henfield school – for ever emblazoned on my memory – I did a great deal of training and usually came in the first three on cross-country runs. At last I was eventually picked to run for the school in the Sussex County Schoolboys' Cross-Country Championship, and came in a respectable seventh. Only one lad from my school beat me.

I could leap like a deer, sprint well and hurl a discus further than most juniors so my House had high expectations on Sports Day. However, a new humiliation lay ahead. The night before, the school's Boy Scout troop leaders erected a high wire from the top of a chestnut tree down to the ground. We had to climb up a ladder, grab hold of a 'T' handle beneath a pulley and do a fast slide back down to the ground. Though terrified at first, I soon got the hang of it, then started to show off by taking a few silly chances. The result was that I pulled a muscle in my shoulders, so could not throw, run or jump and had to withdraw from Sports Day. My disappointment was intensified when I saw the sad look on his face when I broke the news to Mr Smith, my house master. He had been hoping I would win a good few points for the House. He had been good to me and I hated letting him down.

I was in the school's Boy Scout troop, which he ran, so I worked harder from then on and eventually won eleven badges, which I wore with great pride on my sleeves. I think the one for Axemanship was my favourite. One weekend Mr Smith took us on a weekend camp to Wiggonholt, which I thought was a truly wonderful area, full of sandy slopes and pits and pine trees. We soon discovered a huge sandpit where about six feet from the top of the cliff, soft sand stretched down in a gradual decline to the ground. I made a few tentative jumps along with the other boys, loved the feeling of flying through the air, and began taking longer and longer runs, leaping as hard as I ever did in the long jump. I really felt I had become a bird, seeming almost to fly down in slow motion, landing far beyond the marks left by the other boys. I just couldn't get enough of this and didn't realize I was exhausting myself totally. I fell asleep in the car on the way back and was then terrified that I would collapse in that nights prep in Big School and the prayers service. I went and begged Mr Smith to allow me to go to bed early, which he did. I still recall trying to wake up when the other boys in the dorm came in at normal bedtime but I could not, nor could I provide any answers to their questions. I have never, before or since, been so tired.

Another subject I was good at, and loved as much as art and woodwork, was biology, and often my experiences in the wild woods and fields of Sussex came in useful as the master, Mr 'Buff' Bennett, encouraged us to talk about nature experiences. I had just finished talking about my pet Tawny Owl when one of the day boys said he had a Little Owl at home. He brought it in the following day, the day before we broke up for half-term. When I saw its huge, lovely eyes, and the way it crawled and heaved itself up his sleeve to perch on his shoulder and gently nibble his ear, I fell in love with it and wanted one for myself.

Back home for the short holiday, I again tramped around the pine wood, memories of Pergy flooding back, then cycled over to Lock Estate for that special treat – a day's rabbiting with Jim Adkins. As he hiked towards buries near Middle Wood, laden with the guns, nets and box of ferrets, I said that one of the boys at school had boasted he knew of a keeper who could *squeak* rabbit from their burrows. Had he ever heard of such a thing?

'Oh ah,' he replied. 'I can do it. I'll show you.'

We walked along a hedge until we came to a large bury, a big mound with several holes in it. He stopped and told me to stand in front of him and keep my gun at the ready. Then he cupped his hands and produced a peculiar squeaking sound by sucking through his lips against his teeth. Out popped a rabbit, which I shot. Out popped another which I also shot. Then another a few seconds later – which I missed.

'They thought that was a stoat or weasel,' Jim said. 'The sound seems to fascinate them and they come out to look at what's going on.'

Jim wanted to work his ferrets, 'true rabbiting', he called it, and in three hours we had his quota. As we stumbled home under their weight, I told him about the Little Owl at school and how I longed to own one as a pet. Jim told me he would never kill an owl, not even the Little Owl, which he believed came over from Holland about fifty years earlier and which most gamekeepers then believed was an inveterate killer of game chicks.

'Owls may kill a *few* chicks but they live mostly on mice, voles, rats and lots of insects like earwigs, crane flies and beetles,' he said. 'They do far more good than harm. I leave 'em alone.'

That evening he stood me by the shed where he kept his gun dog Sally and told me to watch the coalhouse roof. I was prepared for a long wait, but within minutes of him going indoors, a lovely Little Owl floated down, landed on the edge of the roof and started walking round it slowly, like a small fat parrot. It kept teetering over the edge, peering with the great black pupils of its bright yellow eyes at the ground below, then walking a bit further and doing the same. Every few minutes it suddenly dived silently to the ground.

Finally it came up with a mouse and flew off with it.

'There,' said Jim when I went in and told him. 'Isn't that better than puttin' it in a cage? He's there every night. He knows mice run round the edges of houses and sheds and that they can't see him up there. He don't have to fly around, y'see – just has to sit up there and keep an eye on his territory.'

I went back to boarding school with my usual reluctance, and got a slight shock. Paul, the strong boy who had become quite a pal, had been removed to another school or college, and in his bed opposite mine was a new boy. His name was Eddy, he came from Brighton, and right from the start it was clear he was confident, cocky and talkative. He had the bland, open, blue-eyed face of an angel, and clearly got on better with the other boys in the dorm than I had. My initial dislike of him increased when three of us came back from morning ablutions in the communal bathroom and he deliberately imitated my facial twitch, which I thought I had just about conquered. I could take this from my contemporaries and my superiors in age, but not from a *new* boy. I felt he was out of order, and told him so.

Immediately he came over. 'And what you going to do about it?'

In an instant we were fighting like cats, wrestling rather than hitting. I'd expected a pretty quick victory but despite his angel face he was fast and strong, and was getting slightly the better of me when the prefect entered and hauled us apart. For days I smarted about this for I always tried to repay grudges, and when an argument flared up in a corridor before a history class, we were fighting again. This time I was better prepared and we ended up stalemate, each holding one of the other's arms in an iron grip, while we grabbed our opponent's hair with the other, yanking his head back. Mr Smith, who wore suede shoes with soft soles, came silently round the corner, seized each of us by one ear and led us to a bathroom. We both got two whacks with his cane while bending over the bath, and were told to shake hands before we ran around the playground together, trying to assuage the pain. Oddly, this whacking seemed to unite us a little.

'I thought you were going to tear my hair out!'

'I thought I was going to be scalped!'

We then entered a strange relationship as friends and yet also rivals. Eddy liked both football and cricket and was better at them than me. When, after spending twenty-four hours in the school hospital with some minor ailment, I heard he had won a mile race, I went into immediate training, and made sure I beat him over the distance in the next race. But he took it well. Over the next two terms we were occasional friends; we played marbles together, a shove-ha'penny form of table football, and conkers, but neither of us liked to lose.

At the end of each term Eddy and I competed as to who could get the Last Touch. This involved sneaking up to or behind each other, giving a final tap on the body, shouting 'Last touch!' and dashing away before the recipient could react. If I lost at this, it used to niggle me all through the holidays at home. But honour meant I had to wait till the end of the following term to try for revenge. During two summer holidays Eddy and I joined a few other boys at farming camps in Warwickshire. The first one had us potato-picking and apple-picking, both very hard work. At the end I was packing my bag when I felt a light tap from behind on my left shoulder. I turned left but Eddy, who had been standing to my right rear, dashed off before I could turn round. When I did it was to see him slamming the door of his parents' car and being driven off at speed. Boy, I was mad!

The following summer we were in a school party at another farm but this time we were making stooks of wheat. This involved walking for miles behind a binding machine which threw out bound sheaves of wheat. You had to grab two sheaves and bang their tops together after standing them on end. Then you repeated this with four more sheaves so you had six sheaves standing on end and self-supporting. The sheaves were left to dry out and we then loaded them on to high wagons with pitchforks. The full wagons were driven to the Dutch barns and I learned how to make a rick. I stood at the top of a clattering metal chute while an endless chain driven by a canvas belt from a tractor bombarded the sheaves at me so fast I had barely time to get one in place before the next hit me.

I had never worked so hard in my life and I can still hear that rattling roar, the dust and mist made by bits of straw, and the infernal heat. Eddy and I slept in different parts of the camp and didn't meet much, so I hoped he had forgotten about Last Touch. I most certainly had not! On the last day I kept a distant but close eye on him as we all packed our belongings to return home. I was doubly annoyed that day because his voice had just broken and mine had not and I felt less manly. I waited until he was talking to some other boys on a fairly steep slope. I wheeled my bike to face *down* the slope just three or four yards away, then sneaked up behind him, whacked the top of his head with the flat of my hand, yelled 'Last touch' and dashed to my bike. By the time he had recovered and turned round, I was careering downhill, laughing my head off. Sweet revenge!

As it was wartime all the young fit masters had been called up into one or other of the services and the following term we had a new PT master called Mr Moore. He was old but barrel-chested, thick-necked with a head like a rounded rock. He had been a very good amateur boxer and believed that boxing was good for building boys' characters. When he started a Boxing Club Eddy was one of the first to join. I also joined, not wanting him to gain any more advantages over me, and also because there were still some older boys I was not sure of. I want to reiterate that I did not actually like boxing. It hurt, and each time I climbed into the gym ring for sparring bouts I was scared. I just felt I had no choice.

Mr Moore was a terrific teacher. As long as we didn't hit him full in the face he let us pound at his body and arms to our heart's content, all the while teaching us various basic moves. I slowly learned in the three-round sparring bouts that if I took it easy in round one, concentrating solely on defence, I could lull my opponent into a false sense of security and go for broke in round two and, with luck, Mr Moore would stop it before round three. When he told me I had a very good hard right, I worked out that if I aimed several low left shots in succession at my opponent's solar plexus, he would drop his guard to there and I could sling over a fast right cross or hook. Once that landed flush on a jaw, Mr Moore usually had to call a halt.

What surprises me, looking back, is that I never sparred with Eddy. Mr Moore must have kept us apart. Maybe it was because Eddy was slightly heavier than me, enough to put him up to the next weight group. I must admit that I was never champion material over the two terms but I won more bouts than I lost.

Naturally, when the Sussex Schoolboy Boxing Championships came up, I thought I would be chosen to represent my weight, because I nearly always got the better of the other three lads who were in that category. To my surprise, a stocky, freckled, thick-set but slow lad called Chick Young was nominated. Instead of protesting, I asked to spar with him next time we were in the gym. I had him going towards the end of round two, Mr Moore stopped the bout and I was sure I would then be chosen to represent the school. To my horror they still chose Chick Young. It was like that horrible moment at Worthing High School when Mr Foinett had accused me of having 'Duck's Disease'. The injustice of it! I found out later it was because of my facial twitches. They reckoned I was nervous and too highly strung and as I had a thin face I might get badly hurt if I came up against a really good fighter. As it was, Chick was stopped in the first round of his first bout, but Eddy, to his great credit, battled his way into the semi-finals.

During my next holiday at home I was delighted to see more jays than usual in our hazel woodlands and longed to catch one so I could study it. Surely, along with perhaps the goldfinch and the kingfisher, the jay is our most colourful bird. When I next went rabbiting with Jim I mentioned my wish, but I did not expect much help from him in view of his attitude to my catching a Little Owl. To my surprise he said that as jays, magpies and crows were regarded as pest species, he would show me how to make a trap he used for catching magpies alive. He was sure it would also work with jays. The trap consisted of making a pyramidal cage from lengths of one-inch-thick hazel sticks on a two-foot-square base. The cage was propped up by an L-shaped twig in turn held up by a forked stick. The end of the L-stick was held in place by a bender stick hinged to the cage's base. When any big bird tried to get at the bait, it stepped on the bender which gave way, and down came the cage. Excited, I cycled home and spent almost a whole day making the trap.

Then it hit me: what was I going to do with a jay if I actually caught one? I remembered then that on my last walk in the pinewood I had seen some half-buried small-mesh wire netting. I hurried down to the wood and started hauling the netting from its entanglement of grasses, nettles, brambles and other plants. The more I tore away the longer the netting grew, without any gaps. It took me two whole days to free as much as I wanted, to make a big roll. I waited until it was nearly dark, then with a great deal of puffing effort, rolled the whole caboodle home. Two more days and I had an aviary which was five feet high, twelve feet long and six feet wide. In it I put several perches, Pergy's old hay-strewn hutch and some large conifer fronds for natural shelter. Then I set the trap.

The following morning I dashed out eagerly but both the trap and the peanuts bait remained untouched. On the second morning my heart leaped when I saw the trap was down. The nuts had gone but no there was jay. I set the support twig on a knife edge... Next morning a large black beak was poking through various places in the gaps between the hazel sticks of the trap. I had my jay at last! I ran to the house for a small sheet of plywood, opened the gate of my aviary, slid the plywood under the trap and carried the jay into its new home. At first, of course, it flew to and fro, landing on the perches, looking for an escape gap. I put in some food and left it to settle down. The following day the trap had caught another jay, which I put with the first. I made a quick hide from an old child's playpen and set it ten yards away, and as I sat in it watching the antics of my captives I felt like the great white trapper!

I spent many hours over the next few days watching the jays, marvelling at their intricate colours, the way they jumped about, and their broad, blunt but very neat wings. It soon became clear that they would not settle down and regard the aviary as a new home. They were in constant motion in their attempts to escape, and when the time came for me to return to school I reluctantly let them go.

6
Sometimes a Winner

At this time, April 1943, my parents moved home again, to Staplesbarn House on the outskirts of Henfield. It was a big, three-bedroomed house with a large garden, fairly isolated down a small lane, and it sat on a hill high above a railway line. I managed one walk before my return to school, happy to find plenty of wild woods and fields to the north, plus a large stretch of the Adur river.

This was to be my last term as a boarder. On top of buying the new house, Dad's finances were also stretched further as he was sending my half-brother Richard to a private boarding school. Both Maureen and Valerie were at private schools, and as Steyning was now only four miles away as the crow flies, it was decided I could become a day boy, travelling to and from school on the old steam train. I was quite happy about this as I would have every evening at home, and when weather allowed I could be back again in the wild woods and fields, free of the restrictions put on us boarders at school, where junior boys went in a crocodile formation on Junior Walk, while senior boys, of which I was now one, were only allowed out in pairs or larger groups. And many places were out of bounds.

About this time too it had emerged that, of all unlikely things, I was doing well at religious studies, which the school called 'divinity'. Ever since the age of thirteen, when we boarders were marched every Sunday to St Andrew's church in Steyning, down by the railway, I'd found disturbing contradictions in the Christian religion. Even repeating the Lord's Prayer stuck in my throat. The line, 'Forgive us our trespasses, as we forgive those that trespass against us', made me think, 'But we don't forgive those who trespass against us! Not usually anyway.' And my response to the line 'Give us this day our daily bread' was 'No, let us earn our daily bread, don't give us anything.' There was a phrase at the time, 'All is well. God's in His heaven,' and I thought, if he's in His heaven, how the hell can he be down here? And

Jesus saying forgive your enemies, love your enemies, turn the other cheek and so forth. Where were these notions when he overturned the tables of the usurers and threw them out of the Temple? I could never get around the idea that he died on the cross for *my* sins as I wasn't there, and how could he know I'd be here in 2,000 years' time? Or that I'd commit any! And why did God impregnate a married virgin to have His son Jesus? Especially if adultery was a sin! The more I questioned, the more absurd it all seemed to me. I always had my hand up in divinity class, scribbled longer essays than anyone else, and was sometimes invited after class to discuss points I'd raised with the divinity master, the Rev. Parry Jones.

It certainly surprised Dad when my report at the end of one term had me first in divinity and the Rev. Parry Jones had written: 'Excellent. He has an original mind and is a good thinker. I hope he perseveres with religious studies.' Unfortunately religious studies were the last thing on my mind, for only the study of wild nature interested me, and the nearest I could get to that in the school curriculum was my favourite subject – biology. And it was when I became a day boy that I had a unique chance to shine during actual class.

We were on the subject of fish and at one point the biology master said, 'All British fish have two dorsal fins.' My hand shot up. 'Pardon me, sir, but I think the pike has only one.' And in the silence that followed I added nervously, 'Er, I could show you?' Buff Bennett looked at me in surprise. 'Hmm, then do that, Tomkies. Perhaps you'll do that?'

That night I went straight from the train at Henfield station to get my fishing tackle, cycled to a lake a few miles away and caught a small jack pike to show them all next day. I remember it as a minor triumph as many of the boys, who had never seen a pike, crowded round. Buff thanked me and it was the only time I had showed myself well ahead of the rest of the class.

My first, and worst, shock on becoming a day boy was when I missed the morning train. There wasn't another one for three hours. I didn't bother to ring Dad for even if he wasn't at work he certainly wouldn't drive me to school. I decided to start running, and the shortest route was along the railway line. I still recall my exasperation as the sleepers between the rails were too close for normal running, yet too far apart for normal walking. I proceeded at an awkward short-stepping tottery-trot for most of the four miles! I arrived at school just as the first period was ending. I had not been missed by the teacher, so sauntered into the second period with the other boys as if nothing had happened. One of the boys had noticed my absence but I lied that I'd been on an important errand for the headmaster.

Now I was a day boy I could not be in Holland House, which was just for boarders. Instead I was put in Cuthbert House, one of the three for the day boys. I still wanted to do well on Sports Day, so I sometimes got up early and ran down the railway tracks as part of a training programme. I also made a discus on the lathe in woodwork, sank a lead weight into its centre until I got the correct weight and slung it all round the garden in my spare time. I marked out a 220-yard course in the field next to the house and practised sprints, and made a sandpit so I could practise the long jump. Of course, I could not make a full-length sandpit, just a small one, so if I didn't reach it I had a hard landing!

All this work, which I enjoyed anyway, really paid off. Although I had a fairly sleepless night before the big day, I was not as nervous as usual. I came second in the long jump, third in the discus, second in the 220 yards and second in throwing the cricket ball, which I entered at the last minute. It was the proudest moment of my entire school life when the housemaster presented me with my House Colours in front of all the other lads.

It was on New Year's Eve when I was sixteen that I tasted my first alcohol – in fact Dad almost *made* me drink. He and Bettie returned from the Bull Inn at Mock Bridge with the local Canadian Air Force Commander and two of his erks (ordinary airmen). The erks had been hitching a ride, so were amazed when they were invited to a party at our house. I was still up, so Dad said, 'Do you want to join the men and have a drink?' It was like a challenge, to which I said yes. While the others played poker I kept drinking what I was handed but from time to time had to dash upstairs to the loo and bring it all up again. Each time I went back down, Dad said, 'Want another?' I said, 'Sure,' intent on proving that I could take it. I still recall how the two streetwise erks beat everyone else including their own Commander at poker, then lay on their backs in the snow after passing out! I had an awful hangover and felt so terrible the following day that I didn't touch alcohol for all of the next four years, until my last weeks in the Army! In that way, Dad had done me a big favour.

By now I had outgrown the Boy Scouts, so when the school started its own Cadet Force I was one of the first to volunteer, and soon found Scout skills came in useful, especially in subjects like map reading. I enjoyed the parade ground as well as the outdoor Army exercises, and was eventually made up to Corporal. I got a lot of satisfaction from drilling the squad and giving some of my former tormentors a hard time. I loved most the rare night-time exercises up on the hills and in the woodlands of the South Downs where we were even allowed, under supervision, to throw thunder flashes. One of mine gave Eddy a great fright – accidentally, of course.

The last – and worst – days of my schoolboy years were now looming – the examinations for School Certificate. My father had drilled into me the necessity for passing; it would affect my ability to get a good job, in fact the rest of my life. He wanted me to try for a higher qualification, called Matriculation. But I knew I had a poor chance at this for I was hopeless at maths. Dad even hired a private tutor in my last term, and every Saturday I cycled over to the Borstal school in West Grinstead where a kindly Irish maths master tried to drum skills into my head. I could just about understand cotangents, cosecants, logarithms, etc. when he explained them in detail, but I could not remember them. My brain was not geared to making such calculations. The only way I could get near the correct answers in geometry or trigonometry was to draw the problems to scale on separate sheets of paper, and then measure the results.

I recall the four days of the exams, held in silence in Big School, as one long nightmare. Again I had sleepless nights as I tossed about with worry; my eyes became black-ringed. Once I took one look at an exam paper and panicked – 'I can't answer any of these questions!' but I struggled on.

I did enjoy the exams in art, French (especially oral French), general science (because of biology) English, and, most of all, English literature. Looking back, the school had a most enlightened policy on this subject because the three books we studied were Gilbert White's *Natural History and Antiquities of Selborne*, *Travels with a Donkey* by Robert Louis Stevenson, and *Three Men in a Boat* by Jerome K. Jerome ('It was George's straw hat that saved his life that day'). I loved all three books and felt I knew them inside out. I was in exultant mood when the question papers came for they were all easy. I was so confident that I could not resist a desire to show off. Often I wrote, 'If the question means *this*, then the answer is ... On the other hand, if it means *that*, then the answer is ...' And I kept asking for more writing paper. I scribbled away, writing far more than the required amount, and handed in my sheaf of papers feeling smug.

Well, I *did* scrape through School Certificate, despite failing in maths, with credits in art, French and general science but only a Pass in English. I got a terrible shock when I eagerly scanned the results for English literature. I had failed! I could not believe it, but eventually worked out that the examiner must just have lost patience, and possibly his temper. 'Oh, we have a clever little bugger here,' he probably thought. 'The hell with him – FAIL,' and stroke, stroke, stroke went his red pencil.

The odd thing was that after I left school, no matter what job I went for, no employer ever asked me if I had my School Certificate. Certainly, for the job I now wanted School Cert would not have been required, for I was determined to follow my idol, Jim, and become a gamekeeper.

Although Dad had other ideas, while we now discussed what I was going to do with my future, he did not mount outright opposition. He said that if I did my normal holiday chores, like mowing the lawn and feeding the chickens, I should just spend what would have been the school summer holidays as normal – trekking the fields and woods, fishing, visiting Jim – and then we would have a serious talk. An idyllic few weeks followed as more and more of my time was spent with wild nature. One afternoon, when spinning for pike, I noticed there were several moorhens on the river, and that whenever they saw me walking near they quickly swam under the bank. But they gave their position away because the constant paddling needed to keep them under the bank in the slow-flowing water sent out semi-circles of ripples. It struck me that if I lay on the bank and made a quick grab at the epicentre of these ripples, I might catch one. I was amazed to find this ruse worked, and I caught two that very afternoon. I felt that if I could catch large wild birds by hand I must now have the skills of a Red Indian hunter, that I was truly in tune with the wild. I put the birds into my fishing bag and ran home, where I put them in the old jay's aviary which I had reassembled at Staplesbarn. I dug in a large basin and filled it with water, so they would have some of their normal element, and installed Pergy's hay-strewn hutch in a corner under the trees. Although I kept watch most of the next day from a makeshift hide, the moorhens just went into the hutch and stayed there. They did not eat and did not go near the water. Keeping moorhens was as much of a failure as keeping jays, and so, I realized, would keeping any adult wild uninjured birds, so I let them go. But I was still proud of myself for catching them by hand.

By now I was becoming quite a good shot. Dad had acquired a .22 rifle and he let me use it when I visited Jim, who was quite happy for me to plug grey squirrels, crows, woodpigeons and rabbits. but nothing else. One day, when I had taken my young brother Richard with me, a rabbit ran across our path. I followed through as Jim had taught me, pressed the trigger – and blew the running rabbit's guts clean out. Of course, with a rifle, it was sheer luck, but I was glad Richard was with me or no-one would have believed the tale. Richard and I shared a small bedroom, and one evening we looked out to see a small covey of partridges in the next-door field. I quickly got the .22 rifle, balanced it over the window sill, took careful aim, and shot two partridges with one shot, both through the head. Richard couldn't wait to tell Dad, who came with us to pick up the partridges and said it had been a great shot.

I felt all this meant that Dad was coming round to my wish to become a gamekeeper, but when the time came for our serious talk, it was clear he was not. In fact, he was dead against it and adamant he did not want me to take a low-paid outdoor job. He himself had started his own working life outdoors, selling second-hand lace from a barrow in a Nottingham market. He wanted me to have a career with a real future. The fact that I was a dud at maths meant I could not be an accountant or a surveyor or anything like that but I could become an estate agent which, if one was good at it, was 'money for old rope'.

The discussions went on for the next few weekends, as Dad was away selling during the week, and there were occasional arguments. In the course of these I noticed he no longer tried to force ideas on me or tell me to obey. I was over seventeen, almost as big as him, and no doubt was going through the usual stroppy, rebellious stage of older teenage boys. I had also gone up considerably in my own self-esteem because, missing the best side of school Cadet Force life, I had gone to the Commander of the local village platoon, and was promptly promoted from Corporal to Sergeant Major! And how I enjoyed drilling and marching the lads around the village and on exercises over the Common, especially as some of them had given me a hard time at Henfield school. The Bowman twins had exceptionally clean rifles!

When Dad next brought up the question of my future I asked him to try to see it from my point of view. I did not like indoor desk work of any kind, unless I was making my paintings of butterflies, moths and birds, and writing my notes on them. I said surely I would be more successful in a career if I liked what I was doing, and I loved shooting, rabbiting and working with Jim Adkins. I felt sure I could eventually become a very good keeper and land a well-paid job with a top estate.

My father looked at me thoughtfully for a few moments, then said, 'Hmm, you have a point there, Michael.' Two days later he called me into his study and it seemed a miracle when I heard him saying I could have my wish – Jim Adkins had agreed to take me on as an apprentice and I could start next Monday. It would be for a trial period of one month, and I would have to do exactly what Jim told me. As I cycled the seven miles through the Sussex countryside to Jim's rose-covered cottage, I felt this was the happiest morning of my life.

As I stood in Jim's parlour, panting from my ride, my eyes strayed to the gleaming guns in their racks. Jim knew what I was thinking and said sharply, 'There's more to being a keeper than shooting, Michael – and don't you forget it!' He crammed his floppy green cap on his head and said 'We'll just go out and see what needs doin' in the woods.' We tramped on through Calcot Wood, where we saw a fox out hunting and a stoat stalking a rabbit, my happiness increasing all the time. Then Jim came to a small shed, opened its door and handed me a billhook and a huge pair of shears. 'See those overgrown rides? Just trim back the new growth so we can see right along 'em.' I swallowed my disappointment. I'd hoped to spend the day rabbiting with the ferrets, but I hurried to obey. For the rest of that week I did nothing but clear rides.

The following week Jim handed me a large spade. 'You know that marshy part of Calcot Wood? Well, go and clear the ditch so it can drain into the river.' I slaved away for two days, then Jim put me on to shovelling tons of dirt into rabbit holes so he could put traps on the main ones. After that I was ditch-digging in Stony Copse and I was discovering new areas of my hands that would grow blisters. I still wasn't doing the interesting wildlife work I had expected with gamekeeping and was beginning to feel mutinous. Maybe Jim guessed how I was feeling, for late on the Saturday afternoon, he handed me his old .410 shotgun and told me to get some woodpigeons in the copse. (There were thousands that year and farmers complained of their destroying crops.) Joyfully, I set off, stood under the roosting trees and in an hour came back with three birds.

As Jim handed me my week's pay, he said mysteriously, 'Don't tell your dad you've been shooting.' Why this had to be kept from my father I had no idea. My thoughts were more on my pay – a whole ten-shilling note! – which seemed poor reward for all my hard work. But as I cycled home, and recalled the feel of Jim's slim, well-balanced .410, I felt that things were at last looking up and maybe Jim would let me use Dad's .22 rifle ere too long.

The following Monday my new hopes were soon dashed. I was back on ride-clearing, cleaning field drains, trimming hedges, making gun stakes. My feet began to drag across the fields, and the post-dawn cycle rides took longer. On the third Saturday night I got home and told Dad that maybe I was wrong, that I was not cut out for gamekeeping after all.

He said, 'Oh dear, I *am* sorry,' and seemed most sympathetic. But, as he put it, 'Life is not full of gloom and doom.' It so happened he had just had a letter from one of the county's leading estate agents, Harry James Burt and Son of Steyning, who could take me on as an apprentice.

7
The Runaway – into the Guards

My first day as a trainee estate agent and auctioneer was spent in the open-air Ministry of Food animal market near Steyning station. I had to stand at the entrance to some hefty metal pens, help wobbly-legged veal calves off lorries, slap glue on their backsides with a brush and stick on a big white numbered label. I then logged each calf and where it came from on a clipboard, ready to be auctioned later. All the pens were filled with bleating sheep, bellowing cattle and pigs that squealed loudly when a branding device pierced numbers into their ears, and everywhere was the smell of animal excrement. I hated it.

Another task involved driving round the houses of the recently deceased in an old black car with one of the senior partners. My job was to make the furniture catalogue notes as he pronounced sonorously, 'Lot 24 – one ormolu clock. Lot 25 – one dozen bone-handled fish knives and forks in mahogany case,' and so forth. I helped carry and load chunks of Victoriana to be taken to the salerooms. I also helped catalogue old agricultural machinery in the same way, walking from lot to lot in muddy (often rain-sodden) fields, listing tractors, ploughs, trailers and so on. Still, I preferred this to the animal market where I was also required to hold rabbits and chickens aloft so the bidders could get a good look at the creatures. The rest of the time I was just the office boy/dogsbody working in the reception office, filing and the like. My main release from what seemed drudgery was that I had discovered the Brighton Ice Rink where after the usual first-timer tumbles I found I could skate quite fast. That, and the fact that there were some beautiful girls flying past and spinning around in very short skirts, seemed to lessen my boyhood love and need of the wild woods and fields somewhat. I used to wait for the Gents' Speed Sessions, hang back until the first fast men grew tired or left the rink, then launch myself. I tore round as fast as I could go, throwing up shards of ice crystals on the corners, just showing off. My ambition to be a top-speed skater vied with an equally powerful ambition to actually date a pretty girl skater.

I lasted six months in the Steyning job. It ended when the senior partner wrote to my father, 'I am sorry to say that your son shows no initiative whatever.' Perhaps understandably, relations with my dad began to deteriorate from this point. We had bickering rows and the situation was not helped by my being at home so much, with no career ideas or prospects of another job, not one I wanted anyway. I caught the bus to the Brighton rink as often as three times a week as I had a season ticket and wanted full value from it.

One day, as I was about to set off on the mile-long run/walk to the bus, Dad asked me to take my sister's bike to the cycle shop in Henfield High Street for repairs which included a puncture. I asked why she couldn't take it herself. I forget his answer but when he insisted I pointed out that wheeling the bike for a mile would slow me down and I would miss my bus. As there wasn't another for two hours I would lose all that time at the skating rink.

'Damn your skating!' Dad glared at me. 'You should be looking for a job! Look, Michael, while you're living in *my* house you'll do as *I* tell you!'

Without really thinking, I replied 'Well, I'll get out of your house!'

'You wouldn't dare!'

I made no immediate reply but ran upstairs, put all the money I had into my pocket, and then I was down and out through the front door, calling loudly 'I'm going!' As I reached the gate I half expected Dad to come after me and ask me not to go, but he didn't. I broke into a trot and only just made the bus. It wasn't until the skating was over that I fully realized my position. I had run away from home! I toyed with the idea of phoning Dad and eating humble pie, but I didn't want to admit defeat. I loitered around the town streets, then as it was getting dark went to lie under Brighton pier for the night. The pebbles were large and I had to search for an area of small ones beside a girder that I could make into a small trough of a bed. To the noise of waves pounding on the shingle and the shellacking sound of the stones being drawn back by the undertow, I fell asleep.

Around 3a.m. I was woken by the feeling of something travelling over my chest. It was a man's hand and he was whispering something to me. Thinking I was about to be robbed, I smashed my clenched right fist sideways into his stomach, shouting, 'You're not robbing me!' The man sat up fast, coughing and half-winded, stuttering that he hadn't wanted to rob me but to 'like… er, get to know me. I got to my feet, said, 'You're not doing that either. Push off!' And he shrank into the night. After that I couldn't settle so I walked a few hundred yards to a more deserted area and dozed on and off until dawn in the lee of a beached rowboat.

I had very little money but I treated myself to a cheap bowl of soup at Lyons Corner House, then hiked back to the pier. I tried to get a temporary job – any job, anything that needed doing – among the numerous booths, carousels, mirror galleries, amusement arcades, but no one would take me on. In the late afternoon I was walking along one of the main streets when I came to an Army Recruiting Office. Outside, among various notices, was one showing a Guardsman in full regalia pointing a huge finger at me, saying, 'The Coldstream Guards wants YOU!' Then I remembered the splendid Bob Condy, my father's friend and sales colleague, and how he had told me that if I ever joined the Army I should be sure to try for the Guards as if I made it to Sergeant I could come out and snap up a commission in any line regiment, so good and highly regarded was the Guards' training.

Inside, aside from remarking I might be too small (to which I replied I was stronger than I looked), the Recruiting Officer took down my details then asked if I had my father's permission. Startled, not expecting such a question, I blurted out, 'No, er… not yet!' He told me to go and make sure my dad had agreed and to come back next day when he would sign me up. Now, I could not do that. I would have to lie about it. Not wanting to risk another night under the pier, I searched around until I found a Toc H doss-house in a back street. I'll never forget that night. I was shown into a darkened room in which five of the eight beds were already occupied, some of the men snoring away. The room stank of stale urine and when I got into the bed the sheets were damp with it. I slowly sank into a fitful sleep, then was woken up about midnight when two old men, occupants of the remaining beds, came in. They'd been to the pubs and both started pissing into a large bucket in the centre of the floor. One stopped and went to bed but the other must have had a bladder that could contain half the Atlantic Ocean for he went on and on, a loud tinkling cascade that seemed to last a good ten minutes. In the morning, though, he was the one to lend me his razor as of course, in my hurry to leave home, I'd forgotten even a toothbrush.

I wandered about until just before midday (so I would have had time to get to Henfield and back), then went into the Recruiting Office. I lied that I now had Dad's permission, and was signed on for the Coldstream Guards; five years in the Colours and seven in the Reserve. As I was to receive my call-up papers and train travel voucher in a few days I felt I had to ring home so I could pick them up. I also realized my parents would be worried about me, so I could let them know I was okay, and also tell them I'd soon be out of their hair, as I'd joined the Army.

Dad was almost incoherent on the phone but not from anger, I soon realized. 'Oh my God, Michael! Thank heaven you rang! What are you doing? Where the hell are you?'

I said I was at the bus station, Pool Valley, in Brighton.

'Don't catch any bus, Michael. I'm coming in the car to get you. I'll be there in an hour. Have you eaten?' I said I hadn't but was off to Lyons Corner House for another bowl of soup as I'd almost run out of money. 'The heck with the soup, Michael. Eat whatever you want, the biggest breakfast of your life! I'll meet you there and pay for the meal at the same time.'

It was an emotional reunion, both of us saying we hadn't meant all that had been said. Dad even hugged me and had tears in his eyes. When he heard I'd signed on in the Coldstream Guards he was really upset, and tried his best to get me out of it, even speaking to our local MP. However, he discovered that signing on for the Army was the only contract a minor could make that was binding. I had to go.

During my first weeks at the Guards training depot at Caterham, where I and the other rookies were constantly chased about and told to 'get in double time' everywhere we went by Sergeants and Corporals, all of whom seemed to be giants, I felt I must have died and gone to hell! I was seventeen and a half, skinny and long-necked, while most of the other recruits were ex-miners, railway gangers, labourers, and were bigger and mainly older than me. Along with the few recruits that arrived the same day as myself, I drew my two uniforms and kit and we were put into a Nissen hut from where we would do chores until enough new rookies arrived to make us into a full squad (platoon). Then we began formal training. This involved daily kit inspections, periods of drill, weapon training, gym and chores like potato peeling at the cookhouse, and we weren't left alone for one second. We had our own Sergeant and Corporal but the man in charge of our hut was just a full Guardsman called a 'trained soldier'. Every time we wanted to go to the loo or visit the NAAFI in our brief evening break we had to bang our feet together at the entrance door, stand to attention, and ask loudly: 'Permission to fall out please, trained soldier?'

It was like a big, rough boarding school, with the men quickly forming relationships and adjusting to one another. After I lost a barrack-room scrap with a twenty-six-year-old ex-railway policeman, I felt the only way to survive was to get tough or die! I was extremely miffed when I was not picked as one of the squad's three Recruit Leaders. My protest that I had been a Sergeant Major in the Cadet Force was greeted with hoots of derisive laughter. I liked the drill and weapon-training sessions but was less keen on the gym periods as our PT instructor seemed a bit of a sadist. There was one exercise where we dangled from the wall bars by our hands and had to lift our legs out straight in front of us. If anyone dropped his legs before the instructor blew his whistle we would have to do it all over again. The pain could be excruciating. Later, the guilty rookie was taken into the showers by the rest of us and hosed down with cold water as a punishment.

The best thing that happened in my first month was that I won our squad's cross-country race. Due to my boarding-school years I had done a lot more formal running than most of the other lads and I astonished both them and myself by panting in first. My popularity increased considerably as a result. I had a slight setback when I caught a bad stomach bug and had to spend two nights in the Sick Room which was near the Depot's sports field and running track. When I came out my eyes fell upon the empty stadium in the dusk, the dark cinder track stretching invitingly level to the first corner, and I felt as though it was school Sports Day again. I sneaked on to the track, got down in the right position and did a full 220-yard sprint, giving it a really hard go.

As I pulled up I heard a cough in the stands. Sergeant Riddick, the most feared of the Sergeants who drilled us, had been watching me silently in the dark. I was terrified, but to my astonishment he was kind, even gentle, said I could certainly shift and he would see to it that my Sergeant let me represent our squad in any competitions. He also told me I should try to get into the athletics team of whichever battalion I was posted to after my training. We weren't allowed out of the Depot for six weeks but on my first leave I was so proud of being in the Guards I refused to wear civvies and strutted about the lanes and Henfield High Street in my uniform and boots, all my brasses gleaming. I also found I had grown almost an inch.

After Caterham I had a few more weeks' training, more field work and complicated drills and weapon training at Pirbright and was then posted as a fully trained Guardsman to the 2nd Battalion Coldstream Guards in London. At Wellington Barracks I discovered that I was good at drilling my platoon and had an instinctive ability, when the marchers were a fair distance away, of judging how fast my voice would reach their ears. I could turn or halt them on a sixpence as easily at sixty yards as at ten. When the Drill Sergeant singled me out for special praise I felt very proud. At this time my battalion had to send a few selected Guardsmen to Officer Cadet Training Units, to be tested to see if any were suitable for training as officers. Perhaps because I had also been to a public school my application was successful, and, for some reason I never understood, I was made up to Lance Corporal.

Man, was I proud of those twin stripes! I whitened every single chevron with Blanco and spent all my spare time strutting about the West End of

London, proudly showing the world my promotion! At the OCTU in Catterick Camp I did well on things like map reading, marksmanship and drill, but there was a problem. Several of us slept together in a small dormitory and a few of them were loud snorers. I had always been a light sleeper, so by the end of the week I had lost a lot of sleep and was weaker than when I'd arrived. On the last day came the Assault Course, which I normally took in my stride, but – and that day is etched on my memory for ever – I just could not get over the last high obstacle. I threw myself at it three times, failed, fell back to the ground and had to be helped off the field. It was even more humiliating than when I'd come last in that cross-country race at the Henfield school. My disappointment increased a few days later when I was marched into the Battalion Office to learn I had not passed muster and was not considered officer material. I had some consolation over the coming weeks as some of us from OCTU kept in touch with one another – none of the others had passed either and it seemed clear that as the Indian Army was being disbanded at the time, those who had been promised commissions in it were coming back and snapping up the commissions in the line regiments.

At Wellington Barracks I performed the usual sentry duties at Buckingham Palace, as well as at St James's, the Bank of England and on POW Guard, and had done a few stints standing at my post outside the main gates, desperately resisting the impulse to crack into a smile or laugh as passers-by and tourists took photos and made cheeky remarks. If it got too bad we sentries could go into 'march off' mode. You banged your rifle butt on the ground twice, which meant you and the sentry next to you counted a silent 'Toop-three-ONE!', came to attention, took a pace forward, turned left or right with the usual three foot bangs, marched so many paces, performed a smart about-turn and returned to your post, all in twin unison even when many yards apart. I was once on one of these marches when a small black man in a track-suit ran past and turned to face me with a mocking grin as he ran backwards at the same pace as myself, before trotting off fast into the distance. I found out later it was Dado Marino, world featherweight champion!

Being promoted to Corporal had a strange effect on me at first. Apart from sheer juvenile pride, I became for a short while 'dead reg', which meant I enforced discipline when it wasn't really needed. Once, when many of us squaddies were off duty at the Stage Door Canteen, the Queen Mother and the then Princess Elizabeth paid an impromptu visit. I rushed and fussed about and got eight soldiers on to their feet to form a guard of honour. The Queen Mother seemed a lovely woman and she smiled sweetly and went through the motions of inspecting them. Then the Princess came up to me, also smiling, and said quietly, 'Thank you, but that wasn't really necessary!' I felt such a fool.

We Guards had other interesting jobs apart from normal guard duties and in the same year, 1947, I was put in charge of one of the major jumps at the Royal Horse of the Year show at Wembley. Our job was to replace the poles when a horse knocked them off. I distinctly remember how after one of the French riders had shouted something unpleasant at us, we set the poles right on the very edges of the holders when he next came round, but set them well back and tight for the other riders. He knocked them off all right! I was pleased a day or two later that a newspaper photographer must have thought I looked smart because a big picture of me by my jump, and a horse going over it, was printed across four columns of *The Times*.

I was also rather chuffed on my next Buckingham Palace duty to be appointed Corporal of the Guard, which meant one had to march a squad of soldiers around the Palace perimeter and install a sentry at each post with the usual elaborate foot stamps and rifle slaps. The Corporal then had to march smartly up to the Guard Commander in the Palace forecourt, halt, give the rifle salute and shout, 'Order Boards and Sentry Boxes inspected and found correct, SIR!'

All went well, and I mounted all the sentries without mishap. But when I was marching into the Palace forecourt, the only soldier moving from the whole Guard contingent in full public gaze, and was approaching the Guard Commander standing in front of the Palace, now glowing brightly in sudden sunlight, I was overcome with nerves. I slammed my feet into the halt, gave the rifle salute, and shouted, 'Order Boxes and Sentry Boards inspected and found correct, SIR!'

'You bloody fool!' hissed the Guard Commander through contorted lips.

When we dismounted guard and were marching back through the gates of Wellington Barracks, its Guard House on the right, the Sergeant of the Guard shouted, 'Corporal Tomkies... right WHEEL!' I trundled into the Guard House, sure I would be shoved into a cell, but luckily I got away with being held for just a few minutes while receiving a smart dressing-down from the company Sergeant Major.

Shortly after this I found myself transferred to the battalion's Motor Transport section. I thoroughly enjoyed the driving out to the Ruislip area of country roads and learning how to drive Bedford one-ton trucks. My driving skills were soon up to standard but I didn't do so well on the maintenance side, dirty, oily, mechanical work, especially when it had to be done outdoors in an icy winter. I was then put into the motorbike section and was thrilled to have my own wheezy, noisy and rather ancient AJS bike. I loved the training, especially the field work, racing over hilly, sandy ground in Surrey, and also when I had to run messages and packets between various Army units in and around London.

The only drawback now was that the full Sergeant in charge of MT took a dislike to me early on and made it clear he didn't think I had any right to be a Corporal, especially not in his MT unit. I had been put in charge of a barrack room of men, most of whom were much older than me and knew all the 'old soldier' dodges. The Sergeant sometimes flaunted my inadequacies in front of them and, thus encouraged, a few would rebel against any slight command from me. Eventually, I overreacted and reported two of them for insubordination. This probably caused me more worry than it did them for once again I was losing sleep.

One winter morning, with snow falling, I was delivering a packet on a route which took me through Piccadilly Circus. I was going a bit too fast, my mind on my barrack-room troubles, when suddenly the front wheel of my motorbike slid to the left as I was halfway round the Circus. Down I went, and round and round, slithering and sliding in the snow, fearing my head would be bashed in on the kerb, until the bottom of the bike slammed to a halt up against a lamp-post. The bike wasn't totally wrecked but damaged enough to make it unrideable without repair. One of the Bedford trucks had to be sent from the Barracks to pick it up. And who should be driving it but my friend the Sergeant. Shortly after this I was not too surprised to find myself out of the MT and back in my old barrack room, but what I didn't realize at the time – although I should have done – was that I was now a superfluous Lance Corporal in my old platoon.

On my next Buckingham Palace guard I was only Junior Corporal but I got through my duties without mishap. The following day after we had marched back to Barracks I was informed that I was on Company Orders next morning, having been reported by the Senior Corporal, Syd, for having left a dirty bed area while on guard. I knew I had left my bed area pristine and was incensed. I had thought of Syd as a friend and went up to him.

'Did you report me for having a dirty bed area?'

'Yes, I did.'

'Well, Syd, you've had your chips as far as I'm concerned.'

'You heard that!' shouted Syd at two squaddies who were watching all this. 'Fall in and follow me!' And the trio marched out before I could finish what I was saying. Within moments they returned with the Company Sergeant Major who, when I admitted saying Syd had had his chips, refused to listen to my explanation that I only meant as far as our friendship was concerned, and marched me with the two soldiers out over the tarmac to the Guard Room.

The following morning I was marched into Commandant's Orders, found guilty not only of a dirty bed area but of insubordination to a superior NCO, and was stripped of my rank. I was busted, a mere guardsman again, and had lost my beloved tapes. To me, at eighteen, this seemed a total calamity. My troubles continued to an extent when I was back in the Guardsmen's mess and ran into the two older squaddies I'd reported in the MT and one or two others I'd yelled at when I was a Corporal. Suffice it to say that a few 'Montgomery Cliff in *From Here to Eternity*' scuffles behind the bike sheds followed, but as I had taken up boxing training in my spare time, I just about held my own, and escaped with only minor cuts and bruises.

After this my idealistic desire to be 'dead reg' and do everything by the book began to wane, and on my next, and last, stint on guard duty at Buckingham Palace, I did something I would never have done before being stripped of my stripes. For the first time I and another guardsman with whom I was friendly were posted as sentries on the edge of the huge gardens at the rear of the Palace. It was a warm late spring night and overlooked by no one, we relaxed and met together for a chat. We were laughing about how sometimes the two Princesses, Elizabeth and Margaret, used to walk out and back through the gates, to make the guardsmen spring to attention and present arms! They were delightful young girls, and Margaret especially was developing into a real beauty. My pal wondered idly whether if we looked through the rear windows we might be able to see her in her bedroom, maybe getting undressed! Or even having a shower! We could hear water cascading from a waterfall not far away and we knew there was a lake in the grounds and that there were some punts on the water.

'Come on,' I said, 'let's take the slings off our rifles, find one of the punts and paddle out on to the lake. The further away we get, the better the angle to see into the windows!'

We removed the khaki–Blancoed slings, laid them in a dry spot, then stole about carefully until we found one of the punts moored at the water's edge. Feeling like Indian poachers, we silently slid out, using our broad rifle butts as paddles, until we were at the far western edge of the lake. We didn't see Princess Margaret, *deshabillée* or not, nor anyone else. The few Palace windows that were lit had hefty curtains drawn across them. We paddled back, dried our rifle butts before water damaged their hard-won polish, replaced the slings and were back at our posts with no one any the wiser.

About this time, partly because of the occasional barrack-room squabbles and because I was still a bit skinny, I took up weight-training and boxing – not because I liked boxing any more than I had at school, but so that I might better defend myself. And if you were good enough to get picked for the team you could get struck off some duties. I felt one night of pain was well worth missing many weeks of guard duties. I was better than average but certainly not champion material, as evinced by being floored in the third round of my last bout by a fellow soldier called Jerry, who I recall was built like a white Mike Tyson. I took some solace from the fact that Jerry was occasionally taken off duty so he could be one of the sparring partners of Joe Louis, who was training in London and was then the world heavyweight champion.

I still had only one ruse when fighting: spend the first round and a half on the defensive, take a few shots where they didn't do much damage, thus lulling your opponent into thinking he can kill you, make a few plays to his solar plexus with your weaker left hand so he thinks that's where you're aiming for and drops his guard. Then choose the exact moment and let go your hardest right shot to his head. It worked – sometimes! I did learn a ruse that Jerry taught me – three left jabs in a row, on fast-advancing feet. He had apparently impressed Joe Louis with it. I was always scared stiff before a fight and my corner in the ring before the first round was, to me, the loneliest place in the world.

At this time – and after all I was still a teenager – I became over-concerned about my appearance. I wanted my narrow waist and narrow shoulders to become a narrow waist and broad shoulders, and my skinny arms to be muscular arms. Obviously I could not have a set of heavy weights in the barrack room so I invested in a Charles Atlas course and did his exercises in 'dynamic tension', whereby you need no equipment but pit one set of muscles against another. I also bought a three-spring pull-out exerciser which I was forced to use in front of the other soldiers. Mostly, the lads were tolerant of one another's little quirks and foibles. No one laughed at the two lads who knelt by their beds each night and said their prayers. And if one of them accused me of pulling the springs because I wanted to look tough, I could disarm them by saying things like, 'No, I'm just trying to stop looking so weak!' We were now allowed to walk out in civvy clothes and I bought myself a Sherwood-green corduroy jacket, a red bow tie and a bright yellow waistcoat, and strutted about thinking myself quite a dandy! And to disguise my narrow shoulders before all the exercising put on genuine muscle, I sewed little pads on the inner shoulders of my jacket, as I did with my best drill uniform.

I did far better at athletics than I ever did at boxing. When the battalion were putting together a team, remembering my successes at the Training Depot, I put my name down. A group of us budding athletes were trucked out to the Tooting Bec stadium and put through our paces. I did well enough at the half mile, long jump, javelin and discus to get picked for the team. Paradise days followed, for the chosen team were struck off all guard duties for three months. I can still see in my mind's eye that sunlit cinder track in the early morning, pristine because no one had set foot on it, stretching before me with such intense invitation. I was free to jog, trot or hurl myself round it as fast as I could. My best time for the half mile, according to our training Sergeant was 1 min 53 sec. I loved the training, experimenting with different techniques for the long jump, throwing the javelin and hurling the discus, and how glad I was of my months with my home-made discus at school, for they had enabled me to lay down a foundation of tendon and muscle that was easier to retrain than if I'd started from scratch. No one else in our team had even seen a discus, let alone thrown one.

On the big day, before which I'd managed a better fitful sleep than on other such occasions, I came second in the discus, third in the half mile, fourth in the javelin, and can't remember where in the long jump as I was certainly not placed. My most enduring memory was of the 4 by 440-yard relay, for which I had to run the anchor leg. I was terrified of letting my team down but when the other three athletes were haring round the first corner before I was even handed the baton for my leg I felt intense relief, if not gratitude. No one could expect me to make up a good eighty yards to the next athlete, though I like to think I reduced the gap a little.

All this physical activity made me very fit – fitter than I have been before or since – and my weight was up to 13 stone 2 lbs, my heaviest ever, and none of it was fat. My confidence soared, and I had come to love London's feverish city life, so much so that my returns on leave to my parents and village became less frequent and even shooting rabbits and pigeons with Jim Adkins seemed tame. I developed spare time routines: on fine days I'd hike to the Serpentine, hire a skiff and row up and down for hours, surprised to find I was as good if not better at rowing (now called sculling) than I was at running. I won most of the bets with other amateurs, which gave me extra money to go to the cinema or scoff ice cream at a new parlour in Piccadilly started up by a young Tony Forte, who often told me of his ambitions. Little could I have guessed he would become Lord Forte, one of the richest men in Britain and owner of countless hotels, all long after I lost touch with him. On rainy days I'd head for the long cartoons programme at the little News Theatre in Soho and treat myself to a good meal at Lyons Corner House, the epitome of luxury to me at that time. On fine nights I would wander with a pal round Soho, chatting to the younger, amateur 'ladies of the night' in Soho's magical streets, or drift up to Hyde Park Corner, listen to the various orators and try to pick up pretty girls.

I succeeded once and thus met the first love of my life. Her name was Jean and she was a nurse at St Stephen's Hospital in Fulham. She was older than me, had laugh lines round her bright blue eyes, and while not beautiful, she had a bubbly, cheerful nature and was very easy to be with. She used a heady orange-blossom type of perfume and for the first weeks of our romance I wanted only to snuggle up to her soft warm body, cuddling and kissing, while lying under a tree in Hyde Park or amid bushes in Kensington Gardens. In fact I don't recall we ever did anything else. I was sure I loved her and would feel agonized if a guard duty forced me to postpone a date with her.

Eventually, the night came when Jean said yes. There was a half moon in the balmy summer air and a nightingale sang from the shrubbery, but when I climbed clumsily on top of her, I couldn't do it! I was let down, literally, by my wedding equipment, A combination of anxiety, inexperience and even fear had made me impotent. When this happened on our next two dates, I was so worried that I consulted our Army doctor, wondering if I might be a latent homosexual. He just laughed it off, assured me it was quite common for the first time, that I should just relax and it would all just happen naturally at the right time.

It was on my next date with Jean, in a grassy hollow in Kensington Gardens, that I lost my virginity. Afterwards, love-panting heavily, I looked up to see we were only yards away from the statue of Pan, which somehow seemed highly appropriate.

Naturally I felt heartbroken when at the end of the summer, Jean said she could not meet me any more. She had fallen in love with someone else, a young doctor at her hospital, who liked to take her to the cinema or theatre. Looking back, I can hardly blame her. The only place I ever took her was into the shrubbery!

The loss of my first love, combined with a rising, more confident libido, propelled me, a fit nineteen-year-old, to look for sexual gratification elsewhere. Having no other outlets, my pal and I increased our chatting-up of the younger amateur ladies of Soho, who often stopped us and asked if we wanted 'a good time'. Street prostitution was all quite innocent in those immediate post-war years. If one *did* want a 'good time' it was thirty shillings, a quick climb up some rickety stairs into a sordid little room, a short grapple on the bed and 'Thanks dear' and away. This is what some of our fellow soldiers told us but we two had never done it.

One night we were prowling around the darker alleys when we heard muffled voices and giggling. Cautiously we peered round the corner, just in time to see three girls apparently comparing their breasts. As one was pushing hers back into her bra under her jumper, a really beautiful blonde lifted her sweater and bra outwards and up, to reveal the most beautiful breasts I had ever seen, or could even have imagined. They were large and firm and yet also long, and they tilted slightly upwards at their tips. As if to emphasize their charms, the girl gave a little wriggle, and it was the way the breasts swayed, slowly and independently, as well as the girl's beautiful, laughing face that induced in me a rather sudden rampant rise. As my pal and I quickly withdrew we looked at each other and both said it at the same time, 'Bloody hell!'

Despite our excitement we were both too embarrassed to make an approach, apart from our unwritten code that we would not pay for sex – it was a matter of pride – but during the next week of guard duties and drills, I couldn't get this crazy gorgeous girl out of my mind. On my next night out I went looking for her, and I didn't tell my pal, nor that I had a crisp £1 note and ten shillings in my pocket. I soon located her, on a corner of Berwick Street, and as I walked towards her I assumed she would accommodate me. But when I was mere yards away one of her mates further on said something and she turned her head so couldn't see me until I was past her. Now what? I walked on round the next corner, spent a few moments checking that my cap angle and my uniform were as neat as possible, then, heart pounding and desperately hoping, I walked slowly back. This time she did step forward and said, 'Hello lovey, feel like a good time?'

'Er, yes!' I said a bit too eagerly, then blurted out without thinking, 'I've got the thirty shillings!'

'Oh no,' she said. 'I charge more. It's two pounds for a short time.'

'I… I… I've only got thirty bob,' I stammered. 'I'm very sorry,' and went to walk off. But she held up her hand with a slight smile. God, she was gorgeous! She took a step to one side, cocked her head slightly, looking at me intently, then said, 'Will you take your cap off?'

'Eh? Er, what…?'

'Just take off your cap!'

I did as she asked, she looked at me for a few moments more, then her right hand came up and riffled roughly through my thick mop of dark brown curly hair, ending with a slight tug and that airy laugh. 'Oh, come on then!'

What followed was a truly blissful time. Although I was somewhat inept at first, largely because I felt I had to do it fast and leave, she was gentle, whispering, 'There's no hurry,' and she even asked what kinds of things excited me (the phrase 'What turns you on?' had not been invented then!). I was still so inexperienced I couldn't think of anything special, so she performed provocative little poses and movements, and by the time we were making love, it was better than anything I'd experienced in my nine-month romance with Jean. Her name was Betty and she came from Hull of all places, yet her northern accent was only slight, her voice sexily husky. She seemed to take my money with some reluctance and then said she hoped we would meet again. All I could think of to say was, 'You can bet on it.'

It wasn't long before Betty and I struck up an odd relationship, sort of occasional 'sex friends'. The word 'love' was never mentioned and rather than accept money she preferred for me to take her out when she wasn't working – in the mornings and some afternoons. So I took her rowing on the Serpentine and to the cartoons show, and we caught buses to an ice rink as we both liked ice skating. What a sight she was, sailing around in her short skirt, showing off those perfect breasts and legs. Quite a few men tried to get chatting to her.

The only drawback in Betty's life was that a former boyfriend had followed her down from Hull and was trying to be her pimp, both to help find clients and take a percentage of her earnings. Their initial affair had been brief, once she found out that Leo had a tendency towards violence and often drank too much. She was having trouble in shaking him off.

One late afternoon Betty and I were talking on the pavement, about to go to the cinema, when a tall, swarthy man approached us. 'It's Leo' she had time to hiss before he grabbed her arm with his right hand, pulled her towards him and said she was to go with him as he had a 'special' lined up for her. As she protested and tried to pull her arm free, I said, 'Hey. Leave off! She's with me,' and grabbed his arm.

'Get lost, you!' snarled Leo, glaring at me with contempt. As he swept my left hand high into the air with his right arm, I saw his front body was exposed and unprotected, and without thinking I drove a real pile-driver of a right into his solar plexus, powered by the thrust of my right leg. We heard the air burst from his lungs and he staggered away, bent double, seeking a shop's alcove for support. As we walked away and had covered a few yards, he recovered his breath enough to choke out a threat that he would get even.

Over our next few meetings it was clear Leo had not given up, but he had changed tactics, pulling cry-baby stunts, swearing his real love for Betty, and in a final effort to get rid of him she had given him a fair sum of money on condition he left her alone. Even so, she felt it would be safer to change her area of work and would now operate in the Notting Hill Gate area. We arranged that our future meeting place would be outside the gates of St Mary's Hospital.

All seemed well with our occasional trysts over the next month. It was now the end of summer, and on an extended leave, instead of going home to Henfield, I stayed a week with an Army pal in Croydon, partly to be nearer Betty and also so that we, or I alone, could use the nearby Purley Ice Rink. I was still keen on ice-skating. When I phoned her before our next meeting she said she thought Leo had caught up with her. She was sure she had seen him twice, skulking nearby in the dark, but he had not approached her. After we had walked back from the cinema we were lingering, kissing goodnight by the hospital gates as Betty was temporarily shacking up in a small flat with one of her mates, so I couldn't go back with her. Suddenly we heard the sound of running feet.

'It's Leo!' gasped Betty. Everything seemed to happen in slow motion as he ran towards me shouting, 'Bastard! Now you're going to get it!' and I saw him pull out a knife. Terrified, the adrenalin rush must have sharpened my reactions, for I just got my left shoulder up and felt a sharp pain in it from the knife that had been meant for my face. He was still coming forward so I stiffened my right leg and my right fist caught him flush on the side of his jaw. There was a weird scream and down he went, clutching at his jaw with both hands. Then Betty screamed, 'You're bleeding!' Blood was pouring through my best civvy shirt from the wounds in my left shoulder. She helped me stagger into the hospital, my right hand clapped tight over the gashes. The nurses managed to stem the flow and a few minutes later a doctor put five stitches in the wounds under local anaesthetic. The cuts were in the shape of a small cross – a cross that had been meant for my face – and I still have the scars to prove it. I also had a very swollen, painful right hand but luckily none of the fingers was broken.

Before we left we saw Leo being helped into the hospital by two men who'd found him lying on the pavement, but he was taken into a different cubicle further away and he didn't see us. I noticed his bottom jaw was twisted to the right. Betty knew a nurse in the hospital and heard later that Leo's jaw had been broken on one side and fractured on the other. If only I could have found a punch like that against Jerry!

From now on my affair with Betty began to unravel, not only because the Leo incident had sickened me, but she was giving up 'the game', having been accepted as a trainee nurse at the hospital, and I was transferred to the 1st Battalion, which was being sent to Palestine.

8
Shot at in Palestine

It was as our unit sailed across the Mediterranean in the *Empire Trooper* that my spring exercises got me into trouble. We lower ranks were crammed under decks in a fetid hold where there was no room for normal beds. Instead, we had to sleep in narrow, uncomfortable hammocks, often only two feet apart, and many of us were strangers to one another. Tempers were often short. I tried to do my exercises when most of the others were up on deck or at least try to expand the springs between the hammocks rather than across them. But one hefty chap took umbrage one night, accusing me not only of showing off but of invading his bed space. An argument ensued, and I was challenged to a fight.

The other lads welcomed this diversion, quickly unhooked hammocks and formed a sort of ring, and we were at it, my heart pounding with fear. I threw out two tentative lefts which didn't connect, then covered up so that my opponent's blows landed on my arms and elbows, and after nearly two minutes he was blowing hard. I focused on his solar plexus area and aimed three lefts towards it. He dropped his guard and over went my right, to crash on his temple and send him staggering. Instantly two Corporals, both good amateur boxers themselves, stopped the fight. I was relieved, and even more so when my opponent wanted to shake hands. We became quite pally after that and when he asked to have a go on my springs, I let him.

My memories of those first months in Palestine are somewhat vague. At just nineteen I had no political nous whatever, and knew only that we were there to keep the Arabs and Jews apart, mount various guards and patrols, and still do a lot of drills, square bashing. We were installed in a tented encampment at Nathanya and while I loved the continual sun and the huge free Jaffa oranges, the murder of two Sergeants who were strung up in a eucalyptus grove two days after we arrived reminded us we were on serious business. This being so, I increasingly viewed the frequent parades and drills in the hot sun as unnecessary, and I wanted to get out of them somehow. This desire increased when I was put on rooftop guard on a tall square building that housed an armoury.

I was posted by the ramparts on the west side of the roof while another Guardsman, one I knew only slightly, was posted on the eastern edge. We were warned to keep watch but carefully, keeping our heads down as much as possible. I could discern little as dusk came on, just whispering pines and white buildings with pinkish roofs. After about an hour I heard a sudden smack from where my colleague was stationed, then the bang, clearly from a rifle. I looked across, just in time to see the top of the back of his head fly off and hit the floor on which he stood, with a combined thump and plop. It was like a jelly with a crust on it hitting the ground. As his rifle clattered down, he too, or rather his body, fell back and hit the rooftop with a terrible thump. I knew I could do nothing, that he was certainly dead, and dashed down for medical help. One look at my white, shocked face meant that I was taken off duty and no new guard was set on that rooftop that night.

It was only about two weeks later that I too was deliberately shot at. I was on a two-man foot patrol in the back streets of Haifa with Guardsman Davis, who was quite a character. He had the sensitive, aquiline features of an aristocrat, and he also spoke like one. Apparently, he had started out in an officer training squad but for some mysterious misdemeanour had been relegated to one of the other-ranks training squads, He had a fondness for practical jokes and also subtle remarks which took the mickey out of any verbal opponent without that individual quite realizing it. On this day we were nearing a run-down 'red light' area when he lifted his tunic and revealed the handle of a small revolver tucked into a holster. As we were not carrying our rifles, this made me feel a lot safer, and we decided to look further into the area in the hope of a little fun. We were passing a three-foot-high whitewashed wall, just before a left-hand corner, when I heard sudden dull thuds, then saw thick flakes of plaster flying off the wall. I was momentarily perplexed, then I heard the '*crack crack crack*' of an automatic rifle. We realized some rooftop sniper was shooting at us, and we must both have broken the world's 50-metre dash to shoot round the corner, from whence we beat a hasty retreat. Davis then showed me his 'revolver'. It was a dummy, its body made of wood!

It was after I had spent a bitterly cold Christmas Day and night on guard at Lydda airport, when I'd fired a shot over the head of an Arab who ignored my call to halt and tried to climb the perimeter fence, that I got my chance finally to escape all the onerous parades and guard duties.

A vacancy occurred for a clerk in the Brigade Office and as I had more than rudimentary shorthand and typing abilities, due to the weeks I spent at Brighton Technical College, I went into the interview talking my head off. I was sent to the Chief Clerk, a Scot, with the equal rank of an RSM. He told me to take down a long sentence and read it back to him. Luckily, he used simple words and I did it without hesitation. I got the job.

For months I loved the work, the freedom from hard soldiering, the regular hours, and I worked hard, wanting to please my new boss, who was softly spoken and kind for a Guards NCO. I spent as much time in the office as I could, improving my typing and trying to take down shorthand from radio broadcasts. As my work improved I was marched into Company Orders and promoted once more to Lance Corporal. Daft though it seems to me now in my old age, I was delighted at getting my tapes back. The trouble was, there were now no girls to show them off to!

For some reason I hardly ever drank while in the Army, perhaps because of the memory of how awful I'd felt after that New Year's Eve drinking orgy with my dad and the French-Canadian erks, and I spent a lot of my spare time reading. When the Brigade Office was moved to a beautiful white villa amid the pines up Mount Carmel, Haifa, another clerk and I were given a room of our own, small but peaceful. It was after helping in the base library and reading inspiring works by Vera Brittain, J. B. Priestley, Rudyard Kipling, the Myths of Greece and Rome, even superb short stories by Guy de Maupassant, that I decided I wanted to be a writer. I was most impressed by a phrase of Vera Brittain's which went something like: 'The task of the artist is to show – at one and the same time – Life As It Is – Life As It Ought To Be.' It seemed a good formula for a budding author.

By correspondence, I enrolled in the Short Story Course at the London School of Journalism and set to with a will, churning out short stories for the approval, or otherwise, of my mentors. I still have those short stories and cannot read any of them without squirming with embarrassment. I once copied out all the long words I didn't know from a copy of Merriam and Webster's Dictionary, then wrote a short story using as many of these obscure long words as I could, totally out of step with Hemingway's later dictum to any writer: 'Always prefer the short word to the long.' But at least I spent most of my spare time over the next two years learning how to string words together.

These were idyllic days, and I was working as one of the clerks to Brigadier G. F. L Johnson, who was planning the Army evacuation of Haifa, but on the day before we embarked I fell ill. I had a terrible headache and any bright light hurt my eyes so much I had to keep them closed. I was carried on to the ship on a stretcher and taken straight into the hospital ward. I still faintly recall two military doctors standing over my bed and shaking their heads. One, a Captain, said I ought to be taken straight back to the UK as they suspected meningitis. 'Oh yes, please!' I remember thinking, but the other was a Major and he said I should go to the military field hospital in Tel El Kebir, Egypt. To my dismay, the Major's opinion prevailed. I was given a very unpleasant lumbar puncture and the next thing I recall was a long, jolting, dusty drive across the desert in an ambulance, unable to open my eyes for pain, sure I was going to die, and then the blurred days in the primitive ward where I slowly recovered. I was sent to a transit camp in Famagusta, Cyprus, then shipped to rejoin my Brigade Office which was now based in Tripoli, Libya.

Here I began offering to do other men's overnight duties in the Brigade Office so I could not only extend my studies and continue to read what I felt was classic literature but escape having to sleep in the large, noisy barrack room. Although I was a clerk I was the only Corporal in the room and was expected to keep order. This I hated.

Over the months my night-time studies took on a more philosophical bent and the main catalyst for this was Tolstoy's great novel *War and Peace*, especially when I read the line 'A good soldier requires a total absence of philosophical enquiring doubt.' This is what I now had in plenty as I was beginning to question the necessity of having an army at all. I buried myself in some of the works of the iconoclastic philosopher Ralph Waldo Emerson, and began to compose ponderous treatises with titles like 'An Idealist's Survey' and 'The Philosophy of Justice'. I went for long, lonely walks in the desert writing notes, *bons mots*, little essays in philosophy and nostalgic descriptions of the woods and fields of my boyhood. I became more and more frustrated with the regimented, repetitive life of an army clerk, and began writing long, agonizing letters home. I thought I might escape the tedium by applying for a transfer to the Education Corps where I might meet men who had more on their minds than booze and football.

One night the Brigade Major came weaving in from the officers' club and found me engrossed in Karl Marx's *Das Kapital*. When his report on my application landed in the chief clerk's In tray two nights later I surreptitiously steamed the envelope open and was shocked to read, 'Not recommended. I fear this soldier's beliefs will conflict with his loyalty to King and Country...' I had been given no chance to explain I was merely reading the book, that even at twenty I found communism to be a conspiracy against true individuality.

The injustice of the fact that I couldn't even protest as I was not supposed to have read his report, infuriated me.

I had only sold one of the nineteen stories and articles I had written, a nostalgic yarn about an old gamekeeper and a young boy deep in the Sussex countryside. It had been bought by the American *Saturday Evening Post*, of all magazines. They paid me quite well, and by doing other clerks' duties and not going out to bars and clubs, I had saved a bit more, but I was well short of the £97 required to buy myself out of the regular Army. Here, my dad came to the rescue, offering to lend me the balance of £40 (at 5 per cent interest!), and even though I had now been promised I would soon be made up to Lance Sergeant, I put in my application for Discharge By Purchase.

As for my attitude to communism, in one of my short stories I had an American say, 'Communists say the trouble with democracy is that it's just a free for all. Exactly, pal, but say it *real* slow – FREE FOR ALL. Get rid of all the nasty little whip-cracking capitalists on the poor serfs' aching backs, and what do you get? Nasty little whip-cracking commissars on the poor serfs' aching backs. Instead of you having five bucks and him having three bucks, everyone gets TWO bucks! That's communism, buddy.'

While it may appear I had become a real prig at this time, the needs of my young flesh were still there, and once I knew my application was going through, I'm afraid I went a bit mad. I had palled up with another Corporal called Robbo, who was not only more streetwise than I but played a mean honky-tonk piano. I would go with him to the NAAFI club in Tripoli and sit for an hour or more, envying his dextrous finger control and the catchy music he could make. A French ship had just entered the harbour and two of the sailors joined us at the piano, also loving Robbo's playing. They spoke good English and later we all went for a drink in a bar, the first time for me in the Army. We had a few, then the sailors said they were going to a special club in the Casbah where we could meet beautiful girls, quite cheap too! Robbo said the Casbah was strictly out of bounds to us British soldiers but provided we kept a lookout for military police and just took a quick look we'd be all right.

To my surprise the little club was warm, discreet and inviting. Soft music played and the air was faintly perfumed. Two of the girls were very attractive, and one of them came up to me with a big smile and slid her arm through mine. Reluctantly we said we could not stay but I tried to tell her I would return – how, without getting into trouble, I didn't know. That night, before sleeping on the bed I always made up on my desk in the Brigade Office, I had an idea.

The next time I met the sailor with whom I'd been most friendly I persuaded him to lend me his French shore pass/identity card. He agreed, for the equivalent of a fiver, but said he must have the document back by tomorrow evening or he would have trouble back at the boat. I hurried back to barracks and spent nearly all the night making a forged copy. The pass had very small print and the letters were close together. In the office I found a typewriter with the correct-size letters but the gaps between were too large. I had to type one letter, backtrack half a space and type the next, and so on for the whole document. It took *hours*! There was a red seal on the pass which I managed to match with a combination of red ink and correcting fluid of nearly the same colour, slightly smudged when almost dry to give it a worn, authentic look. As for my French name, I finally came up with Jacques Toussin and scrawled it on the document with the thickest nib I could find.

The following evening I found my sailor friend, anxiously waiting in the NAAFI club, and gave him back his pass but was so tired from the tricky, nervy, delicate work of forging the document and my near sleepless night that I didn't go to the Casbah. Instead, on the way back to barracks, needing to complete my disguise, I bought a short length of black woolly material. The following night, with expeditious use of scissors and sewing needle, I made a creditable French beret!

It was on my second visit to the club in the Casbah, when I had just been led into a little room by my girl and was about to follow her into bed, that two British military policemen came through the door without knocking and asked for my identity.

'*Oui, oui. Bien entendu*,' I said with what I hoped was a relaxed smile. '*Je suis un matelot française*.' I handed over my pass and dropped my beret on the bed. Without looking at me again, one of the cops gave me back my pass, winked at the girl, said, 'Enjoy yourself, mate' and left.

I only went to the Casbah once more after that, not only because I needed to save money but because my discharge papers came through, I was boated back to Blighty on another troopship and formally discharged from the Army at Aldershot.

9
Cub Reporter and Cycle Racer

Back in Henfield I felt like an old man, a man who'd been halfway round the world, been shot at twice and had taken his first steps as an author. I bought a walking stick, tried to grow a beard, and walked round the Common feeling like Methuselah!

On my arrival home Dad had initially treated me like the prodigal son. For my twenty-first birthday he not only bought me a smart, discreet grey suit 'for your first job', but took me and Jim Adkins to the greyhound racing at Hove stadium. I put two bob on a hound called Bill's Wish, just because I liked the name and had an Uncle Bill, and won ten bob. I risked another two bob but lost it and decided to pocket the six shillings remaining and not bet any more. 'Very sensible,' said Dad – rare praise.

It was soon obvious I could not earn a living as an author, so I hoped to get a job as a cub reporter on a small provincial newspaper. This was on the advice of J. B. 'Lysander' Morton, who wrote the Beachcomber column in the *Daily Express* and with whom Dad had shared an Observer Corps dugout in the war. My many letters yielded no results as I simply had no experience.

In the end it was my dad who got me my first job. One of his lady buyers in Bognor Regis was the sister of Basil Acford, who owned the *Observer* series of three provincial newspapers in Chichester, Bognor and Midhurst. Before long, wearing my new suit, I was ushered into the presence of Jimmy Neal, editor of the *Chichester Observer.* I followed Dad's instructions to the letter – initially, money was not important. I needed experience, would work hard, and would expect to advance purely on my ability, if any! 'The trick is to try and make yourself indispensable – then hit 'em for more money,' Dad said.

I liked Jimmy Neal immediately, He seemed always to be smiling, had a terrific sense of humour, and even took me for a beer. I was delighted to learn about a week later that I was to be hired as a trainee reporter for a trial period of three months, for the princely sum of thirty-five shillings a week. I located digs at thirty bob a week with a family that ran a grocery shop in Whyke Lane, which was probably why the food was good and plentiful. The only drawback was I had to share a bedroom with a mechanic called Joe who was a nice guy but snored a lot.

I threw myself into this new life with a mixture of fear and a desperate desire to do the work well and please Mr Neal. At first I was put on the routine stuff – calls to fire and police stations and undertakers, taking details of the recently deceased from their relatives, noting the names of mourners at gravesides, just as we had to get all the names of winners at fêtes, flower shows, even whist drives. The theory was that anyone named in the paper would buy a copy.

My first break came at the end of my second week. I had ridden out to Bosham one summer evening on the office bike, a tired old racer, and after a half of beer saw lights twinkling out on the water as a small boat came into the harbour. I suggested it was late to be out fishing to the man next to me. 'Fishing?' he repeated. 'More like smuggling!' My mind latched on to this in a trice and I got a good quote from him, and from the pub's landlord too. I walked round the darkened harbour, getting some atmospheric notes, and back at the office typed out my story which I left on the editor's desk.

Next morning I felt disappointment when Jimmy Neal handed my story back to me, but this changed to delight when he said, 'Get a good quote from the police and we'll use it.' I was delighted when that week's paper came out – my story was the main lead on the front page. My first scoop! We three reporters were encouraged to think up 'readers' letters' in case too few real ones came in. One morning I walked past the big clock at the City Cross when I saw there were different times displayed on two of the dials. My letter was from an 'irate train user' who'd glanced at the first dial (8.25 a.m.) and thought he had a good five minutes to saunter down to the railway station, only to see his train steaming away. The second dial, which he would have had to screw his head round to see, had shown the correct time of 8.30 a.m.

By the end of my first month I was obviously doing quite well as Mr Neal handed me a typed letter which said my trial period was over and I was hired as a permanent staff member at the Union rate of £4 2s. 6d a week. It seemed a fortune at the time, and now I could afford to pay Dad back the £40 he'd lent me – at the rate of ten bob a week. Gradually, I was trusted to cover more difficult jobs like parish councils, city magistrates' court, and annual meetings of bodies like the St John's Ambulance Brigade and the British Legion, as well as the occasional property fire and once even a plane crash. When news was short I was dispatched to the many villages surrounding Chichester to look for stories and dig up special features. Naturally, all this dashing around meant I had to cover many miles on the office's old racer but I didn't mind as I found I loved cycling, and began to develop large leg muscles. One day I was going at a good pace up to Lavant when I heard the swish of wheels and the whirring of a chain, and a cyclist in full racing gear went past me. For some reason I hated being passed on a bike, in fact I was quite obsessive about it, and when I glimpsed this one had grey hair under his racing cap I trod on the pedals, swept past him deliberately with my hands off the handlebars, and made sure I had left him a good distance behind by the time I pulled up outside the church where I was due to meet the local vicar.

To my surprise, instead of just sweeping past, he pulled up with a huge grin on his face and said if I could push my old crate of a bike as fast as that maybe I should take up racing. He was a veteran rider and co-founder of the Chichester Cycling Club and he thought I ought to become a member. I thanked him and said I'd bear it in mind. By now I had realized I needed a far better bike both for my work and pleasure riding and had ordered one to be made to my own specifications from the private firm of Carlton, with twenty-eight inch wheels instead of the usual twenty-seven. It took me many weeks to scrape together the £46 it cost. Just before I collected my gleaming new black and white bike at the shop, I happened to go to the local Odeon, to do a brief write-up of the week's movie for my paper. Before it, on came *Movietone News*, and my first sight of the man who has been my only sporting hero from that day to this – sprint cyclist Reg Harris.

He had just won the world sprint championship for the fourth time (Harris was *five* times world sprint champion, and he came back at the age of fifty-four and won the British pro sprint championship) and he was shown training on the road (apparently being filmed from the back of a truck), winning two sprint races and finally doing extended exercises on a special rollers machine which had a huge dial showing the speeds he was attaining. I had never seen, or even dreamt of, such raw power. His legs were like two pistons, both powerful and graceful, and the huge but oddly elegant muscles bulged and relaxed, bulged and relaxed as if each lived a separate vibrant life. I saw the dial go past the 150mph mark and gasped with admiration. When he said he had been a rather weak and sickly child I dared to wonder if I could become a top cyclist too.

I soon joined the local club and surprised everyone, myself especially, by winning a cup in my first race. True, it was the Novices' Cup, but it was a twenty-five-mile time trial in which everyone goes off at two-minute intervals, and I felt I must have done quite well as no one caught me up and overtook me. My time of 1hr 10 mins was no record breaker but it was quite fast in those days when bikes were heavier than now, and the race was held on public roads with normal traffic to cope with. (I recall that my besttime for 25 miles was 1 hour 5 minutes.) That did it really, and for much of the next two years I spent most of my spare time training. At least four times a week I did fifteen- and twenty-five-mile rides, using the fast new Chichester bypass as much as possible, before breakfast. I would then go into the office for a full day's reporting. I came third in my second race, won the third, and have now lost count for it was all over fifty years ago. How I wish I had a tenth of that energy today!

There was no cycle track in or near Chichester and it wasn't until my second year that the club began entering events in the Portsmouth and Gosport Track League. It was here that I felt I had really come into my own. I came third in the final of my very first sprint race on the banked track. Here the techniques were totally different from road racing. Usually you started slowly, manoeuvring for position and keeping your opponent high on the bank, then at what you judged the strategic moment, you made a dash for the line. I can honestly say I believe that final dash, usually about 200 metres, is the most strenuous few seconds in any 'explosive' event, and that includes the 100-metre and 50-metre dash in running. At top speed your biceps are hauling the handlebars up to counter the thrust of your foot on the same side down on the pedal to enforce maximum momentum and in such rapid succession you are literally wrenching, wrestling the bars so fast and so hard from side to side that you feel you are about to wreck the bike, to tear it in half! It was some time before I realized my road bike's frame was too 'loose', too low-angled to be ideal for the track. I needed a smaller, harder frame with sharper angles but I could not afford a second bike of good quality.

I won a few races and medals but did far better on the short time trials from one lap to one kilometre with both standing or flying starts, and I used the Chichester bypass again to practise specifically for these. When a new boarder who had a motorbike moved into the other room above the grocer's, I asked him to time me. He stayed behind me as I worked up speed and when I shouted 'Now!' and went all out he drew alongside for a few seconds, going at exactly my speed long enough to look at his own speed. When I heard him shout 'Fifty-three' as he accelerated away I thought I must have heard wrong, but when we stopped he assured me I had been going at 53 mph! I recall being very proud of myself and that when I got back to my room I examined my legs in the mirror, flexing and bending them at various angles. They had certainly thickened up but they did not match those of Reg Harris, nor, it was apparent, did my abilities as a sprint cyclist, for during my next main event on the track I had a nasty experience.

I can't quite remember now what it was, but it was a major event, between southern counties, and I'd reached the final after two races. It was a three-up between myself and two top sprinters, Paddy Mullaly and Wally Rigby (their names for ever indelible in my memory). I had kept Wally up on the embankment, with Paddy cruising along quite fast towards the first bend of the last 200-metre dash. I caught him up and had just pulled out to try to pass him and go for broke when Wally swept down fast, the slope giving him additional speed, and somehow his rear wheel swept right across my front wheel. His axle nuts must have hit my front spokes for I shot up in the air and down with a crash. I landed heavily – luckily on the grass at the side of the concrete track – and just lay there for a few seconds, not because I was knocked out but in despair because I'd lost. Two St John's Ambulance men appeared from nowhere, helped me to my feet and asked if I was okay. I remember saying, 'Yes, fine, thank you,' then recalling nothing else until I found myself standing with my bike on the wrong sea ferry going in the wrong direction. I must have boarded it while under the effects of a slight concussion. I felt peeved that none of my club colleagues had come to my aid or showed any concern, although I'd felt for some time that the few who could give me a hard time in the road races were slightly jealous of my success on the track. In fact they had all gone home by train. It was late by the time I left on the right ferry, and I had a lonely thirty-mile ride home in the dark.

I never went back to the club, not even when I slowly realized I could not really race on the track any more. One had to be in an affiliated club to take part in official races. The other reason for my lessening interest in cycling was because my paper's group was sold to the Portsmouth and Sunderland Newspaper group who owned the *Portsmouth Evening News,* and I suddenly had a lot more work on my plate. Jimmy Neal was moved to Portsmouth to edit all the Chichester, Bognor Regis and Midhurst papers, and the *News*'s Chichester man was my new boss.

Geoff White was a short, slightly hunched figure with gimlet eyes and a sharp nose, who rolled his own cigarettes endlessly. He wore a faded check overcoat several sizes too large for him and when he rode to and from work through the city streets on an old upright bike with a basket in front he reminded me of the Wicked Witch of the West in *The Wizard of Oz.* He was also a brilliant provincial journalist, a hard taskmaster, and he taught me more than any other journalist before or since.

One maxim at the time was 'If in doubt – leave out.'

'No,' said Geoff. 'If in doubt – *find* out!'

I now had to give up all my Sundays, which also impeded any cycling. After instruction by Geoff, I had to ring over thirty football club contacts to get the results of Saturday's games in three different leagues, then work out the new league tables. This took from 8 a.m. until late into the night. I then had to cycle down to the station and put the tables, plus short résumés of the main games, on to the 2.30 a.m. milk train down to Portsmouth. This was so they could appear in the following day's Chichester edition of the *Portsmouth Evening News.* Of course it was slave labour, of course I was being exploited, but I wanted to hold down my job, and felt lucky to still have it after the takeover. I was young, keen and had the chance to learn, to earn my own keep. During the next few days, on top of normal reporting duties, I had to write up longer stories on all the games for the *Chichester Observer*, shorter and different résumés for the *Hampshire Telegraph*, plus notes for next Saturday's football rag, *The Green 'Un.* I was just thankful I didn't have to attend any actual games, for I still hated football! Another extra chore landed on my plate was a column called Pulpit and Pew (nicknamed Pulpit and Spew) for which I had to ring up a dozen vicars to gather the weekly news from all the churches.

A job I hated was reporting the local trades union councils. I particularly disliked their notion that if you were not in a union you still benefited from their pay negotiations. In later years, once I felt I was doing a good job I negotiated my own pay, well above the union level, and if the boss wouldn't pay I was ready to leave. I noticed how the militants always came early, to try to form quorums to pass motions before the more liberal members arrived. Yet according to their young treasurer, those who shouted most were the slowest to cough up their subscriptions!

At this time a new young reporter joined our paper. His name was Paddy Welsh but he was Irish and came from Carrickfergus. We hit it off straight away and it was just after he arrived that he saved me some money. The weekly cost of my digs at the grocer's was going up to £2 a week, taking the ten bob I was still paying to my Dad to clear my debt. Paddy, who had moved into digs with a Mrs Carpenter at 58, Whyke Lane, said there was a spare bed in his room and she was looking for another lodger. Her charge was thirty-five shillings a week, so I moved in with Paddy, saved five bob a week and got away from Joe's raucous snoring because Paddy slept as quiet as a mouse. How Mrs Carpenter coped I will never know. Her little three-bedroomed terrace cottage had to house her three sons and daughter as well as herself and Paddy and me. I never did know how the other two bedrooms were shared out. The loo was outside, down the narrow garden path, and we could have one bath a week each by heating buckets of water on the gas rings, pouring them into a long zinc bath (carried in from the loo) and bathing in front of the living-room fire! Years later Paddy liked to regale pals with a recollection about me, one which I had long forgotten. 'Mike was always horrendously strong and liked to prove it. One Thursday night he picked a full zinc bathful of my water to pour down the sink so he could have his bath, but halfway up he yelled, "Oh, my back!" and very slowly let most of the bath's contents go all over the kitchen floor. Mrs Carpenter came down, made us tea and casually mopped the lot up without telling us off at all.'

Mrs Carpenter was one of life's unsung heroines, slight, bespectacled, with straight-bobbed white hair. She slaved for us and her beef stew with dumplings was the best I ever tasted. Her pride and joy was her front room, her 'parlour', which was nicely furnished, and even had an upright piano which was hardly ever used, except on rare special occasions. It took a long time to cajole and persuade her to let me use it, in the hope of fulfilling my new ambition – to be an entertainer.

10
The Darkie

Back in the Tripoli desert, just before I was discharged, I had gone to a NAAFI marquee to see the film *The Jolson Story*, not having a clue as to what it was all about. I was utterly transfixed, not only by Larry Parks's magical performance imitating the great entertainer Al Jolson but also by the Jolson voice. It was harsh but original, full of resonance and emotional power, and the songs, often sentimental and with country themes, appealed to my sentimental nature.

Although during my first year as a cub reporter whenever I hummed or whistled it was usually Jolson tunes, the film began to fade from my memory. Then in my part-time role as film reviewer for my paper, I saw the sequel, *Jolson Sings Again*, with another great performance by Larry Parks. This time I was truly hooked. I'd always had a fair voice (had I not been a choirboy soloist in Worthing?) and I found I could do a fair imitation of Jolson. Could I, even if I only remained an amateur, entertain folks with the songs I loved? The idea of blacking up, so I could hide behind the disguise, also appealed to me. I decided I needed a singing teacher, certainly to find out if I had enough of a voice.

After many enquiries I located a retired voice teacher, a Professor Edwin Pain who had for many years taught in his own studios in Wigmore Street, London, and he had trained, among others, Herbert Simmons of *Immortal Hour* fame on BBC radio, and Arthur Carron, the first English tenor to sing at the Metropolitan Opera House in New York. I cycled down to his home, a large house called 'Tyburn' in Gloucester Road, Bognor Regis. He was eighty-three years old and said he was retired. On the other hand, he did have a little time on his hands and as I was so keen, he would test my voice there and then. We climbed up some narrow stairs to a small attic room. He sat his plump, bespectacled form down at an upright piano, and put me through a few scales.

'Well,' he said, removing his hands from the keyboard to his knees, 'you do have a bit of a voice but you'll never star at Covent Garden – though I might get you good enough for the chorus!' I said that would be fine. It was quite some time before I could tell him I wasn't interested in any chorus, that I wanted to sing like Al Jolson!

I greatly looked forward to my weekly bike rides from my Chichester digs to his Bognor home, and right from the start Professor Pain revealed how seriously he took singing. He told me the truth was that the human singing voice was nothing less than the link between life and death, and was therefore capable of great beauty and great tragedy. The clue, he went on, was the baby's first 'glottal stroke' cry, a sharp 'Ah, ah, ah' when it's smacked on the bottom, and the other was the breathy 'pharyngeal sound', the last sighing 'Err errr err' sound you make when you're dying.

'These are the two distinct outer reaches of the voice. And you have to get a blend between the two, a virtual blend of life and death, to achieve the highest, truest, artistic singing voice, the expression of all of life at its best.' I was enormously impressed by what seemed a Great Truth, and it was here that Mrs Carpenter's precious parlour and its piano came into their own as far as I was concerned. I spent a lot of spare time pounding out the scales and exercises Professor Pain had given me, and singing my head off. The neighbours never complained but I noticed Paddy tried not to look irritated when I announced I was going to 'practise', the two older boys found reason to go out with their mates and the youngest boy and the daughter often retreated into the furthest bedroom.

After a while, Professor Pain put me through some simple songs as I had told him I was more interested in popular ballads than opera. He chose 'The Last Cord' and Harry Lauder's 'To the End of the Road' as being the best for my exercises. I can see him now, his short, plump body bouncing up and down on the piano stool, his fingers pounding out the notes, his eyes bulging behind his 'milk bottle'-lensed glasses, his face getting redder as he sang the songs himself to show me how. And when I was singing and came to the long, high notes, one hand would come off the piano and make violent upward movements to encourage me to build up to the climactic note and hold on to it longer.

By now I was buying all the Al Jolson single records I could afford and was taking down the lyrics in shorthand and writing them down in a little green notebook. I intended to be called The Darkie, a sort of ill-disguised Al Jolson but slightly different, singing the old Dixie songs but not quite so harshly. One afternoon I cycled north of the town to a dark wood I knew, tried to make sure there was no one about and started to practise some songs, with all the Jolson gestures. I had just picked myself up after falling over a stump and was well into my third song, when the bushes parted and a man in plus-fours and holding a shotgun emerged – the local gamekeeper. As he advanced towards me I thought he was going to congratulate me, like in a movie, and say how good I was. Instead, he said, 'This wood is private. Would you mind not making such a racket? You're frightening the pheasants!'

During my next singing lesson I finally told Professor Pain why I really wanted to sing, so I could perform like Al Jolson. He looked blank.

'Who's Al Jolson?'

I told him he was a major singing star in America and next time I came I'd bring one of his records so he could judge for himself. The Professor did not possess a record player, which in those days were quite heavy machines which I could not transport on my bike. I had to bribe my paper's salesman to run it, me and a record round to the Professor's house. I set the machine up and played two of Jolson's most famous songs, 'Mammy' and 'Toot, Toot Tootsie', then sat back, with an expectant smile.

For a few moment the Professor just sat there shocked, as if mummified, his eyes bulging, an expression of total horror on his face, and all he could do was whisper

'He's terrible. The man can't sing at all.' He *squawks*!'

'He's the biggest star in show business,' I protested.

'Well, he's awful.'

Realizing I had fallen right down in my mentor's eyes, I tried to make amends for in that same week I had found another singing hero: *The Great Caruso* starring the new star Mario Lanza was being shown at a local cinema. It wasn't easy but I finally persuaded the Professor to let me take him to see the film. I recall I had quite a struggle to help him up the stairs. As we sat back I was sure he would approve, for Lanza had an exceptional voice. How wrong could I get? The Professor thought he was awful too!

'The man's got a voice,' he said. 'But he can't... technically, he's terrible! He's shrieking not singing... too shrill, far too shrill!'

The Christmas festive season was looming and I felt it would be a good time to try out The Darkie in some small local pantomime or concert. I enquired around and located an amateur group called something like the Bersted Players (it was a long time ago) who were doing a Christmas concert. I managed to persuade them to let me do The Darkie, saying I would give them a big write-up if they did so. I had one practice session with their pianist which didn't go too well but I thought, 'It will be all right on the night.'

I cycled down and put on the black make-up – a mixture of black and dark brown shoe polish – but as I stood in the wings, ready to perform, I suddenly felt terribly nervous. Then I was on! I got through half the first song when my voice went, in that I had to cough because I had phlegm in my throat. I apologized, finished the song, said a few words then with a nod to the pianist launched into my rendition of 'Mammy'. I gave it everything I'd got but noticed my voice was slightly out of kilter with the piano. Trying to correct this while remembering all the extravagant Jolson gesticulations was agonizing but I came to the grand finale, kneeling on the stage, my white-gloved arms held wide, and waited.

There was a hush and I thought, well, this is just the pause before the thunderous applause and they will stand up and cheer. The hush continued. I heard two strangled whispers, 'Oh, my God!' and 'He's terrible!' I stood up and gave an awkward bow, wishing the stage could swallow me up. Slowly I shuffled back into the wings. Without a word to anyone, I grabbed my little make-up bag, jumped on my bike and cycled back to my digs. I think I was in a state of shock, almost as bad as after my bicycle crash on the sprint track. I did go to Professor Pain a few more times but now mainly because I enjoyed his company. But that was the end of my show biz career and The Darkie.

11
A Razor Fight and Tough New Jobs

Because I was now seeing a lot of films – reviewing them was by far my favourite job on the paper – I began to have ideas about becoming a film critic. I hoped that if I was good enough I might get to Fleet Street for I still had a hankering for the fast city life of London. These thoughts crystallized when I bought a copy of Paul Rotha's great movie bible, *The Film Till Now*, which described the best films as being instrumental in changing human thought. I read the accounts of the great films – *Battleship Potemkin*, *Intolerance*, *The Grapes of Wrath*, etc. and all the insightful philosophies in the book and convinced myself that a good film critic not only had a cushy life but could be an important member of society. Accordingly, my reviews became lengthy and ponderous (though I didn't realize it at the time) and I was peeved when they were cut and edited right down in Portsmouth!

I even wrote to the leading film critic of the time, C. A. Lejeune who worked for the *Observer*, who asked me to send some sample reviews, I carefully rewrote three and posted them off. Surprisingly, she took the trouble to reply at length. I can't recall all she wrote but she did say, 'You must never tell the readers what *you* think the director should have done.' Her letter really indicated I was not promising film critic material and to forget it. So – I forgot it! Even so, and even now, I believe the major stars of the Forties and Fifties had enormous influence on our torn post-war lives, when there was very little television and almost everyone went to the cinema. The so-called stars of today don't match up to the likes of James Stewart, James Cagney, John Wayne, Robert Mitchum, Burt Lancaster, Kirk Douglas, Gary Grant, Charlton Heston. I will always be grateful for C. A. Lejeune's kindness – I might have spent most of the rest of my life in darkened cinemas in provincial towns! – the very opposite of how the second half of my life turned out.

I recall seeing three of Kirk Douglas's early films, *Ace in the Hole*, *Young Man with a Horn* and, especially, one of the best boxing films ever made,

Champion. It temporarily revived my interest in boxing and when I was alone I did some shadow-boxing in the bedroom. Maybe this gave me a bit of an edge in the worst incident I experienced in Chichester. One balmy summer night after dinner I suggested to Paddy we take a late-night stroll. We were walking along the High Street when we saw heading towards us a big guy about our own age whom we recognized as a well-known trouble maker. He was not drunk but he had certainly been drinking.

Suddenly he lurched towards Paddy and banged into him.

'Hey, look where you're going, friend,' said Paddy, mildly enough and with a faint smile.

'I know what you want,' said the man. 'A four-incher!' With that he began to pull out a cut-throat razor. I said, 'Oh, go on home,' and started to step around him. His reply was to open the razor and make a lunge at me. As I threw up my arms to protect myself and felt a sharp pain in my right forefinger, the Leo attack in London flashed through my mind, and everything seemed to go into slow motion. As he turned to lunge at Paddy I threw a swift hard right which landed flush on the left side of his jaw, and down he went. I heard his razor clatter on to the pavement and it didn't look as if he was going to get up. Not only was my finger cut but my knuckles were gashed, probably from the man's teeth. We hurried to the City Cross and reported the incident to a Sergeant Reynolds, who took down our details, then told us to hurry up to the Royal Sussex Hospital to get my wounds dressed. They needed two stitches.

It was touch and go the following morning and I felt I was about to lose my job. The police had found my attacker on his feet but he denied having a razor, and as he had got the worst of it – I had in fact knocked out three of his teeth– they were inclined to believe his story that I had been the aggressor. They were not sure who to charge and were considering charging us both with assault and battery. The next few hours were dire but to my great relief the police came round to our office in the afternoon and told us the razor had been found. A clerk in a corn merchant's had found it on top of one of the sacks in their basement, where the man had clearly pushed it through a grating when he had fallen. Two of the man's pals had identified it as his, and said he'd even threatened them with it. I was let off but had to go through the ordeal of being main prosecution witness.

During the hearing the man still had the nerve to say, 'The other fellow should be where I'm standing. I've lost my looks for a while but he got away scot-free!' He was jailed for a year.

Not long after this head office thought I should vary my experience, so moved me down to Portsmouth for a few weeks. I had a horrible little room in a horrible little hotel on a noisy street and didn't like the big city reporting jobs much. The only good thing was that I managed to wangle review tickets for the Saturday night variety shows. I recall tall, gangly Ted Lune, dressed in shorts and schoolboy cap, yelling at an imaginary householder to let him have his ball back. It was so funny I was literally rolling about in the aisles. Then I was sent to work on the *Bognor Regis Observer* for the summer. At least I was back at Mrs Carpenter's but had to cycle the six miles to work every day, not much fun in the rain.

My cycling days came to an end when I was promoted to chief and sole reporter on the *Midhurst and Petworth Times*. I had to write the whole paper, some 13,000 words a week! For this I had to gather the main news not only from the towns of Midhurst and Petworth but also from some twenty villages, and to help me do this, head office bought me a little two-stroke Bantam motorbike. On occasional visits home to Henfield my young brother had coveted my racing bike, so I rode over for the last time and to Richard's delight agreed to leave the bike for him if Dad would drive me back to Chichester. (It was over forty years before I again sat on a bicycle saddle, and then it was on a friend's machine in the south of Spain.) It was on this visit home that Dad jokingly challenged me to an arm-wrestling match. He had always beaten me before and I thought this time would be no different. To my surprise my arm stayed upright but after about two minutes his began to tremble slightly. I heard him gasp with effort – he didn't want to lose – then it gave way and went flat on the table with a discernible crack somewhere in the joint. I was amazed to see a brief spasm of fear in Dad's eyes before we laughed it off. I remembered the incident years later when I read Arthur Miller's immortal line, 'All men grow to fear their sons.' I felt no great joy at beating the man I had respected – and feared – for most of my life. Rather, I felt a little sorry for him.

I nearly lost the Midhurst job after my first week. My predecessor was highly thought of by the bosses in Portsmouth, and was so keen on football that he not only attended every match of the local team but had played for them and become the club's secretary. I hated football and had no intention of attending a single match. As many football fans bought the paper my editor insisted I report the matches. I decided on blackmail. I told the club's chairman, who seemed to take an instant dislike to me, that if he couldn't find someone to supply a write-up of each match, or at least a few salient facts, then the match would not be reported. I was skating on thin ice here and could well have been fired, but luckily the day before the copy had to be put on the train, someone pushed an account of the match through my office letterbox. This worked for three weeks, until I found two football stalwarts whom I could ring each Sunday morning and get enough facts for a report.

Another reason I didn't want to spend every Saturday afternoon watching football was because I now had a girlfriend in Chichester, a very attractive, slim brunette. She always seemed to be with a similar girl and the two were known locally as 'the Siamese twins'. I tracked her down to the cake shop where she worked but I had to go in and buy three lots of cakes on three different days before I dared talk to her. I can't recall we did very much – we'd go to a pub for a crème de menthe for her, and a pint for me (my first since Tripoli!) or visit the local cinema. We spent a lot of time on the sofa in her darkened lounge as her parents always went to bed early and left us to our amorous dalliances. Despite her beauty and physical charms, she was a nice, uncomplicated, small-town girl with no great ambitions, and easy to be with.

Talking of girlfriends, there were at this time two film stars I fell in love with, as many young men do, worshipping from afar. One was Mitzi Gaynor, who gave a fantastically magical and sparking performance in *Golden Girl*. The other was Ava Gardner. In the scene in *Showboat* where she shows Kathryn Grayson how to dance I recall thinking I'd never seen anything more beautiful. Indeed, she was known as 'the world's most beautiful animal'. Not 'woman' but '*animal*'! Little did I know then that Mitzi Gaynor would be the first star I interviewed when I landed a show-business column in Fleet Street, nor that my arms would one day romantically enfold Ava Gardner in her Spanish home.

As the months passed and I puttered about on my village calls, I became increasingly bored and began to long for the big city life. Twice I journeyed all the way to London on the little Bantam bike and went to my old haunts, and spent a night in a B and B so I could row on the Serpentine next morning. I was very peeved when my third intended trip to London had to be cancelled as the King had died and I had to get extensive local reactions for three different papers. I wrote letters to Fleet Street editors, two of whom agreed to give me an interview though they had no vacancies. Two others urged me to stay where I was. One wrote 'We jaded journalists in Fleet Street would love to be working where you are – your village names – Lurgashall, Heyshott, Cocking, Fernhurst – sound wonderful and just the sort of places to which we aspire to retire!'

I did not agree. In my naivety London seemed a magical Mecca where if I succeeded as a journalist I'd be accepted into an exciting world of lords, politicians, movie stars and beautiful women! I decided to go for broke and lay siege to Fleet Street until I got a job. I resigned rather abruptly from the *Midhurst Times* and as I'd had to hand back the Bantam motorbike, took the train to London. To save money I spent two nights sleeping in one of the empty air-raid shelters on Streatham Common. At two papers I couldn't get past the well-staffed reception desks to see an editor, nor even a features or news editor. I was walking to the second of my appointments, with the news editor of the *News Chronicle*, when I saw a splendid cock pheasant walking over a derelict bomb site in Fetter Lane right by the *Daily Mirror* office. The news editor was encouragingly friendly and said he would keep my name to hand and let me know. When I told him about the pheasant he immediately showed me to a typewriter and said, 'Do a short write-up – country bumpkin visits London.' I did a quick 'think piece', handed it in and left. I think he thought it might be one in the eye for the *Mirror* to find a little story on their doorstep.

I decided to spend one more day trying to see editors but as Streatham meant a long tube journey and it was a fairly warm autumn night, I chose a hidden spot by an old wharf on a grassy slope on the bank of the river Thames, and finally dozed off to sleep. A few hours later I woke up as my feet and legs had gone very cold and I heard an odd lapping sound. I had not known the Thames was a tidal river in its London reaches. The tide had come in and I was soaked through almost up to my bum! Obviously, I could not try to beard newspaper bosses with my clothes in that state. All I could do was stumble to the Gents' wash and brush up loo in Leicester Square, wring out my socks and trousers as best I could, and catch the train home. One consolation when I got back to Henfield was that the *News Chronicle* sent me a cheque for five guineas for the pheasant story, which more than covered the return train fare for my abortive journey.

Now that I was back with Dad and Bettie at Staplesbarn House while I tried to land a job on another provincial newspaper, apart from doing a few gardening chores for Dad, I had to earn my keep. The only tolerable job I could find, as I'd always liked working with wood, was in a Steyning saw mill. I thought a spell working with axe and saw in woodlands would be a nice change and good for me physically. But I did not even see any woodland – I was put to work in the timber yard. Together with a local giant called Ralph, I had to work the handles of a huge crane, grab whole trees and swing them round to the circular saw's bench rollers. We had to swing the jib over the trees until the big, heavy calipers were above the trunks at a point we called 'backer', where the tree would be perfectly balanced when picked up. We lowered the calipers, then turned the handles on the big wheel so that they bit into the trunk, and lifted the tree. It was hard, back-breaking work. And if we estimated 'backer' wrong we had to repeat the whole process.

Ralph was the local football team's goalie and three of my hands would not have made one of his! I really had to struggle to keep up with him. I'll never forget one frosty morning when the temperature was well below zero. Ralph clamped his giant mitts on the iron bar of the handle and began to turn. I did the same – and yelped with pain. The freezing metal had 'burnt' some skin off my palms and thereafter I had to swallow my pride and wear gloves on cold days. I was glad on the days when I was taken off the crane and put on to stacking coffin boards.

I was also happy on the day they said I could join the felling squad, for this was the kind of work I'd hoped to do while temporarily working at the timber yard. We drove to some woodlands but as I had no felling axe of my own I was handed a small hand axe and set to work chopping twigs and small branches off the felled boles, mostly ash, birch and hazel and none more than eight inches across the butt. At lunchtime the other three men repaired to a nearby pub for a pint. I didn't drink during the day, so stayed behind to eat my sandwiches. Then I spotted the foreman's gleaming, oiled, well-sharpened axe leaning temptingly against a birch trunk.

Reverently, I picked it up, felt its fine balance, and could not resist the temptation to fell the birch with two, at most three, strokes. Had I not won my Axemanship badge in the Boy Scouts? I swung the axe out to the right, then aimed a blow at the tree with all the force I could muster. There was a sickening crack, but not from the blade hitting the tree. The axe head had gone beyond the trunk. The haft just behind the head had hit the trunk, and snapped almost in half! Gingerly, I forced the head back on to the shaft so most of the torn wooden fibres fitted back into each other again and the break was hardly visible. Then I put the axe back where I'd found it and retreated further away to finish my sandwiches.

The men returned from the pub. With trepidation, I saw the foreman pick up his axe, twirl it with a professional flourish, then aim a terrific blow at the base of one of the thicker ash trees. The axe head stayed stuck in the trunk but the haft carried on with such force that it shot out of the foreman's hands. He strode to pick up the haft, looked at its jagged busted end and said, 'Blimey. I must be stronger than I thought!'

I soon found that common labouring was even more boring than country journalism, even soul-destroying over a long period. The main topic of conversation from Monday to Wednesday at the sawmill was last week's football match, and on Thursday and Friday of the coming Saturday's match.

In my spare time I made frantic efforts to get on to the staff of the Brighton *Evening Argus* group, who also ran the *Sussex Daily News*, by sending them little stories, ending when I witnessed a big car crash. The editor-in-chief Victor Gorringe, called me in for an interview. Great, I thought. It's not London, but Brighton will be 'big time' enough for me right now.

My joy when Mr Gorringe said he could give me a reporting job was diluted when he said I was to be the new district reporter at Littlehampton. But I'd had enough of the sawmill life so showed great keenness. Accordingly, I caught the train to Littlehampton, found some nice digs in a room on the top floor of a house near the rail station owned by two elderly ladies, and set to work.

12
The Mad Adventure

I soon found reporting in the Littlehampton–Arundel area, apart from occasional stories about the harbour and lifeboat rescue, was much the same as at Chichester and Midhurst, and after six months I longed for some kind of adventure. My chance came when I interviewed a local man who was going to try to sail round the world with six other foolhardy characters and he said they were looking for another crew member. This seemed a real adventure back in 1952, long before Sir Francis Chichester made the first solo round-the-world sailing trip in 1967. In fact no one had sailed round the world since Francis Drake. Telling my paper I needed fuller facts, I went with the man to meet the owner and the rest of the crew at Bursledon Harbour.

The stumbling block was that all the other members had contributed £200 towards the trip, and I only had £40 saved up. But by promising to sell stories of the adventure to a major Sunday paper and paying the fees into the boat's account, I talked myself aboard. I resigned from the *Argus*, who let me go after two weeks. I found time to dash by train to London where the features editor of the *Sunday Pictorial* contracted to pay £40 per article, which I would send from the major ports of call. When I got back to Bursledon with the extra £40 for my first story, in which we were called 'The New Elizabethans', and a photographer from the paper, I took a good look at the boat which was to be my home for the months ahead. The *Asta* was an 88-foot gaff-rigged ketch, built along graceful, swan-like lines, and she still held the Bremen to Heligoland speed record. The only trouble was she was rather old, and the plan was to sail to Spain and get her patched up there as the dry docks were much cheaper than in Britain. Romantically, I could see myself on deck, lashed to the wheel as she cleaved through the crashing waves of storms... on, on, ever onward!

I was soon disabused of this notion when the owner, captain and mate called me into the main cabin and told me that since I had put in the least money it was felt that I should be the steward. This meant working with the cook, who'd lost half a leg in the war, and setting the table, dishing out the food, washing up afterwards, and similar chores. Most of my time would be below deck, although in emergencies I would have to help up on deck too. Oh well, at least I would see a lot of the world when we put into various ports.

The owner, Jim, was an American only a year or two older than me: his father ran an important American business office in London. The captain Richard, was French and held the requisite Mariner's Licence, The mate, Richard's pal, was Lucien, a former light heavyweight champion of Argentina, who had been working in London as a sparring partner to Freddy Mills, at that time the world light heavyweight champion. Apparently Lucien, who bore a remarkable resemblance to Rocky Marciano, had put Mills on the canvas more than once when sparring and had been fired. I made a mental note that when this guy said jump, I would jump! This unlikely trio had somehow met up in a Soho garage, where they had temporary jobs, and together had cooked up this sailing venture. The rest of the crew, two of them women, had been recruited through newspaper adverts. None of them had known each other before and in the confined space of the boat, bickering was not long in occurring. Luckily one of the crew was an ex-Commando just a year older than me. Although Peter had been an officer and I a Corporal, our military backgrounds gave us much in common, and we occupied the two bunk beds in the poop deck.

The drawback now was that our departure was delayed by many days because the Board of Trade would not give us the necessary clearance. They said our life-saving equipment was not up to standard. We needed two lifeboats we could sit in, not just rafts to cling to. Why? Because if we just clung to rafts in oceans like the Pacific the carnivorous barracuda fish would chew us to bits!

The one-legged cook and one of the women took a shine to each other and, fed up with the delays, ran off together. I was then promoted. As I had cooked for myself for years in various bedsitters it was clear to all that I should be the next cook, and I was shown the galley.

On rough seas the cook has the worst job in a small yacht because he is trapped below decks in a small. hot space, but luckily I had no tendency to sea sickness. Also, I now had my own small private cabin right off the galley, and Peter was only on the other side of the door so we could still have a natter. Before we set sail I bought a pocket edition of *Mrs Beeton's Cookery Book*. I also stacked up on plenty of non-perishable foods. The crew were going to eat lots of macaroni cheese, for instance!

We set off and I'll never forget seeing the sharp brown rocks around the Needles slip past beneath the surface and only a metre away from our steel hull as we sailed out on a high tide. We lunged through the Bay of Biscay, and when the crew changed tack in the rough January gales up top the yacht veered from port to starboard, then a few minutes later from starboard to port, usually with a shudder and loud crack of the sails. I had to get used to stirring the stew while looking into it at chest level, or staring at the bottom of the pot while I tried to keep stirring with my hand far above my head. The cooker was mounted on gimbals, so whatever angle the yacht took the cooker and its pot remained level – but *I* didn't!

We docked in the port of La Coruña and after the first day, when the owner and captain had failed to find a cheap dry dock, Franco's port police came aboard, said they suspected us of being spies and ordered us to leave. Except for a brief trip to the nearest grocer's to replenish supplies, I had not been ashore. Before we left, Lucien, who spoke perfect Spanish and knew the ports on this coast, came back with three local amateur guitarists. Fuelled by the extra vino they brought on board, we had a noisy musical trip back north to El Ferrol where Jim was sure we would find a cheap dry dock. The party also scoffed in one day most of the food that I had hoped would last a week.

Within an hour of docking in El Ferrol another set of Franco's port cops came on board, arrested the three guitarists as they could have been leaving the country illegally, and even shaved their heads. Richard and Jim were taken away for questioning and I also came under extra suspicion when they saw from my passport that I was a journalist. I managed to talk my way out of it, but when I insisted I had to buy more food, one of the police went with me, to keep a close eye on my movements. Again we were thought of as possible spies.

We sailed to our next port, Vigo, 180 kilometres to the south and did find a dry dock for essential repairs to the hull but the job took several days and the bill made a huge dent in the boat's finances. Jim and Richard decided to try to sell our engine. After all, we were attempting to emulate Drake's voyage, and it would be more honest if we could do this without mechanical back-up; we would then have enough money to get a few more repairs made in the Canary Islands en route across the Atlantic. The yacht was winched back into the water and tied up on its own far down the wharf. These were harder days for me because while the three bosses were touring the bars and cafés trying to find smugglers who would buy the engine (a legal sale would have meant delays to get all the necessary documentation) and the other crew could wander the port or swim on the beaches, I was expected to provide breakfast, lunch and dinner, so was mostly stuck aboard. This did little for my temper.

One night, after a row with some woman he'd met, Lucien came weaving down the steps into the cabin and I could see by his eyes and heavy breathing that he'd been drinking. He glared at me and demanded, 'Miguel – omelette!'

It was about 9 p.m. and I had spent the previous two hours preparing a madeira cake as a special treat when we once again set sail, and while I was scared of Lucien, I felt peeved enough to say, 'You might say please!'

In reply he slammed his big fist on the table and repeated, 'Miguel – omelette!'

'Say please,' I hissed through clenched teeth. Next thing he was coming at me. I knew I couldn't beat him in a fight, that it would be foolish to even try to land a blow on that granite head, that muscled body. Instead I turned and fled! I shinned up the upright ladder in the poop deck on to the main deck and dashed to the guard rail by the boarding ladder that hung over the side. Lucien, who had almost grabbed my foot as I'd climbed the ladder, came out of the hatch saying something like I thought too much of myself, and came for me again. I'd expected a right, so I dodged to my left, but he threw a roundhouse left which just glanced off my right shoulder. I managed to dig him slightly in his side but the impetus of his missed blow swung him round so that his rear legs and lower bum hit the guard rail, and over he went, grabbing my shirt and taking me with him!

I was conscious of the double splash as we hit the sea and that it took only one stroke to get me to the bottom of the boarding ladder where I clutched a rung. I expected Lucien to try to do the same but to my surprise he was splashing about, slapping cupped hands on the surface, head going under and up again, a desperate look on his face as he gasped, 'Can't swim… can't swim!'

He was just within reach, so I grabbed his shirt sleeve as he grasped my arm with an eagle grip. As I hauled him towards the ladder I felt he might try to belt me again but he just clung there, breathing heavily, then climbed up back on to the deck. As I followed him up I was still afraid, but he stood well back, clothes dripping, put his hands on his hips, gave a hearty guffaw and then, with a smile, extended his hand and said, 'Eh, Miguel!'

I smiled too, took his hand and said, 'Eh, Lucien! One omelette coming up!'

We became good friends after that, especially after I was at pains to tell him I knew he could beat me up but hoped he wouldn't, and it was Lucien who was instrumental in my having, at last, a bit of a good time on the trip.

Two mornings later he watched me collecting my shopping bags to go to the port shops. Then he produced two hemp sacks.

'Miguel, you spend too much money! Come, I show you.'

I followed him through a few streets until we came to an open-air market where everything I normally bought in the shops, and more, was being sold at far cheaper prices.

Lucien chuckled. 'You get foods here but charge the boat the same as usual, at the shops. On Saturday we spend what you save!'

We hiked back to the boat with two full sacks.

He was as good as his word for on Saturday afternoon he told everyone I would not be cooking that night as he was showing me the town. No one dared argue with him, not even his pal the captain. We went to a few bars and then to a small nightclub where the dancers were among the most beautiful girls I'd seen. He knew some of them and they joined us between their little acts. I got pie-eyed… no, drunk, for the first time since that New Year's Eve with Dad and the Canadian air force lads. I woke up to find myself in bed with a woman some ten years older than myself but who was most attractive. I recall her name even now – Maria do Carmo Oliveira – and how she kept gaily regaling her giggling sisters in the next room with the naughty things I was doing with her.

I only saw Maria twice more before Jim announced that they had found some smugglers who would buy the engine. They would follow us out to sea and when we were about thirty miles offshore they would come aboard, pay us, and extract the engine. He warned me to get extra food, so I ensured we had enough for four extra mouths for a day and night, and to get us to the Canaries.

The trouble was, the smugglers took three days and nights to get the engine out and into their boat, a severe drain on my food supplies, but we were never to make it to the Canaries. Overnight gales sprang up, and by the morning we were in a full-strength storm and fighting for the boat's life. We tried to run before the storm with just the flying spinnaker out up front, and for extra stability we set a drifting anchor from the stern. The huge waves battered into the hull, first at the bow, then at the stern… BOOMP… BANG… BOOMP… BANG, and with each blow the old yacht shuddered. I went up on deck and saw that with each thump the deck boards were opening slightly, losing bits of pitch into the hold before closing again. I had my turn at the wheel all right as after twenty-four hours everyone was getting tired and they needed an extra pair of hands. As for food, oodles of macaroni cheese was all I could provide as it was fast and easy.

By morning it was clear our situation was serious and Richard and Lucien agreed we needed help. They sent up distress flares and within an hour a Swedish tanker, the *Kalmia*, loomed through the wind and rain. Being the strongest, Lucien threw the ropes until the main hawser was fastened and the *Kalmia* towed us to Lisbon. After some of the tanker's crew helped us tie up in the harbour at the mouth of the river Tagus, we were all so exhausted that we just stayed in our bunks for some twenty hours.

The adventure was over and within a few days the crew began to break up. The woman was flown home. Ex-Commando Peter and I volunteered to hitchhike to Madrid, some 400 miles away, and with the paltry sum of £30 we were each handed to try to get the rest of the way home by train.

I will never forget that long, hot dusty walk beneath the unforgiving sun. We could not afford to eat more than bread and *sopa de verduras* (vegetable soup) and at night we tried to find ploughed furrows in the fields as by widening them slightly they made fairly comfy cradles for our sleeping bags. At the time, unknown to us, hitchhiking was forbidden in Spain, so apart from two short mule cart rides, we mostly had to hoof it at first. Then a couple of German lads in a battered old Mercedes, who obviously didn't know of the ban, drew up and took just over 100 miles out of our trek. As the car wheezed up one steep sierra of mountains the engine got too hot and boiled over. We had to wait for it to cool down again, then, one by one, each of us had to stand on the front fender and pee into the radiator to top up the water level until we reached the next garage! I eventually arrived home with just six shillings left in my pocket.

Of course, I was now too old to ponce off my parents and I lost no time in ringing Victor Gorringe, begging him to take me back on the reporting staff of the *Evening Argus* group in Brighton. He hummed and hahed, said... maybe... well, yes, he could probably fit me in somewhere. Brighton at last, I thought as I journeyed to see him in his office. I was in for a shock.

He sent me back to Littlehampton! But he said that if I did as well as on my first stint there, he would bring me in to join the Brighton staff after six months or so. As I moved back into my old room near the station (the old ladies just hadn't bothered to relet it), it was as if the yacht adventure had never happened. I was back in the old district reporter rut but I now had a big incentive, and I toiled away at my contacts to get the best stories. On the very day Mr Gorringe called me in and said he would transfer me to Brighton in a month's time, the greatest incentive of all presented itself – I had fallen madly in love.

13
New Love – and Fleet Street at Last

I was strolling along the main shopping avenue in Brighton when I saw Mitzi Gaynor walking towards me, a veritable vision of loveliness! But as she passed me I realized it was not Mitzi Gaynor. This girl was even more gorgeous, with long auburn hair, a slight smile on her face and a tiger-like quality in her movements. She sort of strutted, with a girl-happy-confident-I'm-the-most-beautiful-thing-in-the-world way of walking, emphasizing every generous curve of a superb figure. I was hit by what Sicilians call 'the thunderbolt' – love at first sight.

My heart was pounding. I simply could not just go back to Littlehampton. I waited a few seconds, then, like a dog, I followed her through the busy streets for quarter of a mile until I saw her turn into the Essoldo cinema. By the time I got there she had disappeared. I quickly bought a ticket and spent the next hour ignoring the film and trying to locate her in the audience. When the interval came and I still couldn't spot her, I felt I was wasting my time and started to leave. But as I crossed the vestibule I saw she *was* there – in the box office! I joined the queue and bought another ticket. But as she took my money and handed me the ticket she didn't look up. I don't know where the question came from, but I was desperate. 'Are you in the film?' I asked. She looked up then, laughed and said no. I blurted out, 'You should be – you're gorgeous!' She gave a pleased little giggle but the queue was impatient and I could not say more. I sat through another hour of the film, hoping I could catch her as she left work, but when I checked she had gone, and another woman was running the box office. Well, at least I knew where she worked.

I caught the train back to Littlehampton and when I was not working during the next two days I spent agonizing moments writing down a short speech I hoped would attract her interest. When I finally got her on the cinema's phone I was mightily relieved that she did vaguely remember my compliment. I can't recall all I said but at one point I told her I had never believed in love at first sight – until I saw her! We met for lunch two days later and I splashed out on a posh meal at Cunningham's oyster bar on the Brighton front. My initial disappointment when she said she had to meet a male friend that afternoon disappeared when she said I could come too! The three of us sat chatting on the sunny shingle beach and I just outsat my rival, who owned a busy shoe shop and said he had to get back to work. Joy, for that was her name, didn't date him again.

We didn't even kiss until our fourth date when she invited me in for a coffee nightcap in her parents' mews house. I remember going down on my knees, looking up at my princess and telling her she was the most beautiful girl I had ever seen. As she bent down and cupped my head in her hands for that first kiss, I felt I would never be more inspired by female beauty, nor more sexually inspired. My luck was still in the week when I moved to Brighton because I found a fabulous large flat at Marine Gate on the front, which seemed ludicrously cheap. The movie actor Eric Portman had the flat below me.

It was in this flat nearly four weeks after we had met that Joy and I first made love. Ah, the magic… as we lay on the bed we were both trembling, with passion and not a little fear. It was gentle and long, a visit to paradise. So began an intense love affair although shortly after this I had to vacate the super flat. The whole building had been sold before I moved in and I should not have been let it. I soon found a nice, old-fashioned, large and quiet room in the Langham Hotel, and as Joy could also tolerate the downgrade in style I stayed there until I left Brighton.

The reporting jobs were more interesting now and I worked on news diary jobs, features on heroic paraplegics, and even occasionally stood in for the trilby-hatted crime reporter Syd Curtis. I was also sent out to do profiles of surrounding villages, meeting all the local luminaries and trying to bring out the individual spirit of each village in print and photos. The one thing I dreaded was being made to cover football matches. One day it happened: I was sent to cover the away match between Brighton and Millwall. I still recall the long train journey, the grey sky, the rain, a bleak day in a foreign land! I did not deliberately use clichés but I just couldn't think of any other way of describing football. So my report was filled with phrases like 'play swung from end to end' and 'in the second half Brighton had more of the ball' and 'It was a game of two halves.' The good thing was that I was never sent to cover football again!

By now I had acquired my first car, a BSA three-wheeler which had a motorcycle engine and was driven by a chain. I didn't like its square lines, so hired a small garage and completely rebuilt its body with aluminium sheeting and frontal mesh so that it resembled a Bugatti! Poor Joy spent many afternoons shivering with cold as I sawed, cut, hammered and screwed. I did nothing, however, to the old engine. On the day it was complete, resplendently painted bright yellow, we set off for our first drive. We had only got six miles up the A23 when there was a bang: the engine kept revving but we came to a stop. The differential gear had broken completely and I could not find spare parts anywhere. Goodbye to my 'Bugatti'. I think Joy was quite relieved.

In my spare time now I turned to a new sport, swimming, as my costly ice skates had been lost years ago. My new bedsitter was near the King Alfred Baths in Hove and it was easy to drop in for an hour after work and plough up and down, improve my style and enjoy the warm water and an invigorating shower afterwards. I got a bit peeved when a girl went surging past me time and time again, her feet apparently having turned into torpedo propellers. It was Angela Barnwell, training for the Olympics.

I wanted to improve my style and to learn the stroke correctly. So I joined a swimming class, but while I had strong arms and could propel myself well with them, my feet were a different matter. There was one exercise where you held a foam pad in front of you at arm's length and twiddle-paddled your feet to give thrust. Each time, while everyone else in the line made slow progress towards the other end of the pool, I stayed where I was, no matter how hard I twiddled my feet. The instructor said I probably needed some initial impetus and gave me a shove. I twiddled out for about three yards, then started going backwards! Back I came until my feet hit the edge of the bath from where I'd been pushed. No matter how hard I tried I could not get it right. It seemed I had the wrong kind of feet. In the end I found I could go quite fast by making three arm strokes to one scissor-like sidekick based on the one used in the breaststroke. I sort of humped along through the water. I told the perplexed instructor it was probably called the 'trudgeon stroke'! Joy also enjoyed swimming and in summer I liked taking her to open-air pools, proud to show her off and to be seen with such a beauty. She looked as good in a bikini as in her clothes for she had an excellent dress sense.

There were two jobs I coveted on the paper. One was to be the film critic but this was in the distinguished hands of Derek Grainger (who later, for his sins, became pioneer director on the TV soap *Coronation Street*) The other was a humorous Saturday page called 'Good Evening by Tony Miles'. I was proving quite good at getting quirky angles on human stories and sometimes tipped Tony off about some of them. His column was the most popular in the

Argus, so imagine my joy when Mr Gorringe called me into his office, said that Tony Miles was leaving for Fleet Street (he later became editor of the *Daily Mirror*), and would I like, and could I do his column? The name Michael Tomkies or even Mike Tomkies was considered too long, so in the end they made a play on my surname and called the page 'Good Evening by Tom Keys.'

I now had to sift the news and ring around the town and district for short, humorous and true stories which were superbly illustrated with comical drawings by the cartoonist Miller. I did the normal jobs too, but I really relished my page, and even sacrificed some evenings with Joy so I could stay late to ring all my contacts, find new ones, and get the most lively pieces.

This page proved to be my springboard to Fleet Street for after a year in Brighton I still longed for life back in the capital. The stories came to the attention of Arthur Redford, the dynamic news editor of a best-selling weekly magazine *Weekend Mail*, published by the *Daily Mail* group, and after commissioning me to send expanded versions on a lineage basis, he offered me a job. I couldn't get out of Brighton fast enough. I found a rather gloomy bedsitter just off Holland Road, North Kensington, and went to work, taking the tube each day from High Street Kensington to Waterloo.

Nearly every morning Arthur would erupt from his chair with a sort of joyful whoop, 'Oh boy, this is a real cracker of a story,' usually clutching a slip of paper containing a phoned tip-off or some odd advert he'd cut out of a paper. I was sent all over the country covering human interest stories, even whacky ones. I remember a feature on an old vaudeville entertainer who had been a pal of Charlie Chaplin in the Fred Karno days: he had taught Chaplin two special pratfalls, but while Charlie was a multi-millionaire he had fallen on hard times and was broke. Another came after we discovered that the once famous Victor Sylvester, king of ballroom dancing, had become bankrupt and was working as a hotel janitor in Bayswater. Then there was the one about a young man who had retired at twenty-one and how he'd done it. Yet another arose from a letter of complaint in a provincial paper in the Borders from a Highland regiment soldier who said the girls in his local dance hall wouldn't dance with the 'soldiers in skirts'. I was sent up on the train to interview both the soldiers and the girls and get some pictures. When I got to the dance hall there wasn't a single soldier in a kilt to be seen. I rang Arthur at his home.

'Then go to the pub and get some!'

'Can I buy them a drink?'

'Only one!' I duly did so and got the story and the pictures.

I also did exposures of minor crooks or self-deluders. The formula here for constructing the story was: 'I am a crook. I have always been a crook. But now that you have exposed me I will never be a crook again!' There was a man in the Northampton area who was advertising a special new condom for men that he had invented. He told me there was a natural notch about half an inch inside the penis. His invention was a short rubber tube with a small bulge at one end and a little balloon at the other. The bulge fitted into the notch inside the penis and when orgasm was achieved the sperm was ejaculated into the balloon! I stared at the size of the thing with something akin to dismay. It would have been hard to fit it in an elephant! I bought one and took it to the uro-genital unit/clinic of a major London hospital where experts denounced the device as both ineffective and dangerous.

Arthur became news editor of the *Woman's Sunday Mirror*, a new magazine launched by the *Daily Mirror* group, and took me with him. Here the stories were more hard-nosed. When a sixteen-year-old girl was murdered at a gravel pit near a small town in Scotland, Arthur told me to get up there fast. He wanted me to reconstruct the whole murder for a feature to be called 'When Murder Comes to *Your* Town', talk to everyone concerned and build it up fact by fact. 'Murder figures are rising and we want to shock people into awareness,' he said. 'This could happen in *your* town, to *your* child.'

In the dreary, rainy town with its chip shops, factories, men on rusty bikes and black railway station, I knocked on doors trying to talk to anyone who'd known the murdered girl. At first I found folk reluctant but when I rang Arthur he said, 'Tell everyone the paper wants to do a *memorial* for the girl.' Why any national newspaper would want to write a memorial to a totally obscure schoolgirl I didn't know, but to my surprise the ruse worked.

In a steamy council house kitchen a girl called Jean, her eyes red from weeping, said, 'It was just another Saturday night dance. Pat loved dancing but she always wore ballerina shoes because she hated being so tall. No, she never drank, only ginger beer. No, she had no regular boyfriend. No one took her home as far as I know. I always told her she should never walk home alone past those pits.'

At the factory where she had been a seamstress, the foreman told me, 'Oh, Pat was a fine worker, always a sunny smile, always making clothes from remnants in her spare time for other kids.' I noticed that above the girl's bed hung a picture of Christ, – and six of pop stars, which I would not mention! For two days I tracked down all who'd known her, delving for sidelights on her character. When I mentioned the picture of Christ to one of her girlfriends, she told me Pat had wanted to be a nun. I had my angle. The photographer with me, who had photographed the foreman and the girl called Jean, persuaded her to have her picture taken praying in church, asking God to look after her friend.

Two of the young men who had known Pat turned surly and said she had a bad reputation for encouraging men, giving in easily to some but teasing others. At the murder spot I noted there had been no signs of a struggle over the 200- yard field path. She could well have gone there of her own free will. Nothing excuses murder, but she could have been with a man she taunted once too often. When I wrote the story I was told to leave out these latter findings, and it came out stressing the 'quiet sister' who wanted to be a nun. Purity and innocence, cruelly battered to death.

I now realized I was in a hardbitten world and all that mattered when I was sent out as a reporter was that I get 'The Story'. My bosses were tough-minded, uninvolved personally with the dance of tragedy, passion, bereavement and ruin so frequently behind the human-interest stories they handled. Bad news was in fact good news and news was money. They were in business to sell papers. Shorn of both naivety and idealism, they championed causes so that the championed would buy the paper. What they most cared about was winning circulation battles and good exclusives. They ate, drank and slept Fleet Street, manipulating reporters from telephones, but they were men of shrewd judgement, disseminators of life. I found I myself had to be quite ruthless, just in order to survive.

One sensational story I was sent on was about a young wife in the Midlands who had made a miraculous recovery from cancer. She had been told she was dying of the disease and although not being particularly religious, she had made a special pilgrimage to her nearest cathedral and prayed to God. She was said to have woken up the following morning with the marks of the stigmata on her hands and feet – and the cancer had gone. It was being hailed in the media as a modern 'miracle'. It seemed the whole of Fleet Street was after the full story but the couple, on the advice of their priest or bishop, were refusing to talk to reporters. While I did get them to confirm that the story was true, they politely shut the door on me as well.

Quandary! I had to get the story, and this was a big one. I hit on the idea of going to the top, of tackling the bishop himself. Instead of just ringing him up, as many other reporters would doubtless have done, I went to my hotel room and composed a long letter. I recall pointing out that as my newspaper was largely women-oriented we would treat the matter with more sensitivity than the others, and if the facts came from an authoritative source, i.e. himself, it would not only carry more weight and more credibility, but would also have the effect of the other papers calling off their reporters. I also promised to show the bishop anything I wrote and he could correct it, or even reject it, as he wished. I hoped I was not being a bit too cunning when I ended the letter saying that I was a God-fearing former soloist choirboy and I hoped he might feel I was totally trustworthy. I added my hotel phone number, saying that I only had one day left, then hiked to the bishop's palace/residence and personally pushed it through his letterbox.

The following morning I was delighted when the bishop rang me and invited me to visit. The first thing he told me was that he had been pestered by the press, and the most persistent was a reporter from a Sunday paper whom he named. I knew the name well, and the man's reputation for pulling every trick in the book, and some not in the book, to get his stories. He was certainly an opponent to fear, and I'm afraid to say I deliberately badmouthed him to the bishop, adding that the man would certainly not let him see his copy. To cut a long story short, the bishop said he would not see any other reporters, gave me a tremendous human-interest story, packed with detail, and after we had worked on my copy together that very afternoon, it ended up as the major scoop on the front page. And, the following week, because of the bishop's apparent approval and authorization, I managed to get an updating story from the young couple themselves – another scoop.

One tough assignment I was put on at this time was when a photographer and I were sent down in a hired car to a gloomy prison near Portland Bill. Inside the jail was former Queen's Counsel A. L. Waller, who five years earlier had shot and injured a doctor he believed to be having an affair with his fiancée. He was due to be released that very day and we had found out from his fiancée, a former glamorous model, that she was due to meet him and drive him away. And, for a certain payment, she had given us a short story. But she had steadfastly refused to let any reporter accompany her in the Daimler she had hired for the double journey. Our task was to try to intercept the couple to get the story of their reunion and their future plans and so forth.

When we reached the prison I was alarmed to find half of Fleet Street's tabloid reporters and photographers were lined up outside in their cars, all there for the same reason and, like me, all with hastily drawn expenses, cash to help get the story.

Knowing we had published the short story about the fiancée's long, lonely wait for the QC's release, a rival reporter said to me: 'I suppose you've got them all signed up?'

"That's right,' I lied. 'All neatly sewn up at the corners!'

'Give us a break, old boy. We only need a few words.'

'Sure, we'll meet up later,' I lied again. He wouldn't know we had no further arrangements with the couple at all.

Before long, the prison gates opened and the Daimler swept in. There was no sign of the fiancée, who crouched on the car's floor as photographers leaped like frogs, taking shots of the sky, the car doors and of one another. Then the car was inside the prison walls, the gates closed behind it. I'd found out there were three gates and I felt that Waller would look for an unmanned gate to leave by. I told our driver to drive once right round the jail, then go fast up the only single road out and block it, pretending we had a puncture.

We roared off and sure enough, thinking we were going to meet the couple, the other reporters dived into their cars to follow but soon lost sight of us. We shot up the road and blocked it while I leaped out with a foot pump. Soon the Daimler came hurtling along, braked at our car and tried to edge round it. We leaped out with profuse apologies as I showed the couple the pump and said we could shift soon. 'We're from the *Sunday Mirror.* You know us (to the fiancée). Just one picture, please. Flash! Will you tell us where you're going? No? Oh, all right.' Flash! 'It's your business. Look out, here come the other papers. We'll block them for you. Off you go!' Our driver shifted forward slightly so the Daimler could accelerate round our car, then reversed it again while I pretended to be pumping up a tyre as the other reporters arrived. The air was blue with their curses as I smilingly assured them the tyre would be ready soon, and managed to hold them up for a good four minutes, which enabled the Daimler to get well away from them all.

I was very excited now because I had seen on the couple's suitcase a ticket for the Golden Arrow train, which I hoped meant they were going to Paris. At the next phone box I rang Arthur Redford, who took a few minutes to confirm the time of the train, then told me to call at the office for more expenses which I might need and he would have ready, and also to pick up the paper's own glamorous girl photographer, Alma, as he felt it would help if it was one couple interviewing another, rather than two men.

At Victoria we were nearly an hour early. When the couple did arrive we kept our distance, then boarded the train with first-class tickets. On the way to Folkestone we confronted the couple with apologetic smiles. At first the QC was annoyed and wouldn't talk, but I persisted in what I hoped were low, reassuring tones, and Alma's charm was also helpful. We said the whole country would admire their faithfulness and their devotion to each other, would be happy at their reunion, and so forth. Waller softened slowly, then told us they had been married by special licence at Kensington before catching the train.

'That,' I said to Alma, while already envisaging the headlines, 'calls for a celebration.' And I sent the buffet attendant for champagne. By the time we reached Folkestone I had the full story but I said to Alma, 'Fancy a night in Paris?'

'Well, I do need a shot or two in Paris, perhaps posing by the Eiffel Tower.'

I rang Arthur to tell him that we had got most of the story but the couple had invited us to go with them to Paris where they would talk to us again. There was a short pause, then Arthur replied, 'Well go to bloody Paris then. But don't come back without the story!'

Back in the office late the following day, after editor Lee Howard had congratulated me on the story, Arthur shouted to me, 'Hey, Mike, don't put champagne on your expenses! You want us all to get fired? You bought them *lunch*, right?'

I found myself travelling the country; sometimes when I phoned in a story I'd be told to go another 200 miles to tackle another. I found myself occasionally torn between conscience and the necessity to get The Story. Sometimes it was the crime beat, standing under dripping gutters in the East End, talking to resentful wives of underworld men who had just been arrested or to girlfriends of killers, telling all for money while they served in jail. I developed various little ploys, putting on the 'little boy lost' act – if I don't get this story I'll be fired... or this exact same thing happened to my sister, so I think I know how you feel...I had to pursue folk in the news to get them to reveal what they didn't really want to reveal, interview broken-down celebrities wallowing in self-pity for a fee... batten on to big names so fans would buy the paper. I had some extraordinary luck in the early years and in the office I acquired the nickname of 'the Mountie' as I always got my story and brought home the bacon.

The one time I considered I had failed was when Arthur Redford sent me to France to try to track down the former British model Nina Dyer who had married Baron Von Thyssen, one of the world's richest men, but was now going through a messy divorce and was reputedly holed up alone in one of the Baron's castles. It was obvious, if she would talk, that she had a really emotional human-interest tale to tell. All I knew was that the castle was in the Bois de Versailles area outside Paris. I chased around, sure I wouldn't find her, when I struck lucky at one of the préfectures (police stations) where I was given her address.

The castle stood in dark woods and seemed to have a gloomy, almost sinister aura. As I walked along the drive I expected to be accosted by a guard at any moment. But I reached the huge doors unhindered. I pulled the bell and as no one answered banged on the heavy knocker. Again there was no response, so I pushed my usual sort of note through the letters flap in which I said I would return in hope in the afternoon.

When I returned there was still no response to the bell or the knocker. Oh well, maybe she was out anyway. I'd heard that Nina Dyer had a pet panther called Ti Amo (I Love You, in Italian) so I strolled around the grounds until I located the animal in a large, heavily barred cage below the trees. As I walked towards it I glanced back at the castle and saw a tall, slim woman with dark hair looking out from an upper gabled window. I was sure it was Nina. I waved cheerily and continued towards the cage.

As I came closer I was both surprised and alarmed when a beautiful black panther with huge green eyes came out of what looked like cosy wooden sleeping quarters and padded over to the bars. I was even more surprised when it not only didn't try to attack me but made loud purring noises and rubbed its head sideways on the bars. It looked so friendly I could not resist putting my gloved hand through the bars and caressing its head fur. Maybe I touched a sensitive spot on one of its ears for it gave a sudden spitting-flare noise, lashed out with its right paw – and pulled off my glove with its claws! There was no way I was going to try to retrieve it in case the animal struck out again. Baroness Von Thyssen must have seen the incident as I could see she was still at the window. I held out both hands, pointed to the panther, to my gloved left hand and then to my gloveless right hand and made a Charlie Chaplin 'What now?' sort of gesture with my hands by my side. She gave a kind of half-wave and left the window. I decided to try the castle doors again but just as I reached them they opened.

To cut the story short, the Baroness was polite but firm. She could not give me an interview as it was a strict condition of her divorce settlement that she would not talk to the press. But I did get a few facts when she admitted she was very lonely, had to get a friend to do her shopping because of the occasional invasion of photographers, cooked for herself, and so forth.

When I handed in my story Arthur made a mock grim expression and a thumbs-down gesture. 'Not up to your normal standard, Mike,' he said, but we sat together and managed to add a few bits, mostly atmospheric, and it made a nice little piece with a picture of Nina in her prime. It was when I handed in my French expenses that Arthur yelled at me again.

'What in hell's name is this? "Reimbursement for pair of leather gloves ruined by black panther"?' I told him the full story, showed him my single glove, and finally he signed my expenses sheet.

I should record here that during these new, exciting, testing times, when

I was sent all over the place on stories (and I'm rather ashamed now to admit it), the main victim of my frenetic life was my love affair with Joy. She came up some weekends but I began to find her talk of what she had done in Brighton during the week, to be very 'small-town' and rather boring. She once hired a bedsitter near me and told she had got a glamorous job as a model at Debenhams, and my interest rekindled a little. But I found out she had been turned down as a model simply because she was too curvaceous and a little too short, and she had been spending her days in libraries until such time as she could meet me in the evenings. In the end she sort of faded from my life. I just let her go. At the same time my social life in the evenings had turned, if briefly, somewhat bizarre. I had developed a liking for coloured girls and had joined the well-known coloured Sunset Club in Carnaby Street where some nights I seemed to be the only white man dancing and drinking. I had a brief affair with one of the two leading limbo dancers at the club, a tall, lissom, coloured girl called Beryl, and one Saturday night I took her back to my bedsitter near Holland Road for the rest of the weekend, and we had a mildly riotous time. After I returned from seeing her off at South Kensington tube station for her home in Brixton on Monday morning, I was met by my Irish landlady who was angry with me for bringing a black woman into her house and the noise we had made, and she wanted me out. I wasn't going to argue – her husband, an Irish labourer, looked like Burt Lancaster, and was almost twice his size. I hated the gloomy room anyway, and through an ex-Brighton pal who worked as a sub-editor with the Press Association I found a super top-floor bedsitter in Hampstead, in a classy leafy avenue.

The one thing I did not allow to deteriorate or suffer at this time was my work. The job I coveted on the paper was that of the show-business writer. He wore a monocle and a rose in his lapel, and was always coming in from film previews or premieres and cocktail receptions for movie stars at the Dorchester or the Savoy, which seemed a lot easier and more enjoyable than the tough, hard stories I was sent on. Also, I didn't think much of his stuff – he never got any really gutsy, true-life material from the famous names he met, and I was sure I could do better.

I thought my chance to possibly unseat him had come when Arthur Redford sidled over to my desk speaking sotto voce, as if confiding some great state secret, and said, 'Well, Romeo, I've got a real test for you – Eva Bartok...' I was startled for at the time Eva Bartok was a famous actress who had starred in films with the likes of Burt Lancaster and Dean Martin and was currently conducting an affair with the Marquess of Milford Haven, who was third in line for the British throne. She had given birth to a daughter out of wedlock a year before and the popular press was rife with speculations and were pursuing the couple everywhere they went. At the time she was rehearsing a TV play in a hut in Fulham and Arthur felt I might just get a good interview with her there. When I suggested it was more of a job for the show-business writer, Arthur made a derisory gesture towards the man's empty desk. '*You* have far more chance of getting her than that berk!'

I have written a whole separate chapter about my work – and later romance – with Eva Bartok elsewhere in this book, so suffice it to say that not only did I get a great interview with Miss Bartok but she invited me to fly to Frankfurt with her, to see the premiere of her newest film. It was a major double-page scoop, after which I received an increase in pay, but it did not win me the paper's show-business page.

After a few more weeks of my usual sort of hard stories, my ears pricked up when I heard Arthur discussing with his co-editor who to send to try to get to the then world's major female movie star, Ava Gardner, who was staying at the Savoy. Suddenly the office wag, top features writer Duggie Howell, shouted over to Arthur, 'Send the Mountie'

Arthur gave him the thumbs-up sign, said, 'Exactly', and came over to my desk...

The new lace-making machine invented by Grandpa David, my father's father, and made entirely of wood. He had to sell the patent for £30.

My paternal grandfather, David Tomkies, with his son Vincent (my father) and his wife, Florence, whom we kids knew as 'Granny Mimi.'

My father Vincent, holding me at one month old, with my mother and Grandpa Jack.

Myself at one year old with my mother.

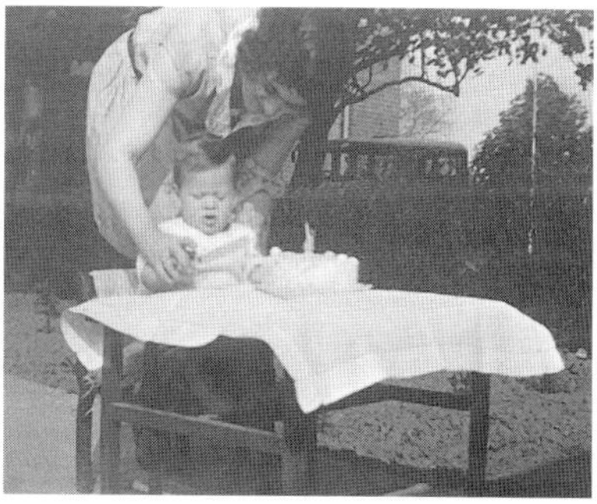

My first birthday party.

I recall nothing of my mother, yet family photos show I was often in her arms.

ABOVE, LEFT: *I spent all of two minutes marvelling at the beauty of a daisy. 'I'd never known you stay still so long,' said Dad.*
ABOVE, RIGHT: *I loved my sister Maureen, always the calm, quiet one.*

My dad, Vincent, at the age of thirty in Beadnell Bay.

Sunny beach days, with, from left to right, Valerie, Grandma 'Mimi,' Maureen, Dad and myself, very skinny at nine.

Vincent Tomkies marries his vivaceous secretary Bettie Mathieu in her home town of Whitley Bay on 20 March, 1937.

In the garden of our new home in Worthing. BACK ROW: *Grandpa Jack Stewart, Dad's new wife Bettie, and Dad who, under great work pressures, had become more of a disciplinarian.* FRONT: *Maureen, Valerie and myself, aged ten.*

In my Coldstream Guards training squad at Caterham (top right). *I ran away from home to join the Guards where my long neck and narrow shoulders began to fill out from the age of seventeen.*

Constant work with spring exercisers helped me gain some bulk.

Boxing training on the barracks' rooftop at Mount Carmel, Haifa, in Palestine, at age 19. Wide open to a left hook!

After leaving the Army I enjoyed considerable success as an amateur cyclist, winning several cups and medals. With my reporter pal Paddy Welsh.

Starting my first race – I won the cup.

In the race for another cup.

After landing a job in Fleet Street I bought my second car, a rakish but rather clumsy old Triumph Roadster, and often drove to Brighton at weekends for dates with Joy.

After a beauty queen surprised me by saying I was good looking, I spruced myself up considerably. Here is my trademark bow tie — which TV star Robin Day copied after we'd met in St-Tropez.

My first real love Joy (centre) who had just won a Brighton and Hove fashion contest.

The Asta, *a sleek but old 88ft gaff-rigged ketch which still held the Bremen to Heligoland sailing speed record. Our motley crew planned to go round the world in it.*

Lucien, former light heavyweight champion boxer of Argentine hands a coil of rope to would-be girl crew member. After a scuffle on the boat in dock in Spain, he and I ended up in the sea – but became good friends after it.

The crew of the Asta. *We were called 'The New Elizabethans' by the Sunday* Pictorial.

As a show business columnist my life was one hectic round of previews, cocktail parties and receptions. Here shaking hands with actress Patricia Bredin. Terry Thomas looks serious in the background.

Gia Scala, star of The Guns of Navarone, *said she could row a boat – so I let her do so on the Serpentine.*

Possibly the greatest female star, beautiful and delectable Ava Gardner, was enormously influential in my life – scoop interviews with her landed me the fabulous show business column – and got me out of it when the job turned sour. Like Eva, Ava told me I ought to do something more intelligent than talk to movie stars for a living. And I'll never forget the night we kissed!

In Hollywood after a fine interview with Dean Martin.

The film studios often used my columns prominently in their publicity campaigns.

My first job in Hollywood was to write a feature on the most popular TV series of the late fifties and early sixties – Wagon Train. *Here I'm talking to the early star of the series Robert Horton (right) and Ted Kotcheff, the Director. Over a beer later, Bob said he was getting fed up with the role and wanted something more challenging!*

After a revealing interview in which Rock Hudson told me the only reason he took up acting was to cure his shyness, he drove me to his yacht for lunch. And I had to cook it!

At Heathrow airport after movie star Eva Bartok had invited me to fly with her to the premiere of her new film in Frankfurt. It was the start of our romance.

One of my first jobs as show business editor of the best selling Weekend *magazine was to get stories from the two 'Kings of Horror' in those days – the fabled Boris Karloff (Frankenstein and others) and the versatile actor Christopher Lee, initially famous for his Dracula roles.*

I flew to Vienna to meet Yul Brynner, sensational star of The King and I, *when he made* The Journey *with Deborah Kerr. I managed to overcome his initial slight hostility to get a fabulous interview, beginning with his days as trapeze high flier, and he even gave me a treasured smoking pipe.*

With the treasured pipe Yul Brynner gave me in Vienna.

For too long I was arrogant, conceited and selfish, and must have been totally insufferable.

My beloved Jaguar XK120 sports car – with girlfriend Paula sitting on it.

My dad at fifty-four has just enjoyed a run in my sleek new rare Healey Elliot car. I later wrapped it round a bollard outside Buckingham Palace.

Jilly – (left) fabulous showgirl and dancer, and wonderful girl. She wouldn't marry me! And fresh from her dancing triumphs in Paris – even my poor photography (right) cannot disguise her beauty.

I went through sports cars like a frustrated racing driver.

I tried to recapture the joys of boyhood by returning to shoot on Jim Adkins' Sussex estate.

Lovely Alexandra — as I first met her.

14
Ava

I had no experience whatever of pursuing world-famous movie stars, and while I had adored Ava Gardner's image from afar as a youth, as I had to a lesser extent Rita Hayworth, Ginger Rogers and Mitzi Gaynor, I very much wanted to get a good story from 'the world's most beautiful animal' or even just to meet her. Approaches to her agent and the publicity folk on her last film yielded no result. Miss Gardner was not giving interviews, was here to discuss a deal and not to promote a film. In fact Ava Gardner had not given a single interview to a journalist since her divorce from Frank Sinatra five years earlier. It was clearly a very tough assignment but, if I got lucky, a major scoop. I decided to approach her from a position of deep respect.

In the *Daily Mirror*'s extensive cuttings library, I prepared my list of careful questions after noting the salient facts of her life. Born Ava Lavinia Gardner in 1922, to a poor share-cropping family in Grabtown, North Carolina, she was the youngest of seven children. Her arrival in Hollywood was purely fortuitous. An MGM executive happened to see some photos her elder sister's photographer husband took when she had spent a short holiday with them. At first, until she was schooled out of her strong Southern accent, her superb figure and alluring beauty were used in parts where she played dumb girls who said little but looked wonderful. I came across this quote: 'I was promoted as a sort of siren, played sexy broads, and people thought I was like that off screen. They couldn't have been more wrong. I was not at all sophisticated. I was born a country girl and still have a country girl's values.' Aha, I thought, maybe if I could get to meet her, this country boy might just have enough in common to get on with her.

Ava had found herself plunged into a world she hardly understood. By the time she was twenty-two in 1946 she had been married and divorced twice, from the then major star Mickey Rooney and the leading bandleader Artie Shaw. She remained single for the next five years, turning down marriage to the billionaire aviator and producer Howard Hughes, despite sumptuous offers, and her career began to improve, with meatier parts opposite Burt Lancaster in *The Killers*, Clark Gable in *The Hucksters*, as the tragic Julie in *Showboat*, with Humphrey Bogart in *The Barefoot Contessa* and James Mason in *The Flying Dutchman*. Her third, and last, marriage to Frank Sinatra lasted two years but it was stormy, beset with frequent rows, mercurial moods and raw jealousies, followed by romantic makings-up again. It was well chronicled that Sinatra made two suicide bids, once when she jilted him before the marriage and again after she split from him for his unfaithfulness, and was filing for divorce. Both had truly loved the other and although they could not live together, they remained friends. Even if I did manage to meet her I doubted I would extract much about deeply personal matters, so unless she volunteered some I would not broach them.

The following morning I went to the Savoy Hotel where she had hired the sumptuous River Room Suite, and found out from the floral desk that Ava Gardner's favourite flowers were yellow roses, although she had not ordered any on this visit. I forked out £3 for a bunch, attached a brief note that said simply, 'From one of your thousands of admirers, Mike Tomkies – journalist,' and asked them to be delivered to her suite. I hoped that would make her curious. Knowing she was now in a Hispanic period, in that she loved and lived in Spain, I went to the British Library and copied down a few verses from the great Spanish poet Garcia Lorca, one of which was entitled, 'A las cinco de la tarde'. I wrote a longer note (I can't recall the exact wording now) saying that I was a young journalist who greatly admired her acting, was working for the *Woman's Sunday Mirror*, part of the *Mirror* group, and that we concentrated on the feminine aspect in our interviews and wanted nothing of a sensational or too personal nature. I had also walked across Spain! I added that if she would grant me an interview I would guarantee to show her the copy so she could correct and alter at will before it was published, or she could even cancel it altogether. I signed the note, knowing I was taking a big risk, but I hoped that the last promise might be enough of a hook. I added that I would telephone her after midday (I imagined she probably got up late) and she could agree to meet me or not.

In the morning I returned to the Savoy, bought another bunch of yellow roses – £4 worth this time! – and had them and the new note sent up. I returned to the office to finish another story I'd been working on, and when Arthur asked me how it was going with Ava Gardner I said I had reasonable hopes but would know by tonight. When I told him what I'd paid for the flowers, and expected to recover it from my expenses, he said, '£7 for bloody yellow roses? You better get the story!'

Wearing my only suit, I returned to the Savoy just after midday and waited on tenterhooks in the reception lounge. Ava's phone was not answered until 3 p.m. but then a soft but direct voice asked if I was the person who kept sending her yellow roses. When I said I was she said she could not guarantee giving me an interview worth publishing but if I was prepared for that I could come up later.

'At what time, ma'am?'

'Why – *a las cinco de la tarde*, of course!'

After nervously knocking on the door of her suite at the appointed time I was surprised when it was opened by Ava herself, who was quite alone, with none of the hangers-on I'd anticipated. Immediately, I took in the thick, glossy dark hair and the beauty of her large green, almond-shaped eyes. I can't recall what she wore, probably because with really beautiful women I tended to try to guess, or visualize, what was behind or beneath the dress. She didn't look quite like the gorgeous young Julie in *Showboat* as she wore almost no make-up and was eight years older than in that film, but she was still stunning. She poured us both a gin and tonic and we sat down on a huge white sofa. At first, when I produced my long list of questions, she objected, but when I said I wanted to make this the best and most accurate interview she had ever given, and reminded her that she could check it herself, she relented. She even seemed impressed that I'd gone to the trouble of doing such full research.

The interview that followed could fill half a book, so suffice it to say, I found her totally honest and frank. We went through most of her life, how she was born a blonde and stayed one until she was fourteen, her country-girl childhood, insights into her early career, how she felt about her best-known films and that she had not been really good in any of them. I even managed to get some glimpses into her three marriages:

'Where I grew up in North Carolina, people got married and stayed married. That's what I grew up hoping to find – a good man I could love and marry and cook for, who would stick around for the rest of my life.' Although her first two marriages lasted less than a year she had initially loved both Mickey Rooney and Artie Shaw. She told me that when she had fallen in love and married Frank Sinatra she had 'truly hoped it would be love eternal but it was like mixing two volatile chemicals in a jar.' She also revealed that unless she was really in love with a man she found physical relations difficult. After nearly two hours of talking, I was quite surprised how she had told me more than I'd expected, or even hoped for, and I knew I had one major scoop on the great star in my notebooks.

We had quite a few laughs and I recall how if one of my remarks or jokes impressed her, she had a way of throwing her head back to look at you in a supplicant manner, exposing the exquisite curve of a beautiful neck. It was a tremendously feminine movement, but she could sometimes swear like a trooper too. As she smoked a lot she didn't mind me smoking my pipe. She showed interest and wanted to try it. She took three puffs, blowing the smoke out again, and said, 'Hmm, quite nice. A bit strong!' When she handed the pipe back to me I put it straight into my pocket – to kiss later. It had been embraced by her lovely lips! As I kept looking at her, still hardly believing I was actually sitting close to a star I'd worshipped as a callow village youth, I thought she had a really lovable beauty. As she shook my hand with a firm grip when we said goodbye, she told me I'd have to wait until 10.30 the following night to show her my written story as she was going to an opera. We could meet in the foyer of the Savoy at that time. I raced back to my bedsitter in Belsize Square and spent the rest of the day typing out the entire interview from my notes.

In the morning I presented a copy of the notes to Arthur Redford, who read them through with several happy expostulations, then rushed them in to editor Lee Howard. When he came back he was ecstatic, saying I'd got my greatest scoop ever. We spent the whole day working on the final story, then I took it to the Savoy at 10.15 p.m. in case Ava came back a bit early. I waited anxiously in the foyer, clutching the copy, expecting her to appear with her male escort for the night. But she swept through the revolving doors on her own, seized my hand with a big smile and led me to the lift. We went up to her suite and she found someone had sent her a crate of champagne. We went through the story quaffing it and Ava became ever more relaxed. She changed very little of the story, and even improved it. On the first morning of their honeymoon Ava had left Frank in bed and taken some trouble to make him a fabulous breakfast – ham, eggs, hash browns, hominy grits, the lot. When Frank finally came into the dining area he looked at the hearty breakfast and growled, 'All I want is juice!'

I had quoted Ava as saying, 'Oh, you do? Okay.' And she threw the fruit juice at him. Ava crossed the line out and substituted: 'And she threw the whole breakfast at him!'

It was well past midnight when Ava congratulated me on the accuracy of the story and said she was happy for it to be printed. As we said goodbye and she presented her face for a quick peck on the cheek, I saw the crate of champagne was half empty. I drove back to my little bedsitter in a dank dawn with a stupid grin on my face. I was cold and hungry, for in the excitement of clinching the scoop on Ava Gardner I'd given no thought to food. All I had in my kitchenette was a cold slice of toast left over from breakfast, and a can of spaghetti. I didn't even have a shilling for the gas so I ate the cold spaghetti on the cold toast and went to bed.

The story was splashed over the entire front page of the paper and most of the back page as well. There was even a half-page advert in the parent *Daily Mirror* proclaiming my scoop, the first interview Ava Gardner had given since her divorce from Frank Sinatra. I sent Ava two copies of the paper and received a lovely little note from her giving her phone number in Madrid and offering to meet up again if I was ever in Spain and wanted another article.

A few days later I was in a pub in Hampstead when I met a work acquaintance, John Knight, who was assistant editor on the most popular general magazine of the time, *Weekend*, which sold some three and a half million copies a week. He congratulated me on the Ava scoop and asked if I was interested in doing show business full-time. When I told him I'd put so much effort into the Ava piece precisely because I was after the show-business job on my paper, John said, 'Forget your paper! We need a good showbiz reporter on *Weekend*. If you're interested I'll fix you up an interview with our editor, Howard French.'

He was as good as his word and two days later I was discussing my ideas for a new show-page section with Mr French; basically, that we should concentrate on the truly big stars of film and TV, anticipate when they would visit London and get the stories out first so we could scoop even daily papers whose columnists all rushed at the stars when they actually arrived. We could also have a separate section for up-and-coming stars if they had good little stories, so we could get them sweet for our magazine when they became bigger names. Howard French listened, said he liked my ideas very much and would decide in a few days whether to offer me the job as show-business editor of the magazine. Meanwhile, could I try to get an interview with the new singing sensation, Mario Lanza, now visiting London for his appearance in the Royal Command Show?

15
Mad Mario – and Mitzi and Sophia

Mario Lanza was behaving atrociously, and as it was my first real show-business assignment, I found it quite unnerving. He stormed around his suite at London's Dorchester Hotel, his black eyes seeming to glow with a strange red light. He shouted at the bewildered entourage around him. He knocked a bottle of soda water over the immaculate carpet and ordered his British manager, the dignified Colin Tennant, to wipe it up. He went in and out of the toilet, bursting into operatic arias – to which he supplied his own profane verses. When they embarrassed a chambermaid he had not seen come in, he apologized profusely to her, strangely concerned that she should not think ill of him.

As *Weekend* magazine had asked me to get a good interview with Lanza, then the world's favourite operatic movie star, while they considered making me their new show-business editor, I felt I was on trial. It had not been easy to get to see him as I'd had to go round in person to the office of his agent, who at first tried to fob me off with an invitation to his one general press call.

At first Mario just poked fun at my questions. When I asked him what he liked doing most when he was not acting and singing, he replied without hesitation, 'Fucking!... But you can't print *that.*' He jabbed my notebook with a finger. 'Better say romancing!'

At last, in desperation, I told him how I'd first seen his films in a small country cinema, how *The Great Caruso* had even inspired my cycling twelve miles to take singing lessons for six months. (I did not mention Al Jolson!) I explained how this was my first trial interview on a new job and if he didn't talk to me I'd probably not get the job.

Instantly Lanza's manner changed. I was no longer one of *them*, one of the spiteful press corps who persecuted him for being overweight and for his drinking, or hinted that he was losing his voice. Nor was I like the Hollywood executives who had him under contract and insisted he diet to an unnatural sylph-like figure for films or star in feeble melodramatic stories just to make money while he was a hot property.

He ordered everyone else from the room and invited me to have lunch with him – it consisted of three trays of exotic ice creams, of which I could manage only half a tray, and nothing else! And he answered all my questions so honestly that I knew I had a terrific story for my first show-business pages. He went through the major events of his life, from being a 'no account waterfront boy' by the Delaware river in south Philadelphia, the son of poor immigrant Italian parents, to where he was today. He denied the popular story that he'd been a piano mover who'd burst into song while shifting a piano in the presence of a famous conductor. He told me how he fell in love with his best Army mate's sister, Betty Hicks, and how when his new record chiefs wanted him to move to New York in a hurry, he insisted she marry him at once. Betty agreed, but instead of the big church wedding and honeymoon she had dreamed of, Mario went into a small jewellery store and paid £3 for a ring and they were married the following day, 'unlucky' Friday the 13th, 1945, in the Beverly Hills municipal court.

'She is still wearing that ring,' Mario laughed. 'I keep wanting to buy her a far better one but she won't take it off!'

He went through his rows at MGM, especially when they made *The Student Prince* using his voice on the soundtrack but giving the part to newcomer Edmund Purdom because they felt Lanza had become too overweight and no longer fitted the costumes.

'This just showed what they were like,' he told me. 'How can you take a promising actor you have faith in and let him become the ghost of a voice that has been accepted by the world? Is that the right way to introduce a new star you believe in – let him represent the ghost of a voice?' And Lanza was right. While his recordings sold as well as ever the film was not a big box-office hit. Knowing he had only had formal voice coaching for two years in his youth, I asked how he kept his magnificent voice. His reply astonished me.

'I have done less training than any singer who has ever lived. I never think about my voice. I don't give a damn about it! It's just been there ever since I was born. It is a gift from God which is beyond me. It could have come to you. I am merely the keeper of a voice. I am the man who luckily or unluckily it passes through. People say to me I'm lucky. Lucky! Do you remember that line in *The Great Caruso* where he says, "A voice has to be in one place, but the man wants to be in another."? Can you imagine anything truer than that?'

My new editor, Howard French, was so delighted by my Lanza story that he not only gave me the job but added a fiver a week on top of what I'd asked.

Little could I have guessed as I left him that Mario was just eighteen months from his death. He returned to Rome where he was then living and resumed the overeating and carousing, followed by dangerous drastic diets, which weakened him. When he went into hospital, Betty tried to keep a constant vigil by his side, but one afternoon they quarrelled and she went home. A short time later Mario telephoned her and asked her to come back to the hospital as he was feeling worse. But Betty, hurt, and thinking it was yet another ruse, did not go at once. Some hours later, when she relented and did return to his hospital room, she arrived only to find he had died without her. On 7 October, 1959 his heart had given up the unequal battle. He was only thirty-eight years old. The grief-stricken Betty Lanza died six months later. She was found dead in the home she rented in Beverly Hills. Today Mario and Betty Lanza lie side by side in the family crypt at Hollywood's Calvary Mausoleum.

The tragedy of the Lanzas is one of the saddest in Hollywood's turbulent history. If his voice was God-given it was one the mere man, tragically, could not handle. But he left behind some beautiful records, and the evidence of that gift lives on.

As soon as I was finally offered the great job on *Weekend* I went to resign from the *Woman's Sunday Mirror* and I must say Lee Howard and Arthur Redford were very good about it and let me go in two weeks. It was not until the last night, when Arthur had organized a farewell bash in the office for me that I had a clue to a question I had been idly asking myself. I had noticed in recent months that whenever a tricky story on a beauty queen, starlet or pretty model came up, I was the one who was sent. I assumed it was because I'd been nicknamed 'the Mountie' as I always got my story.

As all the reporters, sub-editors, picture-room and other staff assembled to raise a toast to my future success, I was astonished when Arthur produced a huge white file which had a big photo of my face (boss-eyed) on it and in large black capitals: 'Mike Tomkies – Is This Your Life?' Arthur, who was doing some comedy scriptwriting with the young Bob Monkhouse at the time, had written a long, hilarious speech in a spoof take-off of the popular TV show *This Is Your Life* in which he really, cleverly yet kindly, took the urine out of me! But I was a bit perplexed when he kept referring to me as 'Handsome Harry'.

I duly responded with a little thank-you speech of my own and was especially touched when I was presented with a fine gold watch as a parting gift. Later, we all repaired to Dorothy's Club in Knightbridge for drinks and a buffet party I had organized. Through my contacts with some London model agencies I had invited them to send along any girls who fancied free drinks and food and meeting press types. Naturally, I was on a high that night, in good form and holding animated conversations. Suddenly a tall, beautiful blonde girl called Bridie, who had just won a major London beauty contest, sat down next to me and said, 'You're so handsome! Can I talk to you?'

I nearly fell off my bar stool. I had never regarded myself as handsome – quite the opposite – and felt myself to be gawky and awkward in the company of pretty women; in fact the prettier they were, the more inferior I felt. But it now dawned on me why Arthur had kept referring to me as 'Handsome Harry' and why I'd been sent on all the stories involving young women. It seemed I *was* regarded as being good-looking. Well, I responded to Bridie's advances with considerable alacrity. We had a few too many drinks and she ended up in my car, in my bedsitter, and in my bed. She became my girlfriend for that summer.

After Bridie had left the following morning I took a good look at myself in the mirror. Hmm, I suppose I was not *too* bad! I decided that from now on I would make the best of myself. I bought a new Daks suit, a smart, light grey Harris tweed sports jacket and new shoes. I switched to always wearing bow ties and bought a sunray lamp so I could have a permanent tan. I got my dentist to make a bridge for my missing upper-right-four tooth, which I'd lost way back in Chichester, so there would no longer be even a slight gap when I smiled. I also acquired a barber, Benny, who restyled my hair. I will always remember Benny on the day he tried to sell me some hair preserver.

'If you use this preparation on your scalp you will *never* go bald,' he said.

I said okay, then saw *he* was bald! I said, 'Listen, if it works so well, how come *you* are bald?'

But Benny had the answer, 'Ah, this wasn't *invented* when I was your age!'

The first star I interviewed once I'd actually got the job as show-business editor was one of my boyhood screen heroines, Mitzi Gaynor, who was in London for the premiere of *South Pacific* in which she gave a career-best, barnstorming performance as Nellie. It seemed incredible that I should now be in the Savoy Hotel and extracting vital life-story facts from a star I'd once worshipped from afar as a gawky youth. One of the best bits was when I asked her husband, Jack Bean, how he had won and married her.

'Mitzi fell ill shortly after we met and had to go into hospital. Of course, a gal like her had plenty of boyfriends, would-be suitors. I went to the hospital every day and no matter what other boyfriend might be there, I outstayed them at her bedside. I just outsat them all!' (Just as I had done with Joy.)

When it was time for me to leave I was astonished when Mitzi jumped up, grabbed my very heavy camel hair overcoat from its peg and held its arms out like a valet so I could put it on easily. A really sweet woman.

At the premiere itself I had a few words with the great composer Oscar Hammerstein who was then in his late sixties. I asked him how a man of his age could keep coming up with great romantic songs of great passion and emotion. I'll never forget his reply.

'Listen, son, a man never loses his hopes for romance until the day he dies. All that changes when you get old is you puff a lot more when going up the stairs! Everything else stays the same.'

Being seventy-six as I write this, I can only say how right he was! I had loved his work ever since I heard 'You'll Never Walk Alone', which he wrote in 1945, its upbeat theme coinciding with our rising hopes at the end of the war. It remained one of my favourite songs for years, until football adopted it.

My next interview, again at the Savoy, was with the new screen goddess, Sophia Loren, of whom more later. She revealed her childhood had been poverty-stricken, and her mother had to make sacrifices to look after Sophia and her sister Maria. As a young girl she was so skinny she was nicknamed by her schoolmates 'Little Stick'. She was eloquent, too on the theme that whereas the gods of fate had given her worldly success and riches with one hand they had taken away some of her happiness with the other because she had so far been unable to have what she most wanted – a baby.

While it was now very enjoyable to be meeting some of the world's major movie stars in luxury hotel suites, I really wanted to travel. Most of all I hankered to make a trip to Hollywood and, like I had done as a boy hunting wildlife, hunt down the major names and get meaningful human-interest stories from them. I figured that if I could get to the movie-making capital, where they would be trapped in the various studios working on their films, I could steal a march on the rest of Fleet Street's show-business reporters who waited until stars actually came to Britain to publicize their films. I put these ideas to my editor and he said he would give them some thought.

One morning Howard French called me into his office and said he would grant my wish to go abroad, not to Hollywood but to the south of France – if I felt sure I could get an interview with Brigitte Bardot.

16
Brigitte and Belinda

As my Triumph sports car purred its way south through the beautiful French countryside, I felt a mounting excitement – and not a little fear. This was my toughest assignment to date and if I succeeded, my new career as a show-business reporter would seem to be set in stone. Brigitte Bardot was now the biggest female film star in the world following the release of *Et Dieu Créa La Femme*, the epoch-making film she had made with Roger Vadim. She was only giving group interviews at actual premieres but my task was to lay siege to her at her new home, the isolated Villa La Madrague outside St -Tropez, and try to get as much of her personal story as I could. Then, if I was successful, I had to track down Britain's beautiful new star, Belinda Lee, who was in the middle of a *grand scandale*, having walked out on her husband, Rank photographer Cornel Lucas, to conduct what seemed a hopeless love affair with the handsome Italian Prince Filippo Orsini. He was a famous Roman aristocrat and the Papal Prince, and he was married with two children, so could not get a divorce under Italian law. It was clear that Miss Lee could give a fascinating story but was refusing all press interviews. One tabloid journalist had found her staying at a casino in Cannes but had only got a two-line quote from her.

Two really tough jobs for the Mountie!

On first arriving in St-Tropez I located and booked into a small, cosy hotel called La Michaudière which was off the main promenade but still overlooked the little harbour with its bobbing yachts. It was run by a small, friendly chap who introduced himself as San Tomas. He knew where Bardot's holiday home was and showed me how to get there. Then, before an early supper, I went to the nearest florist and ordered a huge bunch of yellow and red roses to be delivered to the villa at 9.30 a.m. the next day (not too early as the star might be abed). I enclosed a note saying that as her new film was being released in Britain in six weeks' time I would like a short personal interview which would help promote it, adding 'if possible – today'.

At supper I was pleasantly surprised when an attractive, brown-haired young woman sat down almost opposite me on the long bench table. I noticed she had a fine, narrow-waisted body with big, firm breasts. I was deliberately conversing with San Tomas only in French, feeling I needed to rehearse my schoolboy version of it as, if I got to interview her, Bardot would probably not speak any English. So when the girl said a polite good evening, I responded only with 'Bonsoir'. Soon she was joined by her rather loud boyfriend, who had a Cockney accent and was something in advertising. Before long they were having loud arguments in English, the girl wanting to go to a nightclub but the man wanting an early night after a long drive. I pretended I knew no English, only speaking occasionally to San Tomas in French. That way I could be highly amused during my meal as clearly the couple believed we could not understand what they were saying. After a quick large cognac to help me sleep I turned in early, to be fresh for my onslaught on Bardot.

As I approached the Villa La Madrague in the morning, I saw it was surrounded by a sort of screening fence of bamboo, and that there were three men standing by a small gate. In case they were bodyguards I parked my car a good 100 yards away, out of their sight, which turned out to be the first astute move I made. Checking my notebook, pencils and bow tie, I walked towards the gate. There were only two men there now and they were calling out towards the villa. It was soon obvious they were not bodyguards but Italian paparazzi, photographers who had come all the way from Italy trying to get photos of this great new star semi-naked or even completely so, but she was not cooperating! I then saw that the third man was standing in the sea, holding a small poodle-type dog, and the men were calling out in French that if Brigitte didn't come out and show herself they would drown her dog!

I could see that Bardot was at a window in the villa, wearing a green bikini. waving her arms and appearing to be screaming. There seemed to be no one else in the villa which I thought very odd. I looked at the three men: all were smaller than me. I brushed the two aside, shot through the gate and dashed into the sea with my right fist raised, shouting, 'Donnez moi le chien! Donnez moi le chien!'

The man thrust the dog at me. I grabbed it, oddly still dry, tucked it under my left arm, pushed the man over in the sea for good measure, and waded back up with the poodle. As I got near the villa Bardot opened the windowed door but didn't come out. She took the dog from me with what seemed a reluctant smile, then said, 'Who are you?'

'I'm the man who sent you the roses.'

'You also saved my dog. What do you want here?'

'I want to do an interview with you, just talk to you for my magazine.'

'I don't want any pictures taken,' she replied. It was obvious she had not read my note but I was surprised that she spoke quite good English. I said, 'I don't want to take any pictures. I'm not interested in any photographs. I don't have a camera!'

She said again, 'Well, what *do* you want?'

She could not seem to understand that someone just wanted to talk to her. I was in the middle of reassuring her, telling her she could read anything I wrote, when she said, 'Oh, all right. Come in – and you must take off those wet…' I sat down, undid my shoelaces, took off my wet shoes and was pulling off my left sock when, to my surprise Bardot bent down and swiftly removed my right sock! She even rinsed them under a tap, wrung them out and handed them back to me to lay out in the sun. She said she had some spare time as her house guests were not due back until after lunch and in view of the paparazzi outside it might be a good idea if I stayed around until their return. She led me into a small, flowered, sunlit patio in the centre of the villa, positioned me on a seat nearby so the sun could dry my trouser ends, then lay back in a hammock and said I could start asking my questions. I had fifty-seven questions typed out, based on my full research, but I only produced the top sheet for fear of scaring her.

I will never forget the three hours that followed. The world's sex kitten, its newest star, just swung languidly to and fro in her hammock, wearing the briefest green bikini, and answered my questions with such astonishing frankness that I was sure she was not used to interviews. I was so obsessed with getting my story that I was quite oblivious to her charms, although I did notice her superstructure was both large and perfect because occasionally she shifted the top half of her bikini so as to get an even tan.

To cut a long story short, I got the scoop of my life so far. I also got a free beer which Brigitte got up and poured for me. She shrank from no hard questions, even said she agreed with those who claimed that her looks, walk and pouting lips were more important than her talent. She was definitely not an actress. The parts she played, a mixture of innocence and passion, little girl and grown woman, were based on her real personality. She gave me an intensely detailed account of a wealthy but lonely and strict upbringing, of how she met and fell in love with Roger Vadim, how he made her a star, and how and why she left him when she fell in love with actor Jean-Louis Trintignant. She said she and Vadim were better friends now than when they were married, and he was still directing her. She explained in detail the kind of man she loved, that she didn't believe we only fall in love once. She admitted that some days she just felt ugly and wouldn't go out. She even described her feelings before a publicized suicide attempt. It was a truly astonishing conversation and my shorthand was put to its hardest test. And as I pulled on my now-dry socks and shoes, I knew I had enough material for a three-part series in my magazine.

When her house guests arrived and were walking up the path, Bardot saw me to the door, then surprised me even further by saying, 'Michael, tonight I go dancing at the club Whisky A Gogo. You will come with me, yes?'

'Yes!' I replied with alacrity, and when she said she didn't know when her guests would leave, it was agreed I would telephone her later to fix the precise time and place of our rendezvous.

As I jumped into my open-top car, relieved that the now absent paparazzi had either not spotted it or didn't associate it with me as it had not been touched, I was on such a high I could not just go back to my little hotel. It was only 2 p.m. and the sun was high in the sky. This must be one of those golden days when my luck was in. Why not milk it to the full? I decided there and then to immediately pursue my second target, the errant British actress Belinda Lee. After gulping down a quick omelette at a quay side café, I roared off on the thirty-mile drive to Cannes.

I located the Palm Beach Casino easily enough and soon found that Belinda Lee was not in the restaurant or the bar, but when I asked the barman he pointed through the window towards the swimming pool. I walked through the door and quickly spotted the blonde beauty, one of only three people sitting round the pool. She was entirely on her own, half sitting, half lying on a reclining chair under a parasol at the far end, reading a magazine. At this time I prided myself on my swimming prowess and I had a sudden idea. I paid the attendant for my mattress and parasol, changed into my blue swimming costume, then went to stand on the edge at the shallow end. I gave a couple of slight coughs, until Miss Lee looked up from her magazine, then dived in.

I did three fast lengths, complete with professional racing turns, then banged my hands on the side lifting myself out and twisting so that I landed on my backside, splashing water near to where she was sitting. I was sure she would be most impressed. But she had gone! Her chair was empty and her sunglasses rested on her magazine. I rushed over to the attendant who showed me where the star was now – out in the open sea, lazily sculling along on her back.

Pausing only to stuff a few sheets of notepad and a pencil stub into my costume, I ran through the tunnel, dived into the sea, swam underwater until

I was eight yards from her and came up right beside a very surprised Miss Lee. Trying to maintain a serious but phoney dignity, I jokingly produced both pencil and pad while treading water, and asked formally if I, a reporter from the *Daily Mail* group in London, could have an interview. I hoped she would agree as I'd come a very long way. Belinda Lee started laughing so much she seemed in danger of drowning. As we swam back to shore together she did say the tabloid papers had printed 'a lot of lies' about her. I told her my note was very accurate and she could read what I wrote if she wished. She seemed to like the look of me as she invited me to move my mattress and parasol next to hers. We chatted away until she told me that Prince Orsini had left to go back to Rome three days before and taken his car with him. Apart from taxis she was stuck in the Casino while she decided whether to go back to Rome or return to London. She was feeling cold, so we agreed to meet in the bar after we had showered and dressed. We had a couple of cocktails in the bar but I didn't like the atmosphere, and the barman seemed to want to keep within listening distance. I asked Belinda if she would have supper with me somewhere else. It turned out she had a favourite little club overlooking the sea at the other end of town where they served drinks and superb food in a garden restaurant, so should we call a taxi? I told her I had a surprise outside.

She gave a gasp of delighted surprise when she saw my sporty little roadster as it turned out she loved sports cars herself. On the way to the club, as it was still early, she asked me to make a detour up into the mountains so she could feel the wind in her hair, which she had quickly loosened. As I glanced at her laughing face from time to time, I knew I could fall in love with her myself. She really was the most beautiful star Britain had ever produced. But – business is business!

Over drinks and dinner in the romantic candlelit garden of the club, Belinda really loosened up and gave me a marvellous interview saying, basically, that she would never love anyone the way she loved Prince Orsini but she now knew they would never marry and their affair was at an end. Here I had another scoop. We talked and talked, often about general things, even had a dance together and the time went so fast it was 8 p.m. before I remembered Bardot's invitation. It was far too late to telephone her now; she would already be at the Whisky A Gogo club. With a shock I realized… I had stood up Brigitte Bardot, the world's new love goddess!

By now Belinda was getting tired, so I ran her back to the Palm Beach Casino, gave her my London phone number if ever she needed a journalist, shook hands goodbye, and drove back late to my hotel in St-Tropez.

The following day, anguished, I rang Brigitte with profuse apologies, trying to explain I'd been delayed later than I'd hoped on a story in Cannes. She just said, 'Oh, it is no problem. Come tonight! Meet me at the club. I will be there from eight o'clock.' I promised I would not fail again.

I now had two great stories in my notebooks, both obtained in just one day and felt I deserved a break. I wandered along La Croisette looking at the yachts and wondering why it was that almost everyone in the world had more money than me. Thirsty in the constant sunlight, I turned into an inviting little bar for a beer. I sat down on one of the high stools next to a big man with horn-rimmed glasses and suddenly I realized who he was – Robin Day, then making his name as a TV presenter. I had recently interviewed a former Miss United Kingdom, Leila Williams, whom he had dated a few times, so it was easy to get into conversation.

As we talked, he started looking intently at my bow tie (I now always wore bow ties – even with a sports jacket).

'That's a splendid tie,' he said. 'Really splendid!'

It was a silk cream and magenta striped job and it was very striking against the light grey of my Harris tweed jacket. He made several more remarks about it as we sipped our beers. As I was leaving to return for lunch at my hotel we agreed to meet again at 3 p.m., and take a trip out to the Tahiti Plage where there was reputed to be a nudist beach!

During lunch the pretty brunette with the big bosom had another flaming row with her Cockney boyfriend, and I still had not revealed that I spoke English. The row ended with the boyfriend leaving abruptly, saying he was heading home immediately, and if she wanted to stay longer she would have to fly back. The girl, whose name was Elizabeth, did not seem worried by this but just muttered 'Bye bye' and waved her hand. I turned to her and said in my best Cockney accent, 'Cor blimey, love. That was a right ole carve-up!'

'Oh,' she gasped, 'you understood everything!' And with that she left the table. I assumed she was probably going to run after the boyfriend and make peace. As I finished my lunch San Tomas handed me a telegram – a rather frantic one from my editor asking how the two important stories were going. I felt I'd worked a miracle in getting both stories in just one day and that I deserved a bit of fun and a break. I hiked to the post office and sent a reply telegram: 'Both Bardot and Lee stories firmly promised, latter returns three days. Confident can produce.'

That gave me a three-day break and I would enjoy swimming in the sea and sunning myself on the beaches. I met Robin Day as arranged at 3 p.m. and drove him out to the Tahiti Plage where we had a drink at the bamboo bar and chatted. Again he remarked on my bow tie. Later, both admitting we hadn't dared go there alone, we sauntered over to the nudist beach.

'Are you going to take your clothes off?' asked Robin.

'No,' I said. 'Are you?'

'No,' he replied, so we sat there on a sand dune with just our jackets off. I couldn't help noticing how repulsive most human bodies are when naked, especially the overfed middle-aged and the elderly. Only the youthful body, used to great exertion, is beautiful in naked repose, I thought. As we talked it became clear to me that Robin had a great deal more interest in, and knowledge of, the whole political scene than I did and so we didn't really have much in common. I must add here, though, that when I got back to the UK and switched to the news on my TV set, there was Robin Day sporting a big bow tie! And over the years since, when he rose to become the grand inquisitor on the telly and was knighted, the bow tie became his trademark.

After the visit to the nudist beach, I spruced myself up for my date at the Whisky A Gogo with Brigitte Bardot, unable to suppress a feeling of excitement that she must like me or she wouldn't have invited me. I went to the florist and had him make up a bouquet of roses, small enough to be pinned on her dress if she so wished. Imagine my disappointment when I perceived her standing by the bar, for she had three other young men around her, all in close attendance and all more handsome than myself! I, it seemed, would be only admirer number four. It was then that I had a sudden idea. Bardot hadn't seen me yet, so I put the bouquet behind me, backed out through the door again and put the roses in my car. I returned to the Bardot group, made some polite conversation – which was difficult as they were all gabbling away in French – and when she was dancing with one of her admirers I slipped out of the club.

I drove back to my hotel and found out from San Tomas that Elizabeth had apparently not gone off with the boyfriend, and he hadn't come back either. Clutching my bouquet of roses, I knocked on her door, and when she opened it I saw she had been crying. Proferring the flowers, I said I felt very sorry for what had happened and apologized for pretending I didn't understand English. I said I didn't like the thought of her being miserable and alone in her room and would she like to come out for dinner and visit the Whisky A Gogo club? To my delight she thanked me for my kind thought and said she would. What followed was a most enjoyable and totally wild night where Elizabeth ended up in my room, and in my bed. I can honestly say she was a very fit young lady indeed.

It was a good thing she was, too, because in the morning we were woken up rather abruptly. Apparently her boyfriend had changed his mind and returned, and was now stalking the corridors calling her name as he had not found her in their room, which was two along from mine. Quickly, Elizabeth looked out of the window and saw there was a foot-wide platform or shelf running along the side of the building about a yard below window level. When we heard her boyfriend clattering down the stairs, she climbed out and edged her way along the shelf until she could get through the window of her own room. I was terrified she would fall off for if she edged along facing outwards her large bosom might overbalance her. If she faced inwards it might push against the wall and bounce her off the ledge! She managed it, however, and disappeared through her window with a cheery wave and smile to me. Tired, I returned to bed, overslept and was too late for breakfast but San Tomas told me the couple seemed reconciled and had left the hotel to drive back to the UK.

I spent the rest of that day, after checking Robin was not in the bar, sunning myself alone on a beach, and at the end of it I decided there was little more boring than sunning yourself alone on a beach. I telephoned my editor to tell him that I had both major stories in the bag, and the following day I began the leisurely drive home. Years afterwards I had another significant encounter with Bardot, this time in her apartment in Paris, but that story belongs later. I never met Belinda Lee again but I did know Prince Orsini never saw her again after leaving her in Cannes. I felt very sad to learn of her tragic death in a car crash in 1961.

No sooner had I returned to London and written up my stories than Howard French called me in and told me I was going abroad again, this time to try to get the life story of the newest singing sensation in the world – Elvis Presley. He was serving with the US Army in Germany and it had been well publicized that he would be giving no press interviews at all while he was in the Army. This was under strict instructions from his mentor and manager, Colonel Tom Parker.

Clearly, this would be my toughest assignment so far.

17
Elvis

Although at the time I did not appreciate his raunchy style, the pelvic gyrations, the penile guitar, I did realize that Elvis Presley was changing the face of twentieth-century popular music and that he was then arguably the most famous person in the world. When his first main hit 'Heartbreak Hotel' shot up the charts and America's youth could see him on TV, they saw raw passion, great male beauty, an original genius who was able to mix all the sounds of gospel, black and white, country and blues into a revolutionary form that became rock 'n' roll. Some adults were scandalized at first but as more top hits like 'Blue Suede Shoes', 'Teddy Bear', 'Don't Be Cruel', 'All Shook Up', 'Hound Dog', 'A Fool Such as I' followed one after the other, America caved in and so did the rest of the world. Before he was drafted into the US Army, Elvis had made his successful first film, *Love Me Tender*. His manager, Colonel Tom Parker, could have got him an easier job entertaining the troops but he felt, as indeed did Elvis, that he should show a humble patriotism and serve his time as a common soldier.

Through *Celebrity Bulletin* I managed to get the address of the hotel in Frankfurt where Elvis was staying, as apparently US Army regulations allowed him to live away from but within easy reach of the barracks. I realized that if I failed to get him at the hotel, I would have to besiege his barracks, and if I was barred there I might have to find and bribe some of his Army mates in whatever bars or clubs he and they frequented, although my intensive research of the cuttings revealed Elvis did not drink alcohol. Accordingly, when I went to the bank to get enough German marks for my trip I got £50 worth of US dollars too.

I flew to Frankfurt, took a taxi to the hotel – and received a shock. The man at the reception desk, who spoke limited English, told me that Elvis had checked out that very morning. What lousy luck! It was time for quick thinking.

'Oh, gee whiz,' I said, hoping my poor American accent would not be obvious to a German. 'I'm his pal, we drove trucks together in Memphis. I should have been here two days ago but got held up collecting some of Elvis's things.' I briefly held up my small suitcase. 'Please give me his new address.'

At first the man demurred as the hotel staff were under instructions not to give out the new address to anyone. I said that when I had last spoken to Elvis on the phone he had said I should buy the reception desk a drink when I got to the hotel, and surreptitiously produced a $20 bill. The man told me to wait a moment, went into a small kiosk, scribbled something on a piece of paper and returned. The hand that proffered the dollar bill collected the note – with Elvis's new address! The man said he understood that Elvis had rented the top floor of an obscure boarding house and that his father Vernon was joining him there.

I immediately hired a taxi and shot round to the boarding house in the north suburbs of Bad Nauheim, some twelve miles north of Frankfurt and much closer to Elvis's army barracks. It was a modest four-floor detached building, just like the others in the street, certainly not a place where anyone could expect a world-famous star to live. When the landlord came to the door I was careful not to mention Presley at all but said I was an English student and needed a quiet room in which to complete some studies. To my surprise, he immediately let me in, saying there was just one room left, and showed me up to the first floor and into a large, sparsely furnished bedsitter. I had the shrewd suspicion that maybe he did not even know the true identity of the US soldier who had hired the top floor, otherwise he would surely have been warned, and paid off, not to let any strangers into the house. So far, so good. I made a swift reconnoitre, sure from the silence upstairs that Elvis would be at the barracks during the day and would take up residence on the top floor for the first time tonight, but I would not bother him then. I discovered that the stairs had metal edges, and as his apartment was two floors above my room, I thought I might hear him coming down the stairs next morning, especially if he wore Army boots. I went back in to my room, did some more work on the list of questions I had prepared, then retired early.

In the morning I was up at 5.30 and left my door slightly open. When I heard clattering footsteps coming down the iron-clad staircase from above, I pretended to be examining one of the hinges on my door. Not until the tall, well-built man was almost abreast of me could I see that this was Elvis Presley as he had not switched on the stairwell lights. As he passed all I could manage was a friendly 'Hello'. He briefly looked my way, said a cheerful 'Hiya!', with a wave of his hand, and carried on his clattering way and out of the front door. I spent an agonizing day wandering around the streets of Bad Nauheim and went back to compose a short note which I pushed under his door. It just basically said that I worked for the prestigious Daily Mail group, how great I thought he was, and if he gave me a few minutes I'd let him see what I'd written, adding (a white lie) that it was my first major assignment as a show-business reporter. I resolutely resisted the temptation to actually knock on his door that evening, and waited in my room, but he did not contact me.

I repeated the previous morning's procedure and after the same hello and hiya exchange, he paused long enough for me to ask him if he had got my note. I still could not see his face clearly in the semi-darkness but he gave a soft sigh.

'Yes, Yes, sir, I did and would like to help... trouble is, I am under instructions not to give any media interviews while I'm in the army.' I was so astonished that he had called me 'sir' – I was only seven years older than he was – that I was speechless for a moment. I had expected to meet a rowdy hoodlum but it seemed he was modest and respectful of others, and I made another brief beseeching speech emphasizing that if he would only give me a few minutes, and he could read and correct anything I wrote, it could only be good for his new film's release in the UK. Even in that poor light he could maybe see my crestfallen face, for he said, 'Lookee, I can't do anything today ... manoeuvres ... but maybe I could spare a few moments tomorrow afternoon.' I thanked him profusely and he clattered down the stairs again.

After lunch I noticed a tall, good-looking man with short, cropped grey hair sitting in the small lounge reading the American journal *Newsweek*. As we were the only two in the room we soon got talking, and when I asked him what he did he laughed in a modest, almost guilty kind of way: 'You name it, I've done it – farm worker, house painter, truck driver, garments factory'. I told him my dad worked in garments, for the prestigious firm who made Viyella, which he knew about in America, and we laughed at some tales Dad had told me of his selling days. And when I related a few yarns about my time learning to drive trucks in the Army, it seemed we had quite a lot in common. When I asked him what he was doing in a boarding house in a little town in Germany and he said he was waiting for his son to return from his barracks, I knew who he must be.

'Are you Elvis's dad? Are you Elvis Presley's dad, Vernon?'

When he said yes I felt I had no choice but to come clean, and I told him who I was, that I'd been trying for three days for just a short chat with Elvis, and that as it was one of my first major assignments in my new job I was terrified of failing. When I'd finished, Vernon told me to wait in my room after 2 p.m. and he would do his best to get Elvis to talk to me, as his son had this afternoon off and was due to arrive back any time now. He suggested I make myself scarce in the meantime. Excited by this new hope, I hiked about the town and managed to hire a tape recorder which I smuggled into my room and set up on a small table before which I arranged two chairs.

An agonizing three lunchless hours passed – I couldn't even think of lunch, never mind eat any – then came a soft knock at the door. I opened it, and there stood the world's most famous entertainer.

'Hi,' he said, a slight smile on his face. 'I said I'd *try* and come down, and as Dad thinks you seem a regular guy, here I am!' Again I repeated my written promise to let him read and correct anything I wrote, but as he came into the room he raised his hand in reassurance. 'Okay… okay, let's get talking.' Then his glance fell upon the tape recorder and its poised microphone. His reaction surprised me.

'I can't talk into *that*! The Colonel would kill me!'

As I hastily dismantled the machine, explaining I only wanted to be dead accurate, he said he could not run the risk of any tape finding its way on to radio or TV as he had promised Colonel Parker he would do no media interviews while in Germany. I had the impression he was rather afraid of his manager. I carried the tape recorder to the outside stairwell and shut the door on it, so he could be sure he was not being taped.

As I said before, after watching his raunchy stage performances, I was expecting to meet a rather rowdy hoodlum, but now we were in full daylight I was astonished by the sheer sensitivity of his face: his eyes were simply beautiful, and there was a tender, almost babyish texture to his skin. And how modest, almost shy, he was; he often preceded his answers to my questions with the phrase, 'Well, sir …' I also noticed he did not have bitten nails, in those days considered a sign of a disturbed personality. His hands were immaculate. His answers were also disarmingly honest and full. He described in great detail his poverty-stricken childhood after his birth in a two-room shack in Tupelo, Mississippi, when his twin brother Aaron died shortly after birth. His dad had been a house painter by trade, but in that small town where no one had much money, there was little to spare on peeling walls and blistering paint. His mother had to work in a dress factory so they could have enough to eat, and his dad, when he could, got short truck-driving jobs.

'We never actually starved, but we came pretty close to it at times. It may have been very tough but I didn't realize it then as I had no other kind of life to compare it with', he recalled.

What the young Elvis looked forward to most were the family's Sunday visits to their Fundamentalist church. 'I loved the music and sang as loud as I could. We borrowed the style of our psalm singing from that of the early Negroes – a rolling, rhythmic style, with everybody swaying in the church. This was the only singing training I ever had. I never had lessons. I still remember the old church filled with sunlight and my mother and father singing beside me. It helped us forget our problems.'

When Elvis was fourteen the family left the Tupelo shack for a two-room apartment in the city of Memphis, where his dad got a fairly good job in a paint factory. After school, Elvis worked as a cinema attendant, which brought in another fourteen dollars a week. At weekends he mowed lawns alongside Negro labourers at half a dollar a time, depending on the size of the lawn. After school he worked at a 3 a.m. shift in a factory, then became a truck driver, feeling he was then growing into a man. But when he was eighteen his dad had an accident in the paint factory and slipped a disc in his back.

'He came home in great pain and had to go to hospital for two weeks and lie still all day. When he finally came home he couldn't work for weeks. This put a great strain on my mother who had got a job at the hospital, a job she didn't leave for two years. She bathed patients, made beds, scrubbed floors, and worked harder than she'd ever done before. Her health began to fail but she kept at it and came home every evening to do the housework, cook supper and mend our clothes. I used to tell her, " Mom, you shouldn't have to work so hard." And she would smile and say, "I love you both so much I'd sooner work for you than anything in this world."' Elvis's eyes clouded slightly at these memories but he went on.

'In the evenings I tried to cheer them up by playing tunes and songs I'd made up on a guitar my father had bought for my birthday. Actually I had been hoping for a bike, but Dad couldn't afford one – don't put that in! – he had paid eight dollars for the guitar at the Tupelo grocery store, and even that was a stretch. He had to go without smokes for weeks!' Elvis laughed ironically. 'As it turned out later, that guitar was the best present he could ever have bought me!'

Elvis told me he didn't fully realize how serious the family position was until one night when he came home and found his father sitting on his bed with his head in his hands.

'I thought he was just thinking hard. When I asked, "What's up, Dad?" he looked away and he had tears in his eyes. I'd never known my father cry. I didn't know a full-grown man *could* cry. There had been times when he was strict with me, times when he may have been too easy, but he was my father and to see him like that made me scared inside. I knew his injury was worse than he'd told us and he'd tried to laugh it off. But now he turned to me and said, "Look son, it's time you knew the truth. My back is worse than I thought and there may be long periods when I can't work at all. We're going to have a job to pay all our bills."

'I didn't know what to say when he went on, "I never expected to be the greatest man in the world but I wanted to be a good husband to your mother and a good father to you. Now it seems we're in for some real hard times."

'I went away feeling helpless. I was eighteen. What could I do? I did the first thing that came to my mind. I got down on my knees and prayed to God to be shown some way to help my parents.'

One day Elvis was driving down the main street in Memphis when he remembered it would soon be his mother's birthday. He thought he could do something to cheer her up. He smiled as he recalled the moment.

I was just idling along when I saw a sign which said, "Sun Records Ltd, Memphis Recording Services". I had my guitar in the truck so I stopped and went in. The owner, Mr Sam Phillips, and his secretary were sitting at a desk. They said it would cost me four dollars to make a record, so I paid and went into one of the booths.

'I sang the first two songs I thought of – 'My Happiness' and 'That' s Where Your Heartache Begins' – and I remember feeling very silly in there all on my own. When I came out Mr Phillips said, "You got a fair voice. I'll call you some day. We'll try out a number or two."'

Elvis laughed. 'It was a good job I had the truck-driving job because he took a whole year before he rang me!'

He recalled what happened when he returned to the recording studio. 'We tried a few slow ballads for a couple of hours, then during a coffee break I tried to make a few pals laugh by singing a real fast rhythm-and-blues number, 'That's All Right Mama'. They got to clapping and stomping their feet, then Mr Phillips suddenly bounded over and yelled loud, "Boy, that's great; That's how you gotta sing, boy. Let it go. SING UP A STORM!"'

It was the major turning point in young Elvis's life. If I was both delighted and amazed that in response to my carefully researched questions he could open his heart like this, I was even more pleased when he was willing to carry on and give me more highlights and emotional moments from his rise to phenomenal success. It was a full two hours before we finished, then Elvis got up, and as we shook hands at the door he said he had to get ready as he and some pals were going out on the town that night. I thanked him profusely and said I would be around all next day if he wanted to check anything.

I turned back to the table and started going obsessively through my notes, making sure I could read all my own shorthand, as I knew Elvis had given me a major scoop and that it was a story that could run over three issues of my magazine. I also felt exhilarated, and reached for the bottle of wine I'd bought in case I had something to celebrate! After about an hour of slow sipping, I'd just started on my third glass when there was a knock at the door. It was Elvis, now dressed in civvies – smart dark blue trousers and a glorious scarlet open-necked shirt.

'Hey, we're all going to a fair. You want to come along?'

'Sure,' I said. The chance to spend even more time with Elvis was too good to miss. Down went my glass and before I followed him through the door I stuffed all my notes between my mattress and the bedclothes. One can't be too careful. Outside was a large jeep-like open truck with a Corporal mate of Elvis at the wheel and an Army Private next to him, and I was seated beside him. In the back Elvis sat next to a truly gorgeous young girl whom he briefly introduced as Cilla. I noticed she looked startlingly like Debra Paget, with whom Elvis had starred in *Love Me Tender*, and assumed she must be one of his favourite fans. Next to her sat a US airman whom I thought Elvis (again briefly) said was called either Curly or Curry, and he seemed to be chaperoning the girl although he looked too young to be her dad. Elvis jokingly pointed at me and whispered loudly, 'He's a reporter,' put a finger to his lips and added, 'Sssh!'

I can't recall very much of the merriment that followed except that I knew better than to pry about his companions, and Elvis enjoyed himself too much to have time to talk any more at length to me. We hit the big fair, on the outskirts of Frankfurt, and Elvis was intent on dragging us into trying nearly all the rides and slides there were. He was merrily aggressive on some giant-sized Dodgem-type cars and once he hit me so hard from the rear when I hadn't seen him coming that I almost got whiplash. We tried helter-skelters, one ending with a great splash into water, spiral slides, coconut shies and a firing range, and Elvis paid for everything.

Elvis, his driver and I also went on a dangerous whiz-car type of machine which had long arms and circular seat holders at the ends in which you sat. It would dash you round, then pause, then thrash you around again even faster. Elvis loved it, and I noticed he kept leaning out and shouting things like 'Whoopee' and 'Whey-hey' to Cilla, who was standing at the edge with Curly. There were four roof-support pillars around the machine and I was afraid he would lean out too far and break his head open on one of them. I just put my hand up behind his neck and held on to his collar so he could not stretch too far. If he had been brained by one of the pillars as we were swept past at great speed, the world would not have had the rest of Elvis Presley.

I recall I was dropped off at the boarding house first as the rest of them went to take Cilla home, but after such an extraordinary day I could not get to sleep, so I just kept obsessively checking my notes until sheer exhaustion took over.

I had no way of knowing that the beautiful young girl, Cilla, I had met with Elvis was fourteen-year-old Priscilla Beaulieu, daughter of a US Air Force Captain, who had become the true love of the star's life. For two years after his discharge (with the rank of Sergeant) the two corresponded, then Elvis persuaded her parents to let the sixteen-year-old Priscilla go to live on his Gracelands estate, provided she stayed with his dad and Vernon's new wife, Dee. Although, as he admitted to me, he had many lovers among the attractive girls who threw themselves at him, he kept his relationship with Priscilla pure, short of consummation, and the courtship continued for another four years until Elvis popped the question and they were married on 1 May, 1967. It has been widely reported that after the birth of Lisa Marie Elvis lost interest in the physical side of the marriage, Priscilla eventually found solace in her keep-fit trainer and left her husband Elvis in February 1972. They were divorced a year later.

When Elvis was discharged from the Army he returned to a hero's welcome in the US. The fears of some RCA executives that his 'wasted' two years in the Army at a crucial time in his career might have wrecked his voice were fast allayed. Elvis strolled into the recording studio as if he'd never been away and proved that his voice had matured and now had more power, range and confidence. His first disc, 'Are You Lonesome Tonight?' sold a million copies almost overnight. The trouble was that Colonel Parker had signed him up to a long series of cheap, largely banal films, with the arguable exceptions of *GI Blues*, *Flaming Star* and *Viva Las Vegas*. The money was fine but the quality of his work and songs deteriorated, just at the time the Beatles and the Rolling Stones came barnstorming on to the scene. Elvis definitely gave me the impression that he not only respected Colonel Parker but was even slightly afraid of him. He did not see himself as a great star or the original genius that he was, and maybe felt that if he rebelled against the man he thought was responsible for his meteoric rise, it would all end and he would be returned to the poverty of his childhood.

Elvis did no live performances for nine years, during which time he surrounded himself with an entourage of relatives and hangers-on who looked after him twenty-four hours a day. But instead of protecting him from the outside world, they really sealed him off from it, and into loneliness. Elvis turned increasingly to drugs, especially when he began performing live again and needed to get himself up for sporadic tours.

I had been living in the remote wilds of Canada and the Scottish Highlands for seven years, studying and writing books about rare wildlife, my journalistic life long behind me, when I heard of Elvis's death from a drugs overdose on 16 August, 1977. The news hit me hard, as hard if not harder than the deaths of President Kennedy and Marilyn Monroe, for with the exception of John Wayne, of all the major male stars I met and knew, none had been kinder to me than Elvis Presley. I thought it strange and yet fitting that he died at forty-two, the same age as his beloved mother when *she* died, and that his death had occurred within a few hours of the anniversary of her death. Maybe he knew the end was in sight and wanted to be with her again. I have some of his films and concerts on video – especially his last celebrated performance in Hawaii. He was overweight and looked awful, but even to the end of his last US tour in early 1977 his voice never failed him. While some notes were suspect, the increase in pathos and sheer emotion more than made up for this, and he always had me in tears. I bless his memory.

Footnote: It was thirty-one years after his death that it was revealed, through the pioneer research of writer Allan Morrison in Scotland, that Elvis had Scottish roots, and he was a direct descendant of blacksmith Andrew Presley who had lived in the village of Lonmay, Aberdeenshire, 300 years ago. I sometimes wonder if one of the reasons he and I got along so well was because we shared Scottish blood, my mother being a full Highlander.

18
Snapshots One: Tommy, Cliff, Errol, Burt, Yul and the King

To go from the sublime to the... well no, not as bad as that but ironically it was around this time that I think I made a slight contribution to British rock and roll. One of my pals was the London entrepreneur John Kennedy, who had been a contact for a couple of stories when I was with the *Mirror* group. One day he rang up and asked me, as a show-business columnist, to come to the 2Is coffee bar and give my opinion on a young talent he had discovered called Tommy Hicks, who was due to go back to sea as a cabin boy on the *Queen Mary* in two weeks' time. John had promised Tommy to get him stage work before then but Tommy was doubtful. Could I help?

Well, I met them at the coffee bar and Tommy came on with his guitar with all the confidence of a world boxing champion, silencing Wally Whyton and his skiffle group. He sang 'Rock with the Caveman,' and we all knew this was a star in the making. When Johnny asked me what I thought I said, 'He's like a world boxing champion, has tremendous stage presence. This is a big star. You've got to sign him.'

I think that helped convince Johnny he was right – I recall we all argued heatedly on the pavement outside, I urged Tommy to take the plunge and sign with Johnny, but wanting to get back on to the *Queen Mary* where he also entertained, he felt sure that Johnny couldn't get him a good stage job in the West End so fast. He revealed he had to get back to the ship in ten days now, not two weeks. We had to act swiftly.

Through nightclubbing some nights, I had come to know Bill Offner and Al Burnet who ran the Stork Room and, I think, the Swallow Room clubs. We approached them and they gave Tommy an audition and a spot for a week – unpaid. It was just the kind of showcase Tommy Steele (I don't know when his name changed) needed, but we now had to get him some quick publicity to make sure scores of folk went to see him. Johnny hit on the idea of throwing a sort of debs' party at the Stork Room. Through his own girlfriend and my contacts with model agencies we got some pretty debby types together, and Johnny gave some of them a copy of the *Almanack de Gotha* so they could show off their foreign accents and pretend to be debutantes from the Continent. I recall one girl was the Princess of Nuremburg, another a deb from Lichtenstein, and others from 'Wickstein,' and even Paschendaele!

I rang up Derek Agnew, features boss of the huge-circulation Sunday paper *The People*, and Johnny went to see him, saying this fabulous new rock and roll star was already the rage of the debs' set, even foreign debs! Derek sent a reporter and photographer, Tommy performed like never before, and the 'debs' all clapped and yelled their applause. The story made a big splash, then one night the Duke of Kent was in the audience. Johnny Kennedy rushed out as the Duke was leaving and asked him what he thought of Tommy. The Duke replied something like 'Simply marvellous, tremendous,' and that quote appeared in the daily papers via Johnny. Result – the papers were delighted, the Stork Room bosses were delighted, and so was Johnny for he signed Tommy Steele up that very week, and he never went back to the *Queen Mary*. That may seem a shaky start for Tommy's illustrious career, but his great talent ensured he lasted.

It was not long after this that I met another up-and-coming young rock singer who seemed to be vying with Tommy for the title of 'Britain's Elvis Presley' – Cliff Richard. I had been invited by producer Jack Good to do a column on his new pop music TV show 'Oh Boy!'. I watched the first production and it was soon obvious that handsome young Harry Webb from Huntingdon was going to be a big hit. So I did the main interview with him. The first thing Cliff said to me was, 'I read your show page and think it's the best. You've met many big stars so is there any career advice you could give me?'

I replied, 'It may be a cliché but be polite, aim to please whoever pays you, for you can never really earn or deserve the big money you'll get if you make it to the top. Just realize that if you go up like a rocket you can always come down like the stick!'

Cliff laughed at that, but when he wanted to know about my meeting with his own hero, Elvis Presley, it enabled me to explain how Presley was in real life. I added: 'Truly great talent is usually masked by modesty and courtesy and this is always recognised by those who pull the strings. Niceness is the sign of a man who knows where he is going and has no need to prove himself against anyone else. Also, being nice to those you leave behind is a wise policy as the subservient today may become tomorrow's controllers, for their careers follow different and devious paths!'

Cliff said he thought this excellent advice and thanked me. Whether my few words had anything to do with him for ever being known as the 'Mr Nice Guy' of show business, I don't know. Certainly when I met the naive young teenager Harry Webb I never dreamed that he would one day be the millionaire Sir Cliff Richard who would lend his luxury estate in the Caribbean to Britain's Prime Minister and his family for their holidays.

I was in the middle of interviewing Jack Good when he suddenly asked me if I could sing. Taken aback, I said I could – a bit – but why? Jack said 'Well, you're good-looking enough to be a pop star yourself. I could audition you.'

Instantly, I repressed an involuntary shudder as I recalled my disastrous debut as The Darkie, when six months of singing lessons had ended in one night.

'Jack,' I said firmly, 'I have no talent in that direction whatever.'

The fact was I even got stage fright when I had to just announce a few category winners in my own magazine's annual ball for our readers. It was my job to organize this 'Date with the Stars' ball at the Lyceum Theatre, London, and it was quite a production. We had various categories – Actor of the Year, Actress of the Year, Comedian of the Year, and so forth. We canvassed our readers, then made short lists of the names in each category and I had to approach them all. It usually ended with the 'winner' being the one who actually turned up on the night! I remember offering Comedian of the Year to Benny Hill, whom I'd recently interviewed. He could not accept as he had a prior engagement on the night but he did send me an open postcard on which he'd written, 'Dear Mike, which star's ball will you be holding?' I'm glad to say the following year he did attend and performed a little skit on stage which was the hit of the night.

As mine had been the first main show-biz column to praise the new Cliff Richard I felt he maybe owed me a favour, but when I offered him, as our readers wanted, the Pop Singer of the Year award, he said he could not attend as he had an important gig on the night of the ball. But he did suggest his sister could accept the award on his behalf. She was a pretty little girl, and better on stage than I was, and she went down well, especially with our male readers.

My policy of spotting up-and-coming stars and getting their best stories before they became so famous they were hard to get to, sometimes came unstuck. At a preview I saw newcomer Terence Stamp's marvellous first starring performance opposite Peter Ustinov in *Billy Budd,* and was soon round at his Ebury Street, Victoria, flat to get his life story. He was particularly interesting as he came from 'the wrong side of the tracks', the first Cockney lad from the East End to become a serious film actor. As we talked, he indicated his flatmate, a tall, gangly chap with lizard-like eyes and an unprepossessing appearance who was washing dishes in the kitchen, and he said, 'You should write about *him*. He's going to be big.'

'What has he done?'

Terence replied that he was in a play at the Arts Theatre right now. I said I only wrote about major stars or those I felt would become stars. The man served us tea in a pot and poured it professionally like a waiter. He then stood there with the sugar bowl, and asked me politely, 'Do you want sugar, sir?'

I took two spoonfuls, said thanks, and dismissed him from my thoughts. His name? Michael Caine. Now Sir Michael Caine, one of the biggest international male stars Britain has ever turned out.

Another error of judgement on my part was when I tried to set up an interview with Errol Flynn, who had come to Britain to promote his new TV series. Flynn had long been a youthful hero of mine, especially after he made *Gentleman Jim* in which he played James J. Corbett, the Irish dandy who out-footed and out-fought the legendary first world heavyweight champion John L. Sullivan. It was obvious that Flynn really could box, and several times in that film be did perfect 'Ali shuffles' long before Muhammed Ali was born. He was also a keen sailor, and owned his own luxury yacht, so my own sailing adventure and boxing experiences and the fact that I also liked a drink, made me feel we would have much in common. When I heard he was staying at a pub/hotel in Shenley, near Boreham Wood studio, I picked up my office phone in front of all the other reporters and put in a call to Errol Flynn, which made them prick up their ears. When he came on the line I almost felt I was talking to a friend, and I made the mistake of calling him Errol and not Mr Flynn. I was explaining who I was, what big stars had seen me, and that our magazine had over three million readers when, I heard him say, 'Oh shit!' and he banged the phone down.

Not daring to lose face in front of my colleagues, I pressed the phone earpiece to my ear so they would not hear the empty dialling tone, and carried on a conversation as if Flynn was still on the line, saying things like 'Yeah, yeah… could I come and see you?…Well, any time really… you're free now?… the afternoon?… Oh, sure… Okay, I'm on my way.' With a cheery wave to the listeners I shot through the door and down the stairs to my car.

Cripes, now I *had* to get him! I roared through London's northern suburbs and when I reached the pub found that Flynn was in the bar. Politely, I told him who I was, apologized for my crass approach on the phone and said I was also a keen sailor, having sailed through the Bay of Biscay in winter without an engine. He softened then offered me a drink, and was soon giving me a first-class story. I'll never forget his reply when I explained I was shortly to be a judge at a beauty contest.

'Well, sport, be very careful where you place the one you're after! Don't make her the winner because she's got the crown, the car, the big trip to Hollywood or whatever. Don't make her second as she will be so upset at coming so close to winning yet not, you won't get near her. Make the one you fancy third, because she will be happy, and grateful that she even got placed at all!'

I met Errol twice more over the years and he was always fabulous company. It was clear that he was drinking too much as the tell-tale veins were appearing on his face but I was sorry to hear of his death in that Vancouver bedroom at the age of only fifty-one. Mind you, it wasn't a bad way to go – making love to a pretty young woman.

One major slip-up was on my first trip to Hollywood when I was chatting up a girl in the Raincheck Club, frequented mostly by up-and-coming actors and sometimes even a top star. A small man in a smart suit came up to me saying he'd heard I had a big show-business column in the UK, and as his country singer client was due there on a minor concert tour in some two months, would I care to meet him and write about him? He indicated a tall young man wearing black trousers and a black shirt sitting at one of the tables in the smoky interior, who was staring at me with intense black eyes. I said I only wrote about established stars or those I was sure would become major stars.

'Oh, he will, believe me.'

I said, 'What's his name?'

'Cash, John Cash.'

'He won't get far with a name like Cash,' I laughed, and turned back to the girl.

Johnny Cash became one of the greatest country singing stars the world has ever known, and even now I writhe at my own stupidity, for I could easily have got his fabulous, adventurous life story from him there and then. Not only that; when I spent the second half of my life in wild, remote spots studying rare wildlife in Canada, Scotland and Spain, Johnny Cash records formed the backbone of my nightly entertainment on little battery-powered record players.

At this time I was trying to keep fit, mainly to look good for my job – and girls – and was learning judo from world champion Tiger Joe Robinson, who with his brother Douggie gave lessons in their gym in Orange Street, Soho. We amateurs paid our fees and were allowed to throw these two champions about the mats while learning all the various throws like Uchi Mata, O-Soto-gari and Tiotoshi. I recall that once I threw Joe when he wasn't quite ready with a very unorthodox, lucky (for me) move, and as he got up he cracked: 'I know what that throw was called – Oh My Goshi!'

At the time Joe had a contract to teach judo to the girl pupils at the prestigious Roedean School near Brighton. I asked him how he coped with the proximity of all that young, nubile female flesh. How careful did he have to be? He thought for a moment, chuckled and said, 'Well, I don't throw them about much. We do a lot of mat work!'

Joe was a super chap and a superb athlete then – seventeen stone and he moved like a cat. I also thought he was far better as an actor than the critics said when he co-starred with Diana Dors in *A Kid for Two Farthings*.

The biggest disappointment I ever experienced when meeting a movie star came with one I had long admired, and the man I still regard as the greatest screen actor of all time – this may surprise some folk – Burt Lancaster. No star has equalled him in the infinite variety of his roles. Look at just a few of them, the 'beefcake' acrobat in *The Crimson Pirate*...the Olympic athlete in *Man of Bronze* (still one of my favourite sports films)... the brittle, flawed city sophisticate in *Sweet Smell of Success*...the rugged Marine and that famous love scene with Deborah Kerr in *From Here to Eternity*... the ebullient, extrovert Italian truck driver with Anna Magnani in *The Rose Tattoo*... the crippled catcher in *Trapeze*... the gentle, sensitive prisoner in *Birdman of Alcatraz*... his Oscar-winning, barnstorming role as the evangelistic preacher in *Elmer Gantry*... the tragic, dignified Nazi Chief Justice in *Judgement At Nuremberg,* when he acted principally with his face... the doomed sky-diver in *The Gypsy Moths*.

I needn't go on. In most of Lancaster's films, especially *Gantry,* I had been spellbound by his genius, his energy, his authority, his sheer presence.

Naturally, when I met him at Elstree studios where he was filming Shaw's *The Devil's Disciple* with Sir Laurence Olivier and Kirk Douglas, I anticipated an exceptional interview, but it was soon obvious that Burt wouldn't discuss anything at all about his personal life or early struggles. I certainly didn't dare ask him how he had coped when two of his five children were born with club feet and one caught polio. All he wanted to talk about was business, how and why he had been the first studio star to break the mould and form his own independent film production company, and the problems involved.

But I did get a personal story when I asked him about his astonishing friendship with Nicky Cravat, who played his fighting pal in *The Crimson Pirate* and *The Flame and the Arrow*. Burt told me that when he was a skinny kid (hard to believe!) in the hooligan district of East Harlem, New York, he had got into a few street fights; Nicky, a year older, had come to his aid, and they had become pals.

'I lost track of Nicky when I went into the US Army in 1941. After I came out and had made my first film, *The Killers,* I went to Chicago on a publicity tour and ran into him accidentally. We talked over old times – all the laughs and troubles we'd shared – and I invited him down to Hollywood so we could do pictures together. He's never regretted that trip.'

I bet he didn't. Cravat had been employed by Burt's film company ever since. Such a firm friendship was amazing in the film world when so many big names forget the pals they made on the way up. Burt revealed that while he did most of his own stunts he didn't do them all. 'I'm not a very good horse rider, and I sure wouldn't fall off a galloping horse for a film. Stuntmen are well paid for those things.

He also scotched the myth that he had been a trapeze flier in real life. 'I was never a trapeze artist, only a horizontal bars man. I'm too big for trapeze work.'

That was just about all of personal interest that I got out of him. But even now as I write this forty-six years later, whenever I see a Burt Lancaster movie coming on TV I drop everything to watch it. When I heard of his death in October 1994 at eighty, the same age as my dad, it was like another blow in the guts. I was more saddened to learn that he had suffered a severe stroke two years before, had become less active and had lived alone, almost forgotten, up to the time of his death.

One of my next big jobs came when I flew to Vienna and met Yul Brynner on the sunlit set of his new film *The Journey,* in which he was starring with Deborah Kerr. He came over to me still laughing at a small prank he had played on Deborah, and started to answer my questions. It was soon obvious that his story was more fascinating than most movie stars'. Astounding, in fact. Millions of words, largely guesswork, had been written about this phenomenon of thirty-eight who shot to fame after playing in *The King and I*, for which he shaved his head completely bald. Insolently domineering, his movements sensuous, he strode across the screen and into our minds with the grace of a giant cat.

Briefly, Yul revealed he had been born on Sakhalin Island off Siberia. His Mongolian father had owned a silver mine. His mother had been a Romany gipsy who died giving birth to him. When he was seven his grandmother took him and his half-sister to Paris. They had little money, so Yul started earning a living before his thirteenth birthday, playing guitar and singing gipsy songs in the streets, cafés and nightclubs of Paris. After meeting one of the Fanelli trapeze troupe from the Paris Winter Circus at one of the cafés, Brynner braved a frightening trial on the high trapeze, and was trained as as a 'flyer', travelling with the troupe through France, Switzerland and Italy for the next three years. They were tough years and made Brynner a man at seventeen, by which time he had decided he wanted to be a legitimate actor. Then came the night that was to be his last on the trapeze.

'The audience was bored. I decided I would deliberately miss my partner's hands and fall into the net. I had done it many times before. There was no danger,' he told me.

He jumped. He should have bounced safely in the net, but it had been rigged badly. He bounced up, was thrown sideways, and went down out of control to land with a horrid crash on a set of parallel bars left over from a previous act.

'I was still conscious. The ring hands rushed over and carried me to the clown's dressing room, but on the way I passsed out.'

Brynner was taken to hospital, his left leg broken, his left shoulder smashed. He had forty-seven fractures in his legs, arms, ribs and feet. For six months he lay in a plaster cast. Doctors said he would spend the rest of his life a cripple. Said Yul: 'After my stay in hospital I was taken back to my one-room apartment. The circus had paid all my bills. They always did – even if they fired you when you were better! Even today I limp. It does not show until the end of the day when I am tired.'

Brynner spent five years with the Pitoeffs, a famous White Russian theatre team, and was a jack-of-all-trades – stage hand, electrician, carpenter, costume designer, stage manager and eventually an actor. 'I really wanted to be a director. I did not enjoy the acting because all the parts I got were young lovers!'

In 1941 Brynner arrived in America to join the brilliant actor-producer Michael Chekhov, with whom he had been long corresponding, and his touring troupe.

He gained his acting spurs doing 'one-night stands in church halls, high schools and movie houses. I liked America very much.' He often drove the company's old Greyhound bus, and enrolled in a language school to improve his poor English. When America entered the war the troupe broke up, and from the summer of 1942 to D-Day Brynner worked as a French language announcer on the *Voice of America* broadcasts to Nazi-occupied France. He took various TV jobs trying to learn the art of directing when he heard of a producer who was looking for an actor who was also an acrobat and could sing. Michael Myerberg gave him an audition, had him sitting on the floor singing songs for one and a half hours, then cast him to play the lead on Broadway in *Lute Song* with the fabled Mary Martin. His Broadway career didn't last, however, so he returned to Paris, where he spent a year playing the guitar in a nightclub, before heading back to America to get back into TV.

He rose quickly to the top as a director, covering wrestling matches, baseball games, variety shows, fashion parades, drama and even cooking lessons.

'I rated high in insubordination. I became impossible with all executives who didn't know what they were talking about, but respected those who did. I was fired time and time again from shows, but always I was brought back – at a higher salary! I managed to get the results the public liked.'

In 1951 Rodgers and Hammerstein were searching for an actor of 'commanding magnetic personality' to play opposite Gertrude Lawrence in the Broadway production of *The King and I.* Mary Martin told them that Yul Brynner was their man. He went to see the famous producers, who also believed he was their man.

'But I was not keen at first,' Yul told me. 'I would rather have directed the play. I was making more money than any other TV director then, and wanted to stay in that work. Then, as I read the script, I realized that the King was a character who utterly fascinated me. This was a man I would enjoy playing. I accepted, thinking I would play the part for eight months, and I signed a contract for that period.'

Brynner played the part for four years. With his head completely shaven, he was a sensation. Why did he shave his head, I asked him.

'There were two reasons,' he replied. 'One, in assessing the King's character, I bore in mind that he had gone into a monastery to study. He lived among monks as this was the only schooling he could get in Siam. To do this he had to wear the cloth and shave his head like the other monks.

'The head costume woman, Irene Sharaff, said, "It would be a good idea if you shaved *your* head for this part." I said, "All right. I'll try it. It's six weeks before the show opens so I can always regrow it before then if necessary." I turned up at my first rehearsal with my head completely bald. It was a terrible shock to Rodgers and Hammerstein, then they too went crazy about the idea... Now I keep it like this for one reason only – it is much more comfortable than having hair.'

One night in 1953, Cecil B. de Mille saw the *King and I.* He admired Brynner's magnificence, the strength and almost savage animal attraction of his movements. He signed him up for a lead role in his epic, *The Ten Commandments.* The rest is movie history.

Apart from his fascinating life story – and there was a lot more to it than I've written here, I shall remember Yul Brynner for a very kind gesture. He was one of the few stars who took me up on my offer to let them read my copy, and I had to persuade Howard French to telegraph me more money so that I could stay in Vienna an extra three days while I wrote the three-part series. I enjoyed myself at night, twice going to eat at Anton Karras's café and hear him play his famous *The Third Man* theme and other masterful pieces on his zither.

Once my story was written, Yul invited me to bring it to him in his suite in the splendid Hotel Imperial on Vienna's Elizabethstrasse. I entered the lounge, he thrust a large glass of vodka into my hands, took my manuscript and sat cross-legged on the floor with a pen in his hand. From time to time he grunted or said yes or no, while he cut bits out or amended and added. As he worked, my glance fell upon a rack of smoking pipes and there, in the centre of four, was just the kind of pipe I had been looking for for years. It was down-curved, stubby with a stout stem, and beautifully designed. As he handed me back my manuscript, saying it was fine, he asked me what I was looking at.

I pointed. 'That pipe. It's a beauty, just the kind I've been searching for…'

Before I could say more, Yul Brynner snapped it off the rack, thrust it into my hands and said, 'It is yours!'

Although I gave up smoking long ago, and had overbitten the stem before that, that pipe is still one of my treasured possessions.

Before long it became obvious there just weren't enough major stars in Britain, or even in Europe, to keep my top-names column pages going, so we evolved a new idea called 'Personal Call'. I arranged via Henry Gris, the veteran well-connected Hollywood correspondent of the Associated Press, to phone stars at their homes in Hollywood. This, too, got me an edge over other UK show-business columnists. Of course, Henry could not fix up truly top stars in this way – those like Sinatra, Brando and Monroe not only didn't need publicity but actively shunned it! – but he did pretty well with the first one. I was soon putting my personal call through to the then King of Hollywood, Clark Gable! He was about to play a romantic role opposite twenty-four-year-old Sophia Loren. As he was fifty-nine I asked him if he felt he should play lovers any more. His answer, as to my other questions, was unusually frank, 'It depends what the roles are. I certainly don't think I should be playing a Rhett Butler part like I did in *Gone with the Wind.* I couldn't get away with that any more. But there are still roles an older man could play – in comedy, for instance.'

He admitted that his recent film *The King and Four Queens*, when he had been romantic lead to four girls, had been a comedy attempt that had not come off. I asked him what was the biggest lesson he had learnt in life?

'The most important thing I learnt from success is that no one can do it on his own. Every star has a tremendous amount of help the public don't know about. People behind the scenes who write for him, directors, cameramen, the technicians you never hear about. If you make yourself unpopular with them I guess you can say goodbye. I used to be pretty cocksure. Then I made some bad movies and I suddenly found I needed help. Luckily I got it. Once I was successful again, I learned to be more critical of myself.'

I asked him how he got his powerful physique. Was it true or just publicity that he had once been a humble tree feller?

'No, it was true. I worked for the Silver Falls Timber Company in Oregon. I got three dollars and twenty cents a day. But I think any physique I have was formed before that. My dad was an oil man in Oklahoma and he got me working on one of his crews. I was eighteen or nineteen and I was swinging a sixty-pound sledge (hammer), sometimes for two hours at a time. I think that was what gave me a physique.'

I suggested that Hollywood was the home of unstable marriages, and as he himself had been married several times, though he was happy and settled now, what did he, a public idol, feel was important to a happy marriage?

'Appreciating your home and the help and the association and the love you get from your family. There is nothing in the world quite as good for any man as having the love and affection of a wife and children. If he doesn't have that, he hasn't very much of anything... I haven't always felt that. There were times when I wasn't capable of thinking that way because I got rather inflated ideas about myself.'

We talked about his happy family – his wife Kay and two children, Joan and Bunker, but they were Kay's children by a previous marriage. I asked Gable if he hoped to have his own children one day. His answer was brief but to the point: 'I do, but I'm very happy with what we have.'

In a sad and ironic twist of fate, Kay fell pregnant when Gable went to make what was to be his last film, *The Misfits* with Marilyn Monroe and Montgomery Clift. It was an intensely physical role, where he had to fight and tame wild horses, and he refused the use of a stuntman. He died shortly after the film was finished, and never saw his son to whom Kay later gave birth, the child he had so long craved.

19
Hollywood at Last: Deano, Debbie, Rock and Frank

It was another three months before my editor agreed to let me make my dream trip to Hollywood, when I was to try to get good stories from major stars over a ten-day period. Henry Gris fixed up a few interviews but the rest I had to get via agents and studio publicists. I took a taxi from Los Angeles airport and booked into the Knickerbocker Hotel, largely because I'd discovered it had not only a good pool but also a gym run by Joe Leigh, a Cockney ex-boxer from the East End, who knew many stars. I was now in a different world: near the hotel was a garage with a lurid neon sign which said, 'Have Gun – Will Lube'. The streets were all highways with huge, flashy cars and when I toured the areas like Beverly Hills where the stars lived, I saw immaculate lawns with sprinklers keeping the grass green but never saw a soul walking. Garage doors would elevate and out would come a limousine to purr silently away with some celebrity or other, sealed off from the real world. I'd never even seen a colour TV set before but there was one in my little suite on which I could get thirteen channels, unlike only the two I could get on my little black-and-white set in my bed sitter in Hampstead.

Somehow, over those ten days, I interviewed the stars of the TV series *Wagon Train*, then the world's most popular show, Dean Martin, Debbie Reynolds, Rock Hudson, Stephen Boyd of *Ben Hur* fame, Dale Robertson, star of TV's *Wells Fargo* series, Clint Walker and John Saxon. I even flew to Las Vegas and met Frank Sinatra, who wouldn't grant a full interview but was extremely kind to me in another way.

I first met Dean Martin, who turned out to be wittily honest and a scriptwriter's dream. I knew he loved golf, so I asked him if he ever played with his 'Ratpack' friend, Frank Sinatra.

'Frankie? Man, he couldn't even hold a caddie. I *used* to play with him but he plays *at* it. We'd load one cart with golf clubs and the other with beer. Frank called it golf. I called it "afternoon drinking on wheels". No, I play to a handicap of four, but then I've been playing over twenty years.'

Whose swim pool do you all use?

'Well, I've only got one. Frankie's got two – one to rinse in!'

I asked him about his image as an easygoing, popular drunk.

'It's true, you know. They all think I'm drunk half the time. If I really drank as much as people say nobody would hire me. If there's a drunk act anywhere you can bet my name creeps in somewhere. I don't know how it began. I guess I just *look* drunk when I wake up! Jerry Lewis and I did drunk acts in clubs and I did the drunk bits I guess because of my looks. My eyebrows go down and my eyes go down at the corners, so I guess people reckoned I was *really* drunk all the time.'

'When you split with Jerry Lewis when you had been the top comedy duo in America for ten years, weren't you scared you might not make it on your own?'

'Scared? I was terrified. I didn't even have a job. I had done my first solo film, *Ten Thousand Bedrooms*, and it was a flop. I thought, "You've had it, pal." I had nothing to turn to but one singing job in a Pittsburgh nightclub. I worked there two weeks fully believing at the end of it I was through. On my second to last day my agent called and said I was being offered a part in *The Young Lions* with Montgomery Clift and Marlon Brando.' I thought he was putting me on. He said he wasn't but I'd have to take a drop of 225,000 dollars in my movie salary. "Drop?" I said. "I'll do it for nothing!"' (In fact he got $25,000.) I realized after the *Bedrooms* movie I should not do or try to do star roles but aim at secondary male roles.

'The next thing was Frank making *Some Came Running* with Shirley MacLaine. I said, "Frank, I hear you're looking hard for a guy who can play a drinker and a gambler. You're out of your mind – you're looking at him!" Frank just said, "You've got the job." That's all there was to it. From then on I got all the movie breaks I needed – without singing a note.'

At this time Dean Martin was happily married to the beautiful former model Jeanne Bieggers, and the father of seven children, four by his first marriage. He was already a multi-millionaire, with large landowning interests in Ventura County. He gave me more than an hour of his time and described many dramatic times in his life, but it is beyond the scope of this book, as with all other star interviews, to reveal them all in detail. I was surprised after we finished talking when a studio photographer arrived and asked us to pose together for some pictures. This happened at other studios, too. I never asked for or expected this, but now, in my mid-seventies, I am grateful to have these photos as they remind me of years long forgotten.

The following day when I went down to the hotel gym for my usual morning workout, I found Joe Leigh pummelling a black guy whose face was extremely familiar. It was Sidney Poitier, who had just finished his major role as the crippled Porgy in the hit musical *Porgy and Bess.* Between clumps and slaps, Sidney tried to tell me how much he owed to Joe.

'Man – *thump* – I want you – *thump* – to meet – *thump* – the man – *thump* – who kept me – *thump* – fit during *Porgy*,' he gasped. 'Hey Joe, stop that.'

'This guy kept my circulation travellin', man. I spent all day with my ankles strapped up and went round on a platform with wheels. At the end of every day my legs were numb!'

I was excited that day as I had been promised an interview with Debbie Reynolds, who was making *The Rat Race* with Tony Curtis. This had been difficult to arrange as Debbie was big news. She was just divorced from Eddie Fisher, who had left her for Elizabeth Taylor, and had thrown herself into her work, having made no fewer than five pictures in the year since they first separated. She was currently No. 1 female box-office star in America. The studio were handling her with kid gloves and I'd been warned not to ask her anything about her failed marriage to Eddie Fisher. I met her press agent at the studio, who promptly drove me to Lucy's, a top Hollywood restaurant, saying Debbie would probably join us there. What would I like to drink? I chose my usual then – a gin and It. He returned with a glass the size of a grapefruit bowl. I was halfway through the drink when up came Jim Ameche, brother of the once-famous Don Ameche, who ran a radio programme from Lucy's. He persuaded me to go on it, so for the next twenty minutes I was on the air, plugging Britain, my magazine, plugging Hollywood and Debbie's new picture, plugging Lucy's, then I was released back to the press agent, who said, 'Sorry, Mike but Debbie just rang. She can't make it today. I'll try and get you to her tomorrow. Have another drink!'

With no other interview lined up that day I had another bowl of drink, and was very glad I had not hired a car because I was no longer capable of driving safely. The agent called me a taxi with a strange sort of smile on his face, and back I went to my hotel room. I woke up three hours later feeling I'd been shanghaied! I was now worried I'd been out-manoeuvred and would never get Debbie. I decided to go back to my hard-nosed days as a crime reporter, go round to her house and knock on her door, which would be an unheard of crime in Hollywood. But what if she wasn't *in*?

I composed a careful note, enclosed a copy of one of my best sympathetic columns which had my best-ever photo on its top, so she could see I was not an ogre, and grabbed my Map of Movie Stars' Homes. I hired a taxi and swept round to her imposing mansion where I caught a glimpse of her through a window. She was wearing curlers! No girl would answer her door or, more likely, send her maid to answer the door, then do a press interview in her curlers. My courage failed me. I wrote, 'Daren't ring your bell' on the envelope and posted my note into her mailbox.

The following day I spent two hours in the studio on tenterhooks, sure I would somehow be stalled on Debbie again. Suddenly in burst her press agent. 'Debbie wants to see you! She will see you now. She seems to have heard of you!' It was obvious she had not told him of my note though she must have got it. I was shown into her dressing room for an amazingly frank interview, and how she laughed when I said I hadn't dared ring her bell after glimpsing her in curlers. I'd been warned not to mention Eddie Fisher but she brought him up herself. We were talking about the conflicts between making movies and being a wife and mother. I reminded her she had said before her marriage that if it and her work didn't mix she would give up that work, but she hadn't done so. She looked at me in protest.

'Oh but I did. I worked very little when I was married. I had two children. You *have* to restrict your work if you're a mother, and I did. I really did. Some husbands' positions allow them more free time at home, in which case you stay home with him. Some travel a lot and the wives can work while they are away. My husband is an actor and singer – my ex-husband, I mean. Eddie had to travel and do tours – he was in England three times, in Florida scores of times, and in New York too. But when he was home I restricted my film work because I far prefer a home life.'

When I asked why she had worked so hard the past year, she sighed a little and replied, 'Because it was good for me. The jobs kept me busy and stopped me thinking too much about myself.'

We talked more about her career, her personal ambitions, money. 'I may make a lot of money but I don't get most of it, not in such a high tax bracket as I am.'

We were talking about happiness when I tried another personal question. Did the idea of falling in love again fill her with doubts or fears or any definite emotion?

'Yes, I have many doubts and reservations about falling in love with anyone, but since I have no particular interest in anyone right now it doesn't bother me.'

Even if the right guy came along.?

'Even if the right guy came along I would not be able to recognize it at this time. I really could not accept it. I have been married but it didn't work out. Look! Analysing my own situation… although eventually I may get married again it won't be for a number of years.'

Although she was earning big money before she was twenty, she was astonishingly frank about her abilities.

'My story is a Cinderella story, I know that, but talent is not enough, you must have the right breaks, luck and good directors, I've had a combination of all of these. There are many girls more talented than me but I got the breaks and I worked hard. I'm not a great singer, actress or dancer. I've never pretended I was. But I *can* sing. I *can* dance. And I *can* act. So the fact I can do a bit of each makes me a saleable commodity. That's all.

'My father is like me, can do a bit of everything. He can do anything with his hands – plumbing, electrical work, woodwork. So is my mother – she paints the houses, fixes the wallpapers, makes small furniture. They are both more clever than I!'

When I reminded her that her dad had been a railway man in El Paso, Texas, where she was born, and asked what he did now, now that she was a star, she replied, 'He still is! But he's here with me. My parents moved to California and my father works on the Southern Pacific railroad as a carpenter. He fixes everything. He had been a boiler-maker, a wheel-tapper and a mechanic too. They both live only five minutes from my house here, so I'm never lonely.'

Debbie gave me freely of her time and of her emotions, and I came away with another rattling good piece.

'Come on,' I said to her press agent afterwards, 'I'll buy you lunch!'

This turned out to be a lucky move because that afternoon the agent was driving out to the huge ranch of top wrangler Glen Randall, who not only taught many movie stars to ride but had organized the incredible twenty-minute-long chariot race in *Ben Hur*, still regarded today as a film action masterpiece. Would I be interested in meeting him? Well, would I!

We drove out and Glen proved an interesting character who gave me enough good yarns about the stars he worked with to make half a column. We were watching two of his wranglers putting horses through their paces in an enormous hangar-like building and the animals were walking, trotting or running around a large oblong track.

'Do you ride?' Glen asked me.

'I've never been on a horse in my life,' I admitted.

'Well, now's your chance to try. Want to have a go?'

Now, I was rather frightened of horses. They seemed such huge, powerful creatures, and I recalled an old Henfield school pal, now a farmer, once describing the horse as being 'uncomfortable in the middle – and dangerous at both ends!' But I said I'd have a go. Randall went over to one of the wranglers and said something, and the man went to one of the side stables and emerged with a magnificent glistening black stallion.

'This is Midnight,' said Randall as he helped me up into the saddle. 'He is the horse Tyrone Power rode in *The Mask of Zorro*. One of our prize beasts.'

Following his instructions I went round the track three times until something I'd heard about Randall came into my mind. I asked him, 'Is it true you can make a horse fall without whistling or shouting instructions?'

I didn't see Randall make any specific movement but almost instantly Midnight just crumpled below me, and a wrangler rushed to pull my right foot out of the stirrup. Otherwise I could have been split in two if the horse had also rolled over.

That was the first horse I ever rode. It was also the *last* horse I ever rode.

The following morning I got another great interview, this time at Universal Studios with Rock Hudson. His first comedy, *Pillow Talk* with Doris Day, had been a great success and he was currently No. 1 box office male star in America. He told of his early struggles, how he left school at eighteen, not brainy enough for college or university, and became a mechanic in the Navy during the war. On discharge, he worked as a postman in his hometown before moving to California to stay with his father. He then became a truck driver. 'What else? I had no qualifications. I knew no one. I had no money. I would work in gas stations, in a market, but truck driving paid more, so I did that for about six months.' He took up acting lessons to overcome his … shyness!

'I was terribly shy and nervous. I felt very awkward in all kinds of company and I felt learning to act would make me more relaxed and easy with people. Acting forced me to come out of myself, and I did have a lot of help. A powerful studio like Universal-International had faith in me from the start. I suppose I first wanted to act to prove something to myself.'

We covered many themes – love, phoney friends, his three-year marriage to his agent's secretary Phyllis Gates, life as a bachelor, how he cooked for himself 'mostly out of cans!' and his love of sailing. It was when I told Rock about my own sailing adventure, including going across the Bay of Biscay in winter without an engine, that he looked at his watch and suddenly clapped me on the knee.

'It's only 11.30. Come on, I'll show you my yacht. We can have lunch there!'

It was forty-five miles to Lido Island where Rock kept his yacht and he kept his huge car's needle near eighty mph all the way, so it seemed we arrived at the harbour in no time. I'd expected one of those luxury motorized 'yachts', but while his boat had the ultimate in luxury, it was a real sailing machine with sleek lines, big furled sails, and shining brass everywhere. When I told him I still didn't know a great deal about sailing as I had been shanghaied to be the cook on my yacht, he just said, 'Well, that's great' and led me to his galley and invited me to whip up the lunch! Well, I rustled up a salad and chose from cans of tuna, salmon, caviar and swordfish for the main ingredients while Rock served soft drinks only, as we, or rather he, had to drive back to his Hollywood bungalow. We chatted on and on, and I got a few more good yarns from him, then we were on our way back, and he dropped me off at my hotel.

'Don't forget to call me next time you're in town,' was his parting shot.

When I, and the world, learned many years later that Rock Hudson was gay, I was truly amazed, Never at any time, for one moment, had he given me a reason to suspect he was homosexual. He certainly never made a pass at me.

I got through my remaining interviews with four more leading actors of the day, and found I had two days to spare before my flight back to the UK. I was not one just to lounge around the hotel's pool. Reading in the *Hollywood Reporter* that Frank Sinatra was currently performing at the Sands Hotel, which he co-owned, in Las Vegas, I caught a plane to the gambling town. If I could 'bag' Sinatra, arguably the world's greatest singing star of the time, I would have pulled off a big personal gamble of my own. I booked myself into one of the little bungalows in the hotel grounds, then searched out Jack Entratter, Sinatra's partner in the hotel and a man I'd once interviewed by phone on a general piece about gambling. Jack was friendly but shook his head when I asked if he could help me get to Frank.

'Frank doesn't do individual press interviews, not any more. There's a queue of guys who want to talk to him, press guys he knew in the past. If he gives a reporter from London a big interview, he lets *them* down. But ... go to the bar in the salon over there and I'll tell him you're here. I can't do more than that.'

I went to the bar, ordered a small St Miguel beer and positioned myself so I could see Sinatra, who was playing at the new Baccarat game. Jack told me the guy on his right was none other than the famous gambler, Nick the Greek, and that in one week the Greek had cleared more than $750,000! For the hour I watched, Sinatra looked extremely serious; he didn't smile once. At last he got up and walked towards the bar, then turned, intending to walk on past it. I plucked up my courage and as he came abreast of me I managed to blurt out, 'Good evening sir, world's greatest singer. I'm from the *Daily Mail* group in London. Is there *any* chance at all of a short interview...some time...please?'

I tried to look beseeching and respectful at the same time but Frank's glare could have turned me to stone. Those large bright blue eyes bored into mine as he said, 'Sorry, feller. Not a chance. You'll have to get way back in line. I don't do personal interviews… and now I have to get ready for my show.'

As he turned to leave I just said, 'Well, a long way to come for nothing! Maybe I'll have better luck on the machines.' As I turned back to the bar to order another beer I found I was trembling slightly. I also felt I'd made a damn fool of myself. I spent the next half-hour or so at the bar, just looking around and seeing what celebrities I could spot, when I felt a tap on my shoulder. It was Jack Entratter and he thrust a ticket into my hand.

'Frank wants you to know he's sorry he can't talk to you. But he doesn't want your trip to be a total waste of time. He wants you to have this – a ticket for his show!'

It was for a seat at a much sought-after stageside table, and must have been worth several hundred dollars. Jack escorted me to the small table, at which sat two multi-millionaires, one of whom introduced himself as Joe Blaustein, who ran the Cincinnati Ford agency. His pal had a similar position. When they told me they had had a hard task to get *their* tickets, so how did I get mine, I couldn't resist the airy reply:

'Oh, my pal Frank sent it round for me, just a few minutes ago!'

I had expected Frank to come on, sing a few songs in his unique, inimitable way and that would be that. But he proved to be a great showman and an excellent stand-up comedian. His act was great. It looked casual but had obviously been well rehearsed. He came in like a waiter, from the back of the auditorium, walking through his audience, a spotlight bouncing off his bald patch as he climbed up on to the stage. He broke off in his first song to say, 'Boy, it's early,' and shook his head. He made cracks like: 'I had a deeper tan but I lost it at Los Angeles airport – waiting for my luggage.' 'Dawson Halt, eh? I remember that place. The train stops there for laughs. Everyone gets out, gets hysterical, and gets back on board.' He sang up a storm that night and got his usual standing ovation.

The following day, while waiting for the taxi to take me to the airport, I shoved my last silver dollar into one of the machines. There was a pause as I turned away, then a quite deafening crash, as dollars fell into the maw of the machine, then cascaded over the floor. I'd won the jackpot! There was enough in it not only to pay my air fare to Las Vegas but almost enough also to cover my return flight from the UK. But when I got back, my editor was so pleased with my bag of stories from Hollywood that I somehow forgot to mention this fact when putting in my expenses.

20
The Hedonist – and Jayne, Kirk, Dirk, Paul and Cary

I was back from Hollywood, with eight columns about big names in my notebooks. My show pages had now settled down to a fixed formula – one big human-interest story from a major star, then I had a separate section called *Showbuzz* which was for short stories on smaller stars, aspiring starlets, beauty queens and the like, whose glamour pictures embellished the pages. I also had a records section in which I reviewed the best of the week's pop singles which both EMI and DECCA sent to me. My life was full of parties, cocktail receptions, film premieres and previews.

With eight columns lined up I had time on my hands and, apart from making business calls and attending the weekly editorial conference, I had no need to go into the office every day, and Howard French agreed to this. Naturally, this created some competition among the other reporters and feature writers for my fine desk. I put up a mock fight to retain my desk but secretly I was only too glad to get rid of it! I could then operate from home, just going in to hand over my copy when it was ready.

I was now flying between glamorous cities like Paris, Rome, Athens, Madrid, Vienna, New York and Hollywood, mixing talk, drinks, life, copy and even love with famous names I had once worshipped as a gauche village youth. Meeting and writing about whom I chose, my name at the head of widely read pages which, apart from two women's magazines, were then the only colour spread in Fleet Street, I became the complete hedonist. Most summer days I would take a beautiful girl to the Ruislip Lido or, more often, the Nordic Club in Esher which had a fine swimming pool and a great buffet bar run by owner Bobby Vaughan-Jones, and after a great day out many of the girls were more than happy to return with me to my flat and stay the night.

Unwittingly – and I truly mean that – I had turned my bedsitter into a real boudoir for seduction. Right from the start I had installed a large tropical fish tank on top of the fitted wardrobe and shelves complex that ran from the kitchenette almost to the door. Around the tank I had erected a long bamboo cage that reached up to the ceiling and installed pots of climbing vines and flowers that entwined with the bamboo uprights. When the main room light was switched off and the tropical tank's lights switched on, with the brightly coloured fish swimming between the water plants and rising bubbles from the aerating pump, a soft and romantic light suffused the room. It was perfect for amorous dalliance.

I must say I never set out just to make love to a beautiful woman, never plotted seduction. I always wondered is this the one, the one I could marry? But I seemed to have developed a low threshold of boredom – her top lip was too close to her nose...she had a slight double chin... her nose was too big... the eyes that had seemed doe-like now looked cow-like...there is too much flesh behind the knee. I hardly ever tried to meet girls on a mental or spiritual level. At that time in my life I sought only great physical beauty. I must have been arrogant, smug, conceited and totally insufferable! In my old age I look back on that period, which lasted far too long, with something akin to horror. I have to admit my teenage adolescence lasted until I was about thirty-five! The only thing I could boast about is that I never made love to a married woman.

I went through sports cars like a frustrated racing driver, especially after I first became a freelance and money simply flooded in – Triumph, Austin Healey, Healey Elliott, Mini Cooper, Jaguars XK120 and XK140. I wrote off two of the cars, including wrapping the precious Healey Elliott round a bollard outside Buckingham Palace on New Year's Eve! I emerged unscathed from the crashes, which made me feel I must be protected by some special force. I think the zenith of my hedonistic period came when I bought the Jaguar XK120. I saw it in a second-hand car salesroom in Finchley Road. It was magnificent, sleek, and snow-white with little Union Jacks on each side of its long bonnet. It sat tense, leashed, as if waiting to launch itself. I whistled in admiration, and after a brief test drive, rushed to my bank for a loan to pay the £500 being asked for it. When I first drove it and turned the wheel to the right or the left, the end of the moving bonnet seemed around half a mile away, but I eventually got used to it. I recall the salesman saying as he handed over the keys: 'You'll never find a better bird-puller than that!' And he was right.

Once, I was driving the Jaguar through the London streets feeling happily self-satisfied, no doubt with a smug smile on my face. I was startled when the woman conductor of a double-decker bus in front of me suddenly swung out, holding onto the bus's boarding pole, and shouted, 'You're not half as good as you think you are!'

If a girl I had taken home couldn't understand why I drove such a magnificent car yet only had a bedsitter, I would airily explain, 'Oh, this is just a stopgap. I'm having a new house built up in Hampstead Garden Suburb!'

Some girls accepted this but if one didn't, and wanted to see my new property for herself, I would drive her there, stop outside any posh-looking house in process of erection and point it out. If she then wanted to get out of the car and go over for a closer look, I would say something like, 'Oh no, my dear. I'm dealing with the head of the firm, in his office. These chaps don't know me. Besides, the last thing builders want is the owner walking about, asking questions, when they're working.'

When my younger brother Richard was doing his National Service in the army at Catterick, he sometimes came to spend the weekend in London with me (I had two beds in my flatlet) instead of going home to Henfield. He was certainly surprised at the number of different pretty girls I was seeing. Once, after he'd left to return to Catterick, I found he had penned a note to me, which he had stuck to the inner door. It read:

> 'My brother Mike, how he bustles
> All smiles, white teeth and muscles
> The perfect Adam manqué
> Not for him introspection
> But a woman – erection!
> And one page of copy per day'

The cheek! The truth was I now had easy access to some of the most beautiful girls in the country, even in the world, when I was sent to get stories from the entrants in beauty contests. If I didn't make love to three, or at least two, different beauties in a week I felt hard done by! In old age now I look back almost in disbelief when I recall that among my lovers had been one Miss World, one Miss United Kingdom and one Miss Soho, never mind a few runners-up too. I recall that if any of my pals tried to hide their jealousy while at the same time congratulating me on my good luck with fabulous girls, I would reply with something like, 'Aw, there are better-looking girls standing at bus stops in Regent Street on any weekday night!'

When Jayne Mansfield flew to London to promote her first big film, *The Girl Can't Help It* (who can forget that scene when she sashayed her fabulous figure along the pavement and milkman Phil Silvers' glasses shattered?), I got her to agree to have breakfast in bed with me! Admittedly, she was under the sheets in her bedroom at the Dorchester Hotel while I was perched on the edge of the bed with biro and notebook sharing her cornflakes, but it made a cracking photo to go with a revealing interview. She had a great sense of humour and we had a lot of laughs.

When I told owner Bobby Vaughan-Jones about this at my favourite Nordic Club in Esher, where I took most of my girlfriends for the day, he said the club was holding a big members' party for charity the following week and could I get Jayne to open it? I rang her at the hotel, met her again for a quick drink, and she agreed to do it if Bobby would send a chauffeur and car to pick her up and return her to the Dorchester afterwards. I have a picture of Jayne enjoying herself at the club after opening the barbecue but am now ashamed to admit that I was busy elsewhere with some beautiful girl or other and didn't even bother to attend myself. How arrogant can one get?

One person in my immediate working life who I was beginning to realize did not like my easy hedonistic playboy lifestyle, though he could do little about it while I was securing good stories from major names, was the magazine's deputy editor, David Hill. Once, when I was taking beautiful British actress Dawn Addams to lunch, I parked my Jaguar with her in it below the office windows while I dashed up to hand in the week's showbiz page. David Hill looked out of the window, showed surprise and said, 'Hey Mike, that looks like Dawn Addams in your car.'

'It is, dear chap. It *is*! And I mustn't keep her waiting.'

As I turned to leave I saw a grimace come over his face, a hard look in his eyes. Could he be jealous? Well, it didn't matter – I always dealt with the editor, Howard French, not him. Anyway, in my next major interview I had a hard nut to crack – Kirk Douglas. And after that I had to try to get something new from Dirk Bogarde who had recently attained international star status.

After Kirk had given me a fabulous interview, and knowing how fast he really was with his fists, I took a furtive step backwards before asking him a last tricky question: How did he feel about the many folk in Hollywood who said that when he had shot to stardom after his classic fight film *Champion* he had become a 'right son of a bitch'?

To my surprise he just laughed. 'They're wrong! I was a right son of a bitch *before* that but I was too obscure then for anyone to notice! What's more – I'm still a right son of a bitch!'

It was a few weeks before his smash hit epic *Spartacus* was to be premiered in London and I had tracked him down to Chicago so I could steal a march on the rest of the British show-business press who would descend on him when he came to London. I could thus scoop the lot of them. To my mind

Kirk Douglas has always been a prince among movie stars. Whether as the violent, obsessed fighter in *Champion*, leaping with sword in hand from ramparts as in *Ulysses* and The *Vikings*, or as the neurotic Vincent Van Gogh in *Lust For Life*, the twisted 'tec of *Detective Story*, or the dramatic heroes in *Paths of Glory* and *Lonely Are the Brave*, he was always vital, lusty, alive and compelling on screen. He had also become a brilliant businessman off it and had gambled his entire fortune several times to make box-office hits like *The Vikings* and *Spartacus*, as both producer and star.

While Kirk's humble origins are well known today (largely through his own autobiography) they were not when I first interviewed him in 1960. I found his battle up from the gutters astonishing. He was born Yssur Danielovitch on 9 December, 1916, the son of a poor emigrant Russian street pedlar, in Amsterdam, a small manufacturing town in New York State. He was the only boy among six house-proud girls.

'My father was a poor man,' he told me, 'an ordinary street pedlar who worked hard all his life yet never made it. Every so often he would grow bitter about his misfortunes but in the mornings he would always wake up in the best of spirits and yell to me, "Okay son, Rabotat, Rabotat..." Rabotat is Russian for work and I never forgot that battle cry of his. It's one of the few Russian words I know, but by heaven, it's a slogan I've tried to follow.'

It was clear to Kirk from an early age that sheer hard graft was the only way to succeed. He told me that whenever he has had to play 'tough guy' parts it is the image of his father he draws on for inspiration. Even as a schoolboy he helped eke out the family finances, rising at 5 a.m. to run both morning and evening newspaper rounds. As a kid he knew what it meant to be 'hungry-poor'. 'Unless you've been hungry-poor you don't know what the word poor means,' he told me.

At school he took part in school plays and the debating team and did odd jobs to pay his way while graduating from St Lawrence University, where for three years he had been undefeated intercollegiate wrestling champion. When he tried to get into the American Academy of Dramatic Arts in New York there was no immediate vacancy. Douglas persuaded the Head to let him do a reading, and the Head was so impressed that he created a special, albeit small scholarship for him. It was only enough to pay his fees, so Kirk lived in a tiny room in a hostel in Greenwich Village and worked as a night waiter. I asked him about the lowest period in his life.

'It was at that time. During vacations from the Academy I wandered round the streets of New York trying to get a job as an actor but agents didn't want to know. One Thanksgiving Day, a big American holiday celebrated with a feast of turkey and pumpkin pie, I was absolutely flat broke. I remember walking round the Bowery, the Skid Row of New York, without having eaten for two days, and I stood in line at a Salvation Army place to get one of the free Thanksgiving dinners.

'But by the time I got to the window to get a ticket, they had run out of dinners! I didn't get one. Looking back, I can laugh, but at the time it was a very low moment.'

After a few tiny Broadway roles, he served two wartime years in the US Navy on anti-submarine patrols in the Pacific, and was discharged as a Lieutenant. He made straight for Broadway again. 'I only wanted to be a stage actor. I had no desire or interest in making films,' he said. 'After a few plays I was offered several screen tests but turned them all down. In the end, however, I had no choice. I did about ten Broadway plays, six of which were flops. After the last flop I took a chance and went down to Hollywood to do a test for producer Hal Wallis. He gave me the lead opposite Barbara Stanwyck in *The Strange Loves of Martha Iver*.'

Kirk Douglas was on his way, but while he made seven films in the next three years and was doing all right, he was hardly shaking the film world. He decided he needed a part with real guts, a role with real dynamite. When MGM offered him $50,000 to co-star in a movie with Ava Gardner and Gregory Peck, they were astonished when he turned them down. Kirk had decided to make *Champion*, a Ring Lardner story about a prize fighter, which the then unknown Stanley Kramer had offered him. His pay was to be just $15,000 plus a percentage of the profits – if there were any. What was more, no screenplay had been written for it and his agents told him he must be out of his mind.

Kirk, who had never boxed in his life, trained in the gym with professional fighters. He got knocked out once but became so good with the gloves that the pros had to work hard to stay on their feet, Midge Kelly, the hero of the film, was a fighter to whom nothing was important except winning. In a way Kirk Douglas *was* Midge Kelly in those days. He shared the same philosophy. He played the vicious hero with such depth and insight that audiences round the world were electrified. He was nominated for his first Oscar and from that film onwards has been a major star in the Hollywood firmament.

With the bit at last between his teeth, Douglas knew only one way to maintain success – compound it. He worked for total realism. For his next film *Young Man with a Horn*, he took professional trumpet lessons. For *The Story of Three Loves* he learned to fly on the high trapeze. For his first western, *Man Without a Star*, he learned to play the guitar. For *Detective Story*, another milestone in his career when he played a tough cop, he spent many nights on duty with New York police. Before playing the ruthless reporter in *Ace in the Hole* he wangled a genuine job as a reporter with a Los Angeles paper.

Early in 1955, with his magnificent portrayal of Vincent Van Gogh in *Lust for Life* under his belt, he put his late father's advice into effect: 'Son, when you go out into the world, work for somebody else only long enough to save money to go out on your own. Be your own boss and you'll be a success. Let somebody else boss you and you'll stay just another face in the crowd!' He formed Bryna Productions, named after his mother, and began to produce and star in hit epics like *The Vikings* and *Spartacus*. Audaciously, he sent *Spartacus* screenplays to leading stars like Sir Laurence Olivier, Charles Laughton, Peter Ustinov, Jean Simmons and Tony Curtis: to his own amazement they all said yes. It was one of the greatest casting coups in film history.

Kirk told me: 'I had to make *Spartacus* so good it would get people to leave their TV sets and buy seats in the cinema to see it. It had to be a good *show*.'

His determination showed again before he married his second wife Anne Buydens. He told me the story.

'I was in Paris for a picture called *Act of Love*. I needed someone to help me with public relations, especially when I was dealing in a language I was just starting to learn at the time. Someone suggested Anne because she had experience of co-ordinating American and foreign productions, and spoke four languages. I got her in for an interview. We talked, but to my surprise she said she did *not* want to work with me, although she could maybe help me find someone else!

'This annoyed me, made me real mad, so I kept after her until she gave in. Now I'm working for her!'

The marriage has lasted over fifty years to the present day, or to the time I'm writing this. In old age Kirk Douglas, top producer, director and star, remained at the top of the Hollywood tree, even playing frail old age pensioners in top films like *Amos* and *Greed*, still true to his father's battle cry, 'Rabotat, Rabotat...'

I went to interview Dirk Bogarde shortly after he played composer Franz Liszt in Song Without End, the film that first elevated him to international stardom, and halfway through he told me of the most tragic incident in his life. This was why he would never drive a car as long as he lived, retaining a chauffeur instead. He had never told the story to the press, so it was another minor scoop for me. It concerned the time his Army car killed three army deserters in India in 1945 and injured several others.

It happened on VJ night, nine days after the atom bomb that ended the war was dropped on Hiroshima. Bogarde was then a Captain interpreter in Calcutta. He had been right through the war in Germany with front-line troops, and was awaiting orders to go to Singapore. With his secretary and his Indian Army driver he was driving towards Bogarde's house outside Calcutta. The monsoon was at its height and rain was pouring down. As Bogarde told it to me, 'We had been warned never to stop for anyone on these lonely roads. Above all we were to avoid a certain gang, a band of American Army deserters who used to hitch rides, then beat up the occupants of the car and take all they had. Two of them would thumb a lift while the rest hid. As soon as the car stopped, the rest of the gang would rush out, block the way, hit you on the head, strip you and take the car and all your belongings.

'We were driving along in the pelting rain when we suddenly came upon a double line of men who were standing across the road. The driver didn't see them in time. There was a terrible bumping sound and a man's blonde head smashed through the windscreen, with his body following. The jeep killed three of the men and injured others.

'I jumped out to find a terrible scene. It is a memory I shall have to my dying day. It seemed hours before we could get any sense out of the others. They were all so shocked. So were we. Men who might have survived if the weather had not been so bad, and we could have got help quicker, were bleeding to death. But the driver and I did all we could.

'My secretary was covered in blood from the dead man who came through the windscreen. By the time the ambulances had come and done what they could I was exhausted. Instead of getting into a car and driving home myself, I had to let someone else drive me. I have never driven a car since. That was the end of my nerve in cars. I lost it completely, although I had driven for years without any trouble.'

That was the most dramatic content of my interview with Dirk but he did tell me of some lighter moments in his career (which by this time included over forty films) describing how he had got his first theatre job after he had failed at art school.

'I took a bus ride to Kew and got myself a job at 7s 6d a week at Kew Theatre. I was assistant dogsbody – boiled glue, painted scenery, made tea, held scripts for the prompter, and slept most nights on a pile of sacks in the theatre's paint shed.'

After a few small parts he won a scholarship to the Old Vic, but war was declared on the day the class was due to start. He went to Amersham Repertory Company, then got a part in a play, *Cornelius*, at the Westminster Theatre.

'I got some good notices and thought I was brilliant. I started overplaying for laughs and mucked up everyone else's lines. Suddenly my co-actor Max Adrian swiped me hard on the head with a heavy book and said, "Don't you ever dare to do that again!" No-one but me and Max realised it wasn't in the play. But from that night on I began to learn self-discipline in acting, thanks to him.'

About a year after the war had started, Bogarde and Peter Ustinov, who were appearing in the London play *Diversion* together, decided they ought to do something for the war effort.

'We both marched to a recruiting centre in Charing Cross Road, and to our intense horror were called up four weeks later!'

At least Bogarde made it to Lieutenant, whereas Ustinov remained a Private, though that was largely due to his own wish.

Over the following months I went from star to star, but of course I can't name them all, still less detail all they told me and shall just mention a few key ones. Leslie Caron told me how she managed to juggle complicated roles as wife to director Peter Hall, mother and star, how she was only paid £80 a week when she made *An American in Paris* with Gene Kelly, but after hits like *Gigi* and *Fanny* could afford to make only films she liked and which did not take her away from her husband for too long.

I flew to Rome to meet Sophia Loren's extraordinary mother, who gave me the dramatic story of how poor she was when Sophia and her sister Maria were small and how they were hastily evacuated from their home village during the Allied advance to Naples, and she had to walk the six miles carrying baby Maria in her arms all the way. 'There was no work, no food and for a time I was forced to beg for bread in the streets. Sometimes my face was red with shame but my babies were starving.' She gave me a detailed insight into the hard early life of one of the world's greatest screen goddesses. As the film *La Dolce Vita*, starring Anita Ekberg, had just come out, I used my time in Rome to round up relevant stars there like Eva Bartok, Dawn Addams, Edmund Purdom and Anita's ex-husband, Anthony Steel, who all gave me stories indicating that life in Rome was *not* so sweet.

In Paris I had a surprising interview with Paul Newman, then top new star of films like *Someone Up There Likes Me*, *The Long Hot Summer* and *Cat on a Hot Tin Roof*. He revealed that he would never have become an actor but for being thrown into jail! After the war, when he had served as a radio operator on torpedo planes in the South Pacific, he returned to college but found he was getting nowhere with his initial subject, economics, so he switched to English and the theatrical arts.

'I was in the college football team and one night five of us went into town and got a little high. We had a wonderful brawl and broke up a bit of furniture in a bar, but we upset the local police who threw us into jail. It was a great experience considering it was a jail. Half the college came down to visit us at four in the morning and even smuggled in a cake with a file in it as a gag. The local paper did a big story about how the college football team was in trouble *again*. Naturally the college didn't like this and threw us out of the team.

'Then I had nothing else to do with my spare time, so I took a real interest in the college's theatrical life. I put my name down for a part in a play, got one, and then I did about ten plays there in two years. I liked the life and decided to have a shot at acting when I left.' To pay his way, Paul ran a laundry business for the other students. 'On Saturdays we'd buy a 15-gallon keg of beer and give it away to the students when they brought their laundry. Some of them finished up so drunk we would shove them into their own laundry bins to sleep it off!' Paul also gave me more insights into the milestones of his life and career – another cracking show page.

It was in my third year on the magazine that editor Howard French called me into his office. He not only congratulated me on my recent columns but showed me some statistics from some body called the Audit Bureau of Circulation. These said that in proportion to the number of readers of various magazines and newspapers I was the most widely read entertainments columnist in Fleet Street, and French was upping my salary. My delight was brief, for he then dropped a bombshell – he was leaving the magazine soon to become editor of the popular tabloid, the *Daily Sketch*. When I asked who was taking over, my worst fears were founded. His deputy David Hill would be the new editor of the magazine. Oh well, I'd have to get along with him as best I could.

By now, in my spare time and at weekends, I was renting a cheap attic flat in a quiet farmhouse in Sussex so that I could read some philosophy and start writing a novel in the hope that I could eventually quit journalism and become a writer. That had been my initial aim right at the start, after all.

At this time the most significant star interview I made was with a man I'd long admired on screen – Cary Grant. I actually learned some important ideas and philosophical themes from him.

Born Archibald Leach, Cary ran away from home in Bristol at thirteen to join a troupe of stilt walkers and acrobats, became a carnival barker, a lifeguard, a painter of neckties, a sandwich-board man, and a burlesque artist, survived three marriages in Hollywood and became not only a major movie star but the very epitome of sophistication, suaveté and style. He had reached the top as a romantic lead twenty-five years earlier and at an age when most of his contemporaries had been relegated to ageing character roles, he was still a romantic lead. Quite a life, quite an achievement.

I met him when he came to London to help promote his new comedy, *That Touch of Mink*, in which he played Doris Day's lover. At fifty-eight he looked thirty-eight, was lean and moved with the grace of an athlete. I wondered if he had found some secret formula for eternal youth! I asked him such searching questions that at one point he jabbed a finger at me and said, 'You're asking these questions because you want the answers yourself!' I had to admit this was true. It had been reported that he had undergone a series of psychiatric sessions involving the use of the mind-blowing drug LSD 25, and I wondered if this was the clue. I asked him about the LSD treatment.

'It is not available normally and was pure experiment in my case,' he replied. 'But I could have tried something else and found the same results. Under supervision LSD helps probe the innermost recesses of the mind, can free up repressions. I used it and found it highly rewarding.'

I asked him, 'How much power do you feel your mind has over your body?'

'Complete power. If you're in charge of yourself, your mind can both cause and prevent illness. There are many cases where prayer has been effective in curing illness. I believe the mind has power to prevent illness too.'

I persisted: 'But surely not power over sickness which is purely physical, like cancer or TB, for instance?'

'How do you know they're *purely* physical? And how do you know someone is *mentally* sick? Because he differs from the normal, the average? Some of the greatest men in the world, judged by history, were considered insane when they formed their theories. I read reports that I do yoga. Apart from watching my second wife Barbara Hutton (the Woolworth heiress) in some rather attractive yoga poses, my knowledge of yoga is nil. I'm supposed to be a health food faddist. This is idiotic. I am a scavenger! When I've finished my meal I start helping myself to bits of food others have left behind. I eat what I like and when I'm hungry.'

'Cary, you've been reported as saying your treatments with LSD had proved to you that the most important thing in life is love, not sex-love, or love based on selfish need…'

He interrupted me: 'I'm glad to hear I said something for once that I agree with! The most important person to love is yourself. Not egotistically, but to be at peace with yourself. When you love yourself in that sense, you love other people too… everyone you meet. Love is a feeling, a still feeling, deep inside one, Other people don't necessarily love back, you know, nor need that be necessary if you're feeling love inside you.

'I feel love in me more now than I used to feel it. It may be called "maturity" or "mellowing", or it may be called "settling for oneself". But I do know this. Once you settle for yourself, you can settle for everyone else.'

I asked him: 'What made you try to find yourself? You had fame, stardom, riches.'

'I had been too distressed by my own troubles and faults to be able to accept them without question. I felt they would not be troubles once I understood them, what caused them.'

We talked on and on in this vein and I really felt I was getting a new slant on life, much food for thought. Cary ended by saying that if he had achieved success – and he was not sure he had – it was by trying to be himself.

'I was not born wealthy and had little real schooling. For years I didn't know what I wanted from life, even questioned acting. But later, by an effort of mind, I *made* what I was doing the thing that I wanted to do. I began to enjoy it then. Everyone can do this.'

Two weeks later, after a show page on British actor Kenneth More, I heard that John Fairbairn, who had been my favourite publicity man at Rank studios, was now working on the new Ava Gardner film, *55 Days At Peking* in Madrid. I could get no response from the number Ava had given me so long ago, so I realized she had probably moved. I phoned John in Rome and asked him to ask Ava if she would give me an interview if I flew over. He said she wasn't seeing any journalists but he would try. I hardly expected to hear any more, but two nights later I was sitting in my flat around 7 p.m. with my first drink when the phone rang. To my astonishment it was Ava Gardner. She said she remembered me well and of course she would talk to me, I should just fix it up through Fairbairn. When she asked what I'd been doing I told her of Cary and other big stars I'd been writing about and added that I was now writing a novel and studying some philosophers. When she asked which ones, I said I was currently ploughing through Nietszche!

'Oh, wow,' she said in that low, sultry voice. 'You better come on out and educate me!'

Naturally, when I went into the usual Monday editorial conference – the last with Howard French as editor –I was all agog with the possibility that I could get another scoop on the great star. Mr French and the features chief were all for it but I heard David Hill mutter that he thought Ava Gardner was 'a bit over the top and not of much interest to our readers'. However, Howard French authorized my trip to Madrid and I was on my way.

21
Ava Again – and the Kiss

I walked into Ava Gardner's dressing room in the Madrid studios. She hardly smiled, but extended her hand coolly and said, 'Hello, Mike, come in. I'm afraid it's not very tidy and God, isn't it hot!' Her coloured maid Renee rushed around clearing up towels from the table and emptying ashtrays and offered me a drink. I said thanks, but I didn't drink when I was working, When Ava, who was sipping a cool gin and tonic full of ice, said, '*Really*?' I said I would have a gin and tonic too, and thanks.

When I told her the publicity staff on the film seemed scared stiff of her, Ava laughed. 'Well, I told them when I came that I didn't want to do interviews. It's over two years since I did any press interview. I don't mind doing photographs – if I'm warned about them and they have a little charm and dignity. But I hate being taken when I'm doing something silly or when I'm trying to relax. I'm sure sick of all this crap without shoes, hair awry, and cigarette ends sticking out the side of my mouth. Why should I put up with that?

'One reason I live in Spain is because I'm left alone here, not like in Italy where I'm trailed everywhere by packs of reporters and photographers. Well, I *was* chased around town in restaurants and shops for a month or two when I first came here but I found out the cause of it. It was someone tipping them off who worked for me but obviously was not working for me. That person is *not* working for me now!'

'Ava, as a woman you are not interested in convention but being allowed what you yourself want to do. But the price for overthrowing conventionality for a single woman must be occasional deep loneliness?'

She blew out a small cloud of smoke. 'Oh, this is the idea everyone has about me. I read all these crazy stories that say I am such a lonely figure, this crap how unhappy, how miserable and how lonely I am. It's not true. My God, if I was as sad and lonely as they have made me out to be I would go and blow my brains out! It's a complete lie. When I'm not working I lead a very quiet and simple life. Sometimes I feel a little bored and that I should be doing something creative but apart from occasional reading I don't know exactly what.'

I tried again. 'The popular concept of Ava Gardner is the lone movie goddess who dances till exhaustion, drinks till the small hours, able to command the attention of any desirable male she wishes, but in fact is a rather lost soul…'

'Oh God… please… that's all a load of bull'

'Well, do you feel sometimes perhaps – three marriages, no children – that you paid a high personal price for your present status as a star?'

'No… You know I trained to be a secretary at Atlantic College? This is better than being a secretary. Only a fool would say otherwise.'

'Does the thought of old age and that you will lose your looks upset or depress you?'

She gave a wan little smile as the cigarette smoke curled round her beautiful face. 'Not at all. Thank God, I can cope with it when it comes. Well, first of all I have *never* been terribly concerned or interested in how I look to the world, because if I did worry I'd go around always looking extremely chic and be done up to my eyebrows all the time. It's a bore and would take up too much time visiting beauty parlours. And make-up I hate. The first time I realized a concern for oneself and one's looks really did not matter very much was about three years ago when I fell off one of Peralta's horses and knocked hell out of my face.

'But I didn't panic or think what a really terrible disaster it was, At the time one of my best friends in Madrid had a stroke and was partly paralysed on one side of her face. I was more concerned about her face than I was about mine. I definitely didn't think it tragic that I might have lost everything because it has not meant much to me to be attractive. I admit it wasn't too pleasant for about six months but I flew to London and Sir Archibald McIndoe put it right without much trouble.'

'Then you don't, like so many women stars, consciously preserve your looks to keep at the top?'

'No, God, no… I never think about it.'

'You never go on a health kick?'

'Oh yes, I go on health kicks constantly. I play tennis like mad, furiously, and I stop drinking – for two or three days. I try to stop smoking but that I can't do. I have no self-discipline really for things like that. I went to a health farm in England but I gained four pounds because as well as eating the diet foods, I went to the kitchens and ate some of the cooks' food too. I was eating four meals a day instead of one or two and I gained weight like mad. I *like* exercise but do little apart from tennis.'

'I heard you once broke a toe doing judo?'

'That was when I was in Honolulu, at the time Caryl Chessman was executed. I was with friends, a Japanese lawyer and his wife, and he said if the woman victim had been able to do judo, Chessman could never have raped or killed her. He started showing us a few passes. I was trying to do the kick-in-the-kidneys one but my foot connected with a chair on the way round. That was the end of my learning judo. It was the first bone I'd ever broken. For four months I had to go around without wearing shoes. Well, I could when a hole was cut in the shoe for my busted toe. The very first night I went out was on the Costa Brava. I leaned over in the car to pitch my heavy bag out and the door closed on my foot – and it broke all over again.'

'Wow, that *was* bad luck. Ava, I believe you once said, "Every woman should be a bride if she finds the right guy. A husband and kids is what a woman wants, not the rat race and the big movie star bit... but where to find the right guy?"'

Ava smiled. 'I'm sure if I didn't say that I said something like it. Yes, I would much prefer to be happily married and have a shoal of kids.'

'Well, if you really want a husband and kids, what stops you?'

She sighed, then said, 'It's none of your affair.' A pause, then, 'I made three mistakes. I'll be very careful... it's much too painful... I'll be very careful next time. Oh, now, now... please. Must we talk like this? It is all much too close.'

'I apologize, I'm sorry, but really, do you feel you need reproach yourself too much? After all, the fact that you had little education and were repressed when young because of a strict upbringing, meant that you could have been little more then a child in your first two marriages at least' (to Mickey Rooney at nineteen and Artie Shaw at twenty-two).

'Well, how many wives do *they* have between the two of them? Eight and five. Thirteen. Between the two of them. My choice was bad... I was a child then... I probably still am!'

'Most people find a maturity through the struggles they have to go through to earn a daily crust, Ava. Most of your life you've had the best and had it pretty easy, never had to really struggle.'

She cut me off. 'What are you trying to say – that if I had to go out and scrub floors I would have found myself? No, it would have made no difference at all. Right on up to the time I was eighteen years old I was brought up in a very poor family, so I was accustomed to all that. I don't think how hard you have to work or struggle for your daily crust has anything to do with being mature. Would you not think the struggle in this ridiculous business was enough? Don't forget I spent seventeen years under contract to Metro, doing many movies I hated and struggling for what I felt was right. Mature you? It can *age* you!'

'Ava, I won't ask this as from your own life but as a theory. Do you not feel the ego that a star has to build up to stay at the top is a barrier to a happy marriage?'

'I don't think so. It's not so much the ego of the star but the whole crazy life surrounding the star that makes such a hell of a barrier.'

'I believe you had great love from your parents, that they loved each other utterly until they died. Don't you ever feel it's sad that, with all your success and riches, you have not achieved this?'

She said quietly, 'Yes, I feel it is – very.'

'Are you, in spite of everything, a little unhappy?'

'Oh God, no. I'm happy. I'm not *completely* happy, no one can be, but I'm happy enough. I'm quite content.'

The dressing-room door opened at this point and the assistant director said Ava was wanted on the set for the day's longest scene in five minutes. I put my notebook away, thanked her and said I would love the chance to talk to her a little longer. To my surprise and delight, Ava said that as tomorrow was Saturday, and she had a day off, I could come to her Madrid house at 4 p.m. and continue the interview in a more relaxed atmosphere. She wrote down her address and as she saw me to the door she asked if I liked tennis. I said I did, quite, and often watched Wimbledon.

'Good,' she said, a slight smile playing around the corners of her lovely mouth. 'See you tomorrow.'

The scene next day was Ava Gardner's elegant six-bathroom, five-bedroom house in a leafy square in Madrid. The luxuriously furnished lounge was cool, the shutters turned halfway so the light didn't glare. There were beautiful dark Moorish ornaments on the antique tables, old oil colours hung on the walls, and the furniture was mostly sixteenth- and seventeenth-century French. Ava called down from upstairs, 'Make yourself comfortable. I won't be long.'

She came down the stairs in a white, loose-fitting dress, and it was like the walk of a queen, and when she held out her hand I felt as much like bowing as shaking it. She made me sit down but the huge red velvet sofa was so big I couldn't get my spine right to the back of it and it was either sit bolt upright or sprawl back and look ready for anything. I sat upright.

'What'll you have to drink? I'm having a long Tom Collins because I'm thirsty. Want to try one?' I said I did and Renee brought the ingredients over in a glass, which Ava promptly topped up with more gin. I reached into my little briefcase for my notes...

Ava reacted in slight horror. 'Oh God, you're not going to get a damn great list of questions out again, are you? Oh, Mike, just sit and talk to me, won't you? We can do that lot later.'

So I sat and just talked to her, about the film, the Spanish way of life, why she had sold *Las Brujas* (the Witch's House) in the country – 'Because the damn place was falling down!' – and I even showed her a photo of the isolated country mansion I was using as a writing retreat. She thought it 'terribly cute' and said maybe she would see it one day. Suddenly she jumped up and grabbed my hand. 'Come on, I'll show you my place.'

It was soon obvious that everything in the Gardner home was as Gardner liked it, different with many pieces out of place but charmingly so – like the quaint lopsided Spanish grandfather clock in the huge hall. She showed me the dining room. It was all dull flame-red, with an old coloured coach light hanging from a pinkish ceiling. 'Maybe it's goddamn awful from an expert's view but I like it,' she said. Her library would have done a small town proud. She had over a thousand books, ranging through Aristotle, Plato, Dostoievsky, Tolstoy, through Shakespeare, Dickens, Brontë, Steinbeck, Hemingway, Ruark, Joyce. There were books on philosophy, art, theatre and scores of well-known literary classics. She admitted she didn't read as much as she should.

'I do try but usually put the book down after a few pages. I don't get the time – and I'm so damn lazy, mentally lazy. I once enrolled at the University of California to study philosophy, history and the arts, but I gave up after a few months. I guess I'm pretty useless at educating myself.'

I commented on the old Impressionist paintings and the faded oils, pointing out that Jacob Van Ruisdale's superb *Waterfall with Trees* was among the prints I had bought at the Tate Gallery for my own flat. She said, 'I love them because they're so quiet and old. I like quiet things around me. I don't think any of them are valuable.'

I said, 'What does the value matter? The value is what beauty means to you, not its commercial profit in the world market.' I laughed at the memory of one of my snobbish lady friends who had criticized my art works as they 'were only prints'. I told her, 'Why should I be deprived of beauty just because I cannot afford the original?'

'Oh, that's excellent,' said Ava. 'You're so right. Beautiful things are in themselves priceless to me. Oh, come on upstairs. Come on, I want to show you something – it's a little statue I'm thinking of buying but I think they're trying to screw me!'

We went upstairs into the main Gardner bedroom. It was something to see. The bed, on a raised dais at the far end on the left, was big enough for six, and it had a headboard made from a small proscenium in a Spanish church. The rest of it, explained Ava, was the sideboard downstairs! On the right of the bedroom was the entrance to her terrace, which had straw Spanish lights and hidden lanterns behind bushes. A green wicker fence topped all the walls so no one could see in.

'We can have our drinks out here later,' said Ava. 'Now, it's too hot.'

Drinks? Later? My mind made an optimistic jump!

Back in the bedroom, Ava showed me a small statuette in wood of a cardinal of the Church holding a figure of Christ on the Cross. 'I think he's beautiful but I'm not sure he's really old, and the little shop wants four hundred dollars for it. That's a lot of dough if it's not genuine. Do you know anything about these things?'

'Not much,' I replied. 'But let's look at it carefully. It could be made of a ship's timber. These village craftsmen collect old baulks of timber and carve them to look like this. The wood is old, true, but the work is relatively new. It could be two years old and it could be two hundred for all I can see.'

'We'll take it over to my friend Luis on our way to the tennis courts. He's a painter, so he should know.'

Tennis? So that was why she'd asked me if I liked tennis earlier. I hoped she had two rackets. I'd only played one game of tennis in my life though I'd bashed balls up against our lounge walls long enough in my youth. Finally we went downstairs to the cool, dark lounge for the last stage of the interview. As I took out my remaining questions, Ava raised a restraining finger.

'You know, Mike, the personal questions you are asking me are unfair to me and to you as I can't really tell you the truth. I have to either lie or say nothing. If I do answer them I give you such a stupid answer I put myself in a bad light.'

'I'm highly flattered you answer them at all,' I replied, 'but all you have to do if I fire one you don't like is to say "Belt up!' "

'Belt up – Oh, I love the Cockney slang.'

'Okay, here goes. In your professional life many things must have annoyed you. How about when you were called "The world's most beautiful animal"?'

'Oh, that title was crazy. Some publicity man thought it up for me in *The Barefoot Contessa*. It was a catchy little thing but it had nothing to do with *me*, only the character in the picture. It certainly isn't something I want to live up to or ever tried to live up to. Frankly I feel all that sort of thing is foolishness.'

'Yes, and I daresay you have many doubts or hates about your own facial or physical defects anyway...?'

'Oh, I have eight million physical and facial things I don't like. What can I tell you that is beautiful about me? My hair perhaps? I cannot think of one really pretty thing. God, I'm bow-legged. My arse is too big – and that you *can't* print...'

'Derriere I can.'

'Bottom then. Oh, what else? I am an extremely healthy animal I would say, and that's all. Beautiful? I don't know.'

'Healthy? Well, surely that itself is a high form of beauty. Good health is beautiful.'

She laughed. 'Oh yes, there I am with you. No, physical beauty doesn't matter much to me. What is beauty, how do you decide, who decides?'

'To twist an old phrase, I think beauty is in the mind of the beholden.'

'Oh, that's deep, but true I think. You know I like myself more – if you want to talk about physical beauty – than I did a few years ago. This will make no sense to most people, I'm sure. But I like the way I look now, I feel I look more mature. As a little girl I was a very perfect, pretty little thing – too much so. I had very blonde hair until I was fourteen, as did my sisters who had very dark eyes. I goofed with the eyes as mine were green.'

I asked her if she still loved bull-fights as much as she is supposed to.

'Frankly, I'm disenchanted with them. I have seen eight thousand bull-fights. No, not that many, but I have seen so many and so few good ones. I'm frightened for the bull, for the matador, for the horses, for the whole damn thing. Really, it all scares me to death these days.'

Ava told me she considered herself a rotten actress but to make up for it she worked 'like a bastard', tried to be professional, be on time and know her lines and do what she was told. 'I love to travel and I make pictures so I can live the way I like, I'm not the dedicated type who just lives to make pictures. I'd like my house here, a small house in London and a small flat in San Francisco, For that I'll have to make a couple more pictures.'

I chided her for believing she was a rotten actress – after all, she'd had two Oscar nominations, one for *Mogambo*, one for *On the Beach.*

'I don't think I'm a good actress, I really don't. There is something terribly lacking when I see myself on screen, it embarrasses me. I realize how much I lack, and yet I can't do anything about it.'

I said quietly, as if musing to myself, 'Strange, how great talent is always shadowed by modesty.' and heard her give a little gasp and briefly touch my hand with hers. I would try my last personal question.

'Ava, the last time we spoke you said you had made three mistakes in marriage and you'll be very careful next time. Do you think you will ever marry again?'

'I certainly hope so. Why? Why? That's right where we should stop this talk!'

'All right. Sorry again. But don't you think perhaps you have been alone too long now, and may be a bit too set in your bachelor woman ways?'

'No, I don't feel I've been alone too long or that I am a perennial bachelor girl. Every woman needs to be married. Oh, not every woman. How can I generalize like that? But I feel I'm much happier as a woman when I'm married, even if it's not the completely happy marriage.'

She took a deep breath. 'I hope some day I might find someone... I can't get married simply because I don't like being lonely, or to have children. I must be terribly in love. Isn't that silly? Sounds like a little girl, doesn't it?'

I asked my last question. 'Ava, now and again in our talks, you've referred to your strict upbringing. If you feel this, together with your lack of education, has repressed you, don't you agree that once you reach maturity you can throw off childish inhibitions or bad influences from early environment?'

'What do you mean – narrow upbringing?' she replied. 'I had a very fine upbringing. There was nothing bad about it at all. It *was* strict, yes, but there was great love between my parents. I think if I had a child I would bring it up just as strictly. I was taught to be a lady. What I did after that was of my own doing. But 'inhibitions'? 'Bad influences'? How can you forget? How can you throw off part of your life? You can't. That's why it is so very important to have a very good beginning – just because you cannot throw it off. If I ever have a child I will make sure it has that good beginning.'

I thanked Ava for her perfect interviews and as I closed my notebook she decided, after Renee had brought us two more small Tom Collins drinks, that we should now take her wooden statue to her painter friend, Luis. I struggled heroically to carry it down the stairs from her bedroom.

'Don't hold it by the neck,' shouted Ava. 'You'll break it and then I'll *have* to pay for it!' I said a meek sorry.

Outside, Ava's chauffeur was waiting and when he saw us coming he started the limousine's engine. I put the statue into the front seat area and as it took a few seconds to set it right Ava climbed into the rear, saying, 'Come on, Mike. Get into the car. I can't wait for our tennis.' I followed and sat next to her, wondering how all this was going to end. And what did Ava mean by that remark in her bedroom earlier when she had said, 'This is my wonderful terrace. We'll have our drinks out here later. Now it's too hot'?

We were driven to Luis's place, with its beautiful walled Spanish garden and small swimming pool, just about big enough for two breaststrokes, I noted. Luis, his two sons and a very pretty nanny were sitting by the pool. I lugged the statue up some long steps and as Ava explained her doubts, Luis took it from me and turned it upside down.

'I cannot say. It may be old wood and new painting or old wood with old painting, If it was left in a dusty cellar for a long time it would look old. But 32,000 pesetas is too much.' He would get one of his knowledgeable pals to look at it and bring it back to Ava tomorrow. After he showed us the painting he was currently doing of Ava, the chauffeur drove the two of us for about five minutes to the outskirts of Madrid.

'Where now?' I asked meekly.

'We are going to swim and play tennis,' said Ava firmly.

Mild panic. 'Er, I can't,' I said. 'I don't have any togs.'

'You only want shorts and there's plenty there,' replied Ava. 'And you can play barefoot, like me.'

We reached the huge iron gates of her friends' pine-filled estate, and one of the servants from the entrance lodge opened them for us, beaming cheerfully at the sight of Ava. She jumped out of the car and ran behind the lodge to meet the servant's family, embraced them all in turn, then spied who she was looking for – their little six-month old brown-eyed baby, Pepito.

Then came the most poignant moment in my visits to Ava Gardner, when all her frustrated mother-love showed in her face and in her actions as she sat down on a primitive settee and played nursery games with the little peasant child. She made a tremendous fuss of him then handed him to me saying, 'You hold him, Mike. Isn't he just gorgeous?'

'Babies scare me to death,' I said. 'I'm so afraid of hurting them, or dropping them.' But I took the baby. Strange how tiny he was. Suddenly the father reached over and patted Pepito on the nose, quite hard.

'See what he does to the poor little thing,' cried Ava, and took the baby back.

As we later walked up the green-lawned hill to the summerhouse to change Ava again confessed she hoped that one day she would get married again and have the child she never had in three marriages. I changed in the men's cubicle but all I could find was a pair of briefs that were really too small and crushed everything and were quite uncomfortable. When I emerged Ava, now wearing an immaculate tennis skirt, recovered her gaiety immediately after laughing at my shorts.

It was certainly a tennis game to remember, both of us diabolically bad, especially me. Ava went red in the face but ran around as if she was twenty instead of almost forty. She sure looked good when her split tennis skirt swirled open – and she knew it, occasionally stroking a shapely thigh as if she had an itch, and making little pirouettes. Arse too big? Arse too damn perfect, I thought. Once I sent down a real corker which bounced and hit her on the shin.

'Oh, you did that on purpose!'

Almost an hour later my bare feet were sore but our sides were aching with a combination of stitch and laughter. Dusk was falling when the chauffeur drove us back to Ava's house where she immediately directed me into one of the bathrooms to have a shower while she had one in hers. When she emerged she had changed into a light grey trouser suit with a high collar which I found somewhat disappointing as I could no longer see her legs! She poured us large gin and tonics, saying we could now have our drinks on her lovely terrace. As she led me on to it I carried with me a small book by a philosopher I admired which I'd selected from her library, to maybe give us useful talking points. I also noticed something was missing. Since Ava had poured the drinks herself, I asked her where her maid, Renee, was? My heart gave another little optimistic jump when Ava replied, 'I gave her the night off.'

Well, we sat, sipped our drinks and talked, and I showed her two passages in the philosophy book that might interest her. Suddenly, and I'll never forget the moment, her hand went briefly on to my knee, she looked me straight in the eyes and said, 'Tell me, Mike, what in hell is a charming, thinking, good-looking guy like you doing interviewing old movie broads like me? Don't you think you should be doing something more intelligent with your life?'

I was a bit thunderstruck, to say the least, but I mumblingly replied I did try to get some meaningful material from stars thousands looked up to. And I reminded her I'd hired my country retreat purely to try to write a novel of merit, and if it was a success I'd be able to break away from journalism. She wished me well with the novel and said that when it was published I must send her a copy. She then stood up.

'Enough of all this serious talk, Mike. Have you heard of this new dance thing, the Twist? I've just got new records of Bill Haley and Ray Charles playing and singing it. Do you know anything about it?'

It just so happened that only a fortnight before I had thrown a special Twist party in a marquee in the grounds of the Sussex mansion, not only for all my friends but to give my father and stepmother a farewell bash before they emigrated to Spain, and I had proved quite good at the dance. I could twist all the way down and back up again on one leg, my left, though for some reason I couldn't on my right. 'Come on,' I said. 'I'll teach you the Twist.'

For the next half-hour we twisted away to the records downstairs in the living room, laughing and panting with the vigorous exercise to the exciting music. Ava was very athletic and gasped that it would be good for her waist. Certainly, her carpet would never be the same – flamenco had nothing on it. Momentarily tired, we repaired back up to the terrace to recover and have more drinks. By now, with Ava's permission. I had switched from gin and tonic, which I didn't really like, to my favourite drink at the time – gin and It, which for me was gin and sweet martini, equally mixed. As we stood there together below a quaint wooden arch, I noticed some lovely exotic flowers hanging in a basket just behind her head. I asked her what they were.

'They're Morning Glories, my favourite flowers. I had the seeds flown over from where I was born, in North Carolina.'

'You grew them yourself, from seed?' I asked, surprised that a movie star like her had green fingers.

'Well, my name *is* Gardner,' she laughed, quick-witted, throwing her head back in that supplicant way she had. 'They're rather romantic, don't you think?'

Just then the moon rose above the parapet, lighting up her lovely face. Without thinking I heard myself say, 'Ava, can I give you a kiss?'

She did not seem very surprised but she murmured, 'What for? You're not exactly my boyfriend, you know.' I wanted to say, 'Because I saw you as the beautiful Julie in *Showboat* when I was twenty-four, I saw you as the tempestuous heroine in *The Barefoot Contessa*, the fiery Kelly in *Mogambo*, the ethereal *Pandora*. and so on. And I fell for you every time,' but I couldn't, so I just said, 'Because when I am a very old man I can look in the mirror and say, "Whatever bad things have happened to you, Mike Tomkies, you old fool, at least you once kissed Ava Gardner!"'

She just said quietly, 'All right then,' and she closed her eyes and lifted her face to mine. I meant to press my lips gently to hers for just a few seconds but as I was about to pull away again I was amazed to feel her hand come round the back of my neck and draw me just slightly closer. It was not a French kiss but very near it, delicate, sensitive and enough to make me quickly feel I was *in*, that we might just end up in that huge bed together. Suddenly Ava sprang back with a gay laugh. 'You said a *kiss*, not a peck!' Then she wagged a finger at me in mock admonition. 'But don't start getting any big ideas!'

I mumbled, 'Wow... of course not... wow, thanks very much. That was terrific.'

Well, we carried on talking, dancing and laughing, Ava made some quick, delicious hamburgers, and amid all the euphoria I'm afraid I drank rather too much. When she said I could put on any record I liked I made the mistake of choosing one of my favourite Frank Sinatra records, 'None but the Lonely Heart', sung to a classic, lyrically sad theme by Tchaikovsky, thinking I might introduce a more serious note to the proceedings.

Almost instantly Ava came over saying, 'I never play Mr Sinatra when there is anyone else in the house. It's taboo.' And she removed the needle from the record, which she put back in its sleeve and up on to its shelf. I said I was sorry and went to sit on the sofa, listening to a Spanish record Ava had chosen. I don't know whether I briefly dozed off while Ava was clearing the kitchen but the next thing I noticed, well after midnight, was that the maid Renee had reappeared and was staring at me, not smiling. And Ava was sitting next to me saying quite gently, 'Mike, I think you've had a little too much to drink. I think you should go back to your hotel. I've called a taxi.'

With her promise we would play tennis again next day, or go somewhere interesting for lunch, I willingly allowed her to escort me down to the taxi, and was driven back to my hotel, no doubt with a silly smile on my face.

I was in for a disappointment. In the morning Ava rang me early to say her great friend, the distinguished author Robert Graves, had rung her, asking her to fly to a big party he was giving for his birthday at his Majorca home, and she would not be back for three days. I had to return to my job in London before that, so I repeated my promise to write and invite her to my country retreat and send her a copy of the printed interview. Then we said our goodbyes. I flew back to London with what I was sure was a fabulous scoop, cherishing the marvellous memories of my time with the world's most beautiful animal.

22
Suddenly Unemployed – and Benny, Claudia and Carlo

When I got back to London with the show-business pages feature on Ava, Howard French had gone and David Hill was now editor of the magazine. He read the story with the deflating comment, 'Hmm, not bad,' and said I could give it to the chief sub-editor to prepare for printing. As I turned to leave he called me back and said in a friendly enough voice, 'Mike, I'd like to make a few changes around here. For instance, I'd like you to spend more time in the office. I hardly ever see you, don't know what you are doing. I mean…er… you *are* on the staff, aren't you?'

'Yes,' I replied. 'But my desk has gone. The features editor's got it now.'

'Oh,' he said with a derisory wave round the open-plan office with its many attentive ears, 'I'm sure we can bung another one somewhere for you.'

I just nodded and left, feeling I had trouble ahead. It was clear that to David Hill I was not, as I had been to Howard French, the 'star' of the magazine. Two days later, when I went in to hand over my pop records column, he called me into his office to say he had a few of his own ideas for show-business pages and we could discuss his ideas and mine before next Monday's editorial conference. I immediately realized that the days of my choosing which stars I wrote about, and how, were coming to an end. Then Hill dropped another bombshell – that I could no longer expect my show-business material to automatically occupy the centre double-page colour spread, still the only one in a general magazine in Fleet Street.

'I intend to use the best story and pictures of the week in the colour spread. From now on you will only get it if your story is better than any other we've got, okay?'

I said okay and left. I knew by now this guy just didn't like me. When my Ava Gardner story came out it *was* on the centre pages at least but had been relegated to black and white photos, and to second place below a big daft colour spread of a girl who had four jobs at the Pigalle nightclub in London

– as telephonist, programme seller, cigarette girl and swimmer in a huge glass fish tank. What was worse, the headline for my piece, obviously taken out of context from a chance remark Ava had made, read: 'AVA HAS NEVER MADE A GOOD FILM – and the first one to admit it is Ava.'

That was the end for me and I was incensed. I borrowed the features editor's typewriter, wrote a letter of resignation saying I wanted to go freelance, marched into Hill's office without knocking and dropped it on his desk before his astonished face. A few minutes later his secretary came to me with a note from him that said if I 'wanted to try and swim the Atlantic' he would not stand in my way, but could we have a chat before I left the office today?

This time I did knock on his door and I was surprised to find he looked nervous, his fingers trembling slightly. Clearly my sudden resignation had been a shock. He said if I wanted to leave right away and not serve out the usual month's notice, he would agree, provided I would still write my column as normal for the next six weeks until he could find a replacement. While it was clear we wanted to see the back of each other, this was better than I'd bargained for. When he said he would pay me the same salary, I agreed with alacrity and we actually shook hands. This would give me a fully paid six-week gateway to prepare stories and build up my freelance contacts.

As I left the office I couldn't help thinking how strange it was – my first scoop with Ava Gardner had got me the great job at *Weekend*, and my second interview with her had got me out of it when it turned sour. How instrumental she had been in my life! I also felt a spasm of fear, for apart from the six-weeks gateway I was now out on my own, unemployed for the first time in my life. I went to my bank to check my balance. Standing at the counter, checking his, was a former features editor of *Weekend*, Charles, who was now editor of the new *Today* magazine. As I checked my balance – £247 – I glanced over to look at his. He was £397 in the red! Heavens, I thought, I'm doing better than *him*.

When he hailed me with 'How's the great show-biz writer?' I said, 'I'm not, not any more.' And I told him why. To my surprise Charles slapped his thigh and said, 'Great. I need good show-biz stuff. Have you got anything that might suit us?' I had been discussing for some time a big feature with Benny Hill, who was going round the world shooting sequences for his TV ads on his £1,000,000 deal with Schweppes drinks, and was also TV's most popular comedian of the time. My idea was that Benny would tell a funny story from each port of call, raking in the different types of girls, food, booze, clubs and habits while ostensibly looking for a likely wife and adding his own jokes along the way. Charles commissioned it there and then, in the bank! He said he would pay £400 if it came up to scratch. £400? That was eight times my weekly salary – and I hadn't been a freelance for one full day! Nor was that all – before the end of the week I'd written and sold two 'think-piece' film stories to a leading fans' magazine, and had sold a story that David Hill had turned down to a rival magazine. In my first week as a freelance I earned almost £1,000 – just the kick-start I needed.

The one bad thing at this time was that the lousy display of the Ava Gardner story probably scuppered my relationship with her. I'd promised to send her the piece but could not inflict the awful headline on her, so I cut it off and sent it to her with my promised invite to my country retreat. I feel fairly sure someone must have shown her the full piece, for I never had a reply, even when I sent a follow-up letter saying I had resigned my job over the matter.

My interview with Benny Hill, however, was a revelation. When I rang him to fix it up he asked if I could bring along a couple of pretty girls as he'd had the idea of *acting out* his stories from the various countries he visited, and he would do it better if he had a small audience to play to. I said I could do that easily enough but surely he could have his own pick of his own girls, from the Hill's Angels dancing troupe in his own show?

'Oh, no, no, no, no, Michael,' he said. 'I never try to date any of them, have them to my flat. I never mix business with pleasure!'

Well, I took two models round to Benny's luxury flat in Queensgate, London, and within about two hours he took us round the world! He twanged his Paraguayan harps, plucked his Greek bouzoukis and thumped his Turkish tom–toms in an astonishing performance, complete with all the correct accents and sound effects as he described the different types of girls, clubs, etc., in Tokyo, Hong Kong, Marseilles, Istanbul, Bangkok and Australia. And throughout he stressed the qualities he was hoping for in a wife. He had us reeling with laughter as he also plied us with home–made soufflé and champagne, and it was all good clean fun. One could have put TV cameras on him and ended up with a top-class one-man show, yet he did it for nothing, just to give me a good article. We became quite good friends after that and over the next three years we sometimes repeated that little party, with different girls of course, and often, if they were French or German au pairs for instance, Benny would get ideas for gags from them. There was never any suggestion of sex; it wasn't even mentioned.

For much of the next three years I widened my markets and drove around European capitals interviewing major stars on various film sets. For instance, I did a profile of the newest girl sex symbol, Claudia Cardinale, when she was acting with John Wayne in *The Magnificent Showman*, and it made a double-page spread in the *Daily Sketch*. I recall with amusement that when I was plying Claudia with my usual hard, searching questions, a loud voice boomed, 'Hey, what's with all these depressing questions? Claudia is a happy, normal girl and doing great work on my movie. Don't go making her unhappy!' Standing behind me was the tough legendary director Henry 'Hank' Hathaway and he was not a man to argue with. I even saw him boss John Wayne about. I was to have a couple more amusing run-ins with Hank years later – out in the broiling Mexican desert – but I shall tell them another time. I had the first major media interview with the new young actor Tom Courtenay for *She* magazine, timed to be printed when his first hit film, *Billy Liar*, was released.

When *Everywoman* asked me to interview Sophia Loren and find out why she married short, plump, balding film producer Carlo Ponti, I said, 'Let's turn that eternal question on its head – interview Carlo Ponti on why *he* married Sophia Loren!' Within half an hour of talking to dynamic Carlo on the set of his and his wife's new film, *Operation Crossbow*, I no longer wondered why Sophia had married him. One of the most important film-makers in the world at the time, he carelessly flicked his pork-pie hat on to a hook, sat down on a little stool and told me the whole fascinating story of how he found Sophia 'too skinny at first', recognized a great natural talent beneath the beauty and set out to make her an international star, how they gradually fell in love, with intriguing details of their life together at their 'most beautiful home in the world', the palatial estate and villa he reconstructed near the Pope's residence at Castelgandolfo.

As he talked, he emanated a devastating charm. His brown eyes flashed with gleeful, impish humour as he rocked back and forth, alternately lifting himself off the stool with his hands or gesticulating to emphasize a point, and he generated the aura of the true *bon viveur*. He and Sophia met when she entered a Miss Rome contest and he was one of the judges. Sophia only came second but he persuaded her to do some film tests. 'Some of them were very bad because she was sixteen years old then and too skinny. Yes, she was too skinny, very thin, and not at all good for pictures from certain angles. But what I saw in her immediately was a fine temperament. She was beautiful of course but this in itself was not what attracted me, for beauty is not enough. In fact it can very often go against a girl in this business. But I could see she had the potential of being a very, very good actress.

'It is impossible to be a good actress without having what I call a wonderful ear. By that I mean the balance of a person. Balance is everything – the voice, the body, the movements, the gestures which are made naturally by a person. The visual impact of a person can tell you many things, the way she makes gestures. They're either right or wrong. If you ask a bad actress to make a gesture she does it badly. You ask a good one and she does it well, but without that wonderful ear it's impossible. It is a born, inherent thing and cannot be learned completely. I could see all these things in Sophia as soon as I watched her.'

Carlo went into astonishing detail on Sophia's qualities as a woman and their domestic life together. 'She loves to cook, which is rare, for I know very few actresses of her ability who bother about cooking, but when we are at home we never go out and Sophia cooks all my favourite dishes – Risotto Milanese, Ossobuco, Cotelettes Milanese and wonderful Wiener Schnitzels with special Milanese sauce. I am Milanese and she cooks my food real good!' He revealed that they gambled every day at home. 'She's crazy about poker. Do we play for money? We play for everything. And I mean *everything*! We even play for the house. Sometimes she owns the house, sometimes I do. The trouble is she wins most of the time. Sophia is very lucky.'

He said that after the dinner Sophia cooks they don't feel like going out. So they watch TV, discuss things quietly, have friends over, or read books. 'As a producer I have to read almost everything that's written. Luckily Sophia loves to read to me, it is good for her voice and her accents, she says. And when she does I don't need my glasses!'

The conversation ranged over many topics, their world travels, their films together, the problems with some of them, 'Money has never been a problem with me. If you have good ideas you have all the money you want. All my life I've never had money problems to solve, only idea problems.' It was when I asked him his final analysis of Sophia as a woman, of her greatest qualities, that his answer astonished me and gave me much food for thought.

'My, what a question!' said. Carlo, pausing to collect his thoughts, then: 'You know the biggest quality for a woman to be a woman is to try to be a man. And for a man it is to try to be a woman. This is surrealistic, profound, but it is very, very true. When one asks what is a great woman one could think, perhaps, of a woman Cabinet Minister who is doing a man's work. She is in many ways a man. It is often the same for great men. You take great actors – well, one has to have many feminine streaks to be an actor, especially a great actor. It is strange, but true. Great people often seem to combine the finest qualities of both sexes.

'How does Sophia stay so young and vital at nearly thirty? It is a question of her approach, her attitude to life. It is not the actual age you are that counts – well, until you are *really* old, perhaps – but to be young and bright inside, in your heart, is very important. And I believe this has a lot to do with your reason to live, why you do what you do, and whether you *enjoy* what you do. If you do, then it is no problem to stay young. If you don't, then you must move the earth to try to do what you enjoy doing, what brings you the greatest sense of satisfaction in life…'

At this point I noticed that Sophia herself had entered the room and was standing quietly, listening in the door way, as Carlo continued: 'Sophia has achieved this of course. This is the answer to the problem – to have a real reason for living and a true zest for life. Nothing ages you quicker than boredom, frustration or a feeling of inadequacy or weakness.'

Sophia nodded, whispered, 'It's true,' then took Carlo by the arm and kissed him gently on the neck and they both looked at me and smiled. At that moment they seemed to communicate a greater love for each other than any show business couple I had met. Carlo Ponti was vital, alive, amazingly articulate – he was talking in what was to him a foreign language – and possessed of a dynamic, laughing energy rarely found in a man half his age. It was easy to understand why one of the great screen goddesses of the time loved him.

My story made the cover and *five* inside pages of *Everywoman*, and was syndicated in many countries. From then on I only sold UK rights to any British magazines, and sent carbon copies to magazines around the world. Ultimately I was selling stories to magazines in America, Canada, France, Germany, Sweden, Australia and South Africa.

23
Snapshots Two: Shaw, Oliver, Joan, Sammy and O'Toole

After seeing Robert Shaw's performance as the cold-blooded killer in *From Russia With Love*, and his classic fight with Sean Connery's James Bond on that speeding train, and then his barnstorming role as Henry VIII in *A Man for All Seasons*, I realized a new British star had burst on to the international scene – at the ripe old age of thirty-eight. Apart from that he had also been acclaimed by intellectuals as one of the finest writers Britain had produced for years. The complex psychological patterns, bizarre, imaginative, moving and profound qualities of such novels as *The Sun Doctor*, *The Hiding Place* and *The Flag* had sent literary critics into rapturous praise. From his cuttings I found he had played rugby for the famous Wasps team, still played squash for Buckinghamshire, was a good swimmer, horse rider and golfer, and played a mean game of tennis up to near professional standard. Adding to all this the fact that he had fathered seven children and was currently married to the beautiful actress Mary Ure, I felt sure he was a real life Superman!

I recall that after convincing *Everywoman* I should do a profile on him, and bearing in mind how I made my own living and my sporadic attempts to write my first novel, I approached him with a distinct sense of inferiority. This feeling increased when I found him living in Edwardian splendour in an eighteen-room country mansion with a sleek red Aston Martin in the two–car garage and a fifty-foot heated mosaic swimming pool in the large walled garden, and even more so when I saw he was as muscled as a prize fighter and greeted me with a handgrip of steel, saying he didn't really like press interviews.

However, he seated himself on a large leather couch near the lounge window and allowed me to tease from him a first-class insight into his life and beliefs, too long to recount in full, but here are some highlights. I put it to him that most men would feel they had achieved more than enough if they achieved top film stardom *or* acclaim as a novelists. How could he manage *both*?

He smiled. 'Writing is a sort of justification, salvation, if you like, to me. I enjoy earning film-star money because money means freedom and time, but you're not in control in filming. You have to work with many other people and often do what *they* want. To be able to turn to writing keeps me better adjusted as an actor. People say I must have tremendous energy to do both, but I don't feel that. I feel a tired man most of the time! But I have a childish, aggressive side. I love to be at the top of anything I'm in. Stardom can give you immediate fame but it can fade, whereas if you slave away at writing you might produce an enduring masterpiece.'

How did he choose which to do and when?

'I combine both and each helps me to do the other better. I know my acting has improved since I wrote these novels. I have a better perspective, a much greater sense of humour. But sometimes I do write while filming. On epic films it's easy to get two or three weeks off at a time. I just retire into the house with Mary and the kids, pick up one of my hundreds of biros and start work. This gives me a great advantage over other actors who get bored, don't know what to do, and either drink themselves stupid, play poker or make love to their leading ladies and half the time mess up their marriages. All because they're bored.

'I always write with ballpoint pens in old exercise books. I can't type and pencil seems so vague. I play music a lot when writing, Beethoven quartets and things like that on the record player. The more complicated the better, but never singers because you tend to listen to the lyrics. I prefer to have quiet but don't insist on it. When I'm really concentrating even the shouting of my children in the garden doesn't bother me.

'Mary says I'm easier to live with when I'm writing, creating something I believe in, and yet writing is very tiring and it's such a lonely thing. Acting is so much easier–everyone else is there to carry you along. It's great fun sometimes. I don't know if I could cope if I was a bachelor. I need the family. And I need my garden. I wander round it for hours, just thinking. No, I never make notes for my novels. I've no notebooks of any kind, no diaries, no plans. I never jot down phrases or file anything. I've a good memory for things I want to remember. My imagination is the main thing. If I lost that I would lose everything.'

As a compulsive note-taker myself I found the above revelations astonishing. (For every one of the seventeen books I was later to write myself, I had a barrelful of notes and couldn't have managed without them.) What kind of mind did Robert Shaw have! He took me up to the cubby hole in which he wrote. It was the archetypical writer's garret – bare boards with just a rug here and there, his Victorian desk ridiculously small and the walls bare and rough. 'It's the only room in the house that's not decorated,' he told me. 'I like to keep it rough and natural.'

After giving me more insights into his writings and even interesting aspects of his courtship and marriage to Mary Ure, he took me outside into the beautiful walled garden where he goes for inspiration. It was a hot day and as we reached the swimming pool I remarked how inviting it looked.

'Do you fancy a dip? Come on then. There are some shorts in the summerhouse.' We changed into swimming shorts and when we got back to the pool Robert asked me if I was a good swimmer. I said I wasn't bad, then he said, 'How far can you go under water?' I said I wasn't sure but I'd have a try. 'OK, you go in first,' he said. I took the mandadatory deep breath and dived in. I breaststroked under water until I reached the far end fifty feet away, made a bit of a hash at the turnaround (it's harder under water than at the surface) but managed to reach the first end again when, with my lungs almost bursting, I was forced to come up.

'Hmm, not bad,' said Robert and dived in himself. He went faster than I had and turned better, but I expected him to emerge as I had, after covering two lengths, so it was with some dismay I saw him make the second underwater turn and reach the far end again to cover *three* lengths!

He walked towards me dripping and shaking his head and not very much out of breath.

'Not so good,' he said. 'Not so good today. I usually do three and a half.' Superman indeed. Many years later I was amazed to read the news that Robert Shaw, after his barnstorming roles as the deranged, obsessive shark-fishing captain in *Jaws*, and as the psychotic General Custer in *Custer of the West*, had died of a heart attack in the garden of his home in Ireland in August 1978at the relatively young age of 51. I had always regarded him as the fittest movie star I'd ever met.

When I arrived at up-and-coming actress Suzy Kendall's flat to take her for an interview over lunch, I was surprised when the door opened before I could push the bell – and out came Dudley Moore. She gave me a fine enough interview and said Dudley was one of her best friends. Back at her flat, knowing she was single, I asked if she would let me take her out for a drinks and supper later. She said she was busy tonight but could make it tomorrow night. As I shut her door and went down the stairs, who should be coming up them but Dudley Moore.

When I called for Suzy the following evening I heard splashing sounds coming from her bathroom. I assumed it was probably Dudley but she said it was Oliver Reed, who had arrived without notice. I knew of Reed's reputation as a boozing brawler, that he had slugged a tough Canadian lumberjack who had tried to take a rise out of him when on location for the film *The Trap*. And it seemed clear he was on familiar terms with Suzy. As we talked, he came out of the bathroom with just a towel round him, glowered at me and said *he* was taking her out to drinks and dinner. I said *I* had arranged to do that. He said, 'You better go.' I ignored that and asked Suzy to choose. Did she want me to go or stay as I would do either? Oliver again said, 'You better go!' and took a step towards me.

I didn't like this one bit. He was a bit shorter than me but burlier, yet I reckoned I could probably see him off as he was naked and only had the towel around him. I took two steps towards him when Suzy shouted, 'I think you should go!'

I thought she was addressing Reed but she was looking at me! Immediately I said, 'Okay, it's your decision,' and left. I didn't think anything much could be achieved by a rough house with Reed when some of Suzy's furniture would surely get damaged. In the morning the doorbell of my top floor St John's Wood flat rang, which was odd because I hardly ever got unexpected visitors. It was Suzy and she was all apologetic. Then she said she wanted to show me something outside. I went back downstairs with her and she showed me a brand-new gleaming yellow E Type Jaguar car!

'Isn't it lovely? It was a gift from Dudley.' I knew I couldn't match *that*. We had a brief coffee in a High Street café and that was the last time I saw Suzy. She did marry Dudley, but as was well reported at the time, the marriage didn't last.

The only other time my doorbell rang unexpectedly was after I'd done a fine interview for a TV magazine with Patrick McGoohan, then star of the *Danger Man* series. He wanted to check what I had written so I posted it to him, expecting he would take about a week to reply. The following morning my bell rang and a small packet came through my letter box. It was the McGoohan article, signed. I opened the door swiftly – just in time to see Patrick pedalling up St John's Wood High Street on a pushbike. He had been banned from driving for a short period following some traffic misdemeanour and had cycled all the way from Mill Hill to deliver the article personally.

I first saw Joan Collins when she was at a show-business bash with her sister Jackie. I caught her half kneeling over a bed to retrieve her coat, and I noticed the superb backside, narrow waist and the swelling rise of her breasts – the sexiest creature I'd ever seen. She was a rising young starlet with Rank, and truly a female physical phenomenon. Weeks later I interviewed her at Pinewood Studios for my column, and we seemed to get on like a house on fire – we discovered we were both Geminis, born a few days apart (in different years of course!) She must have liked me because she invited me to take her to an opera the following week. When I rang the day before she said she couldn't keep the date but would let me know when we could meet again.

Unknown to me, she had gone to see the new stage musical *Stop the World, I Want to Get Off* and had gone backstage to meet its new star, Anthony Newley, then at the height of his career. They fell in love and later married. I was blown out before I could get started!

Many years later, when I went down to Hollywood after my first two years in the Canadian wilderness – so I could earn enough money for another year in the Canadian wilderness – the first star I interviewed was Anthony Newley. He was making *Finian's Rainbow* with Petula Clark. Tony invited me home to his Hollywood villa for a superb dinner cooked by Joan and we all had a big laugh about my date that never was. This was before Joan got the top part of the super-bitch in the international TV series *Dynasty* and became an international star.

When I went to his hotel room to interview Sammy Davis Jnr., then billed as 'the world's greatest entertainer' I was somewhat disconcerted when I entered his room. With him, all engrossed in animated conversation, were the great base singer Paul Robeson, William Warwick who sang *Ol' Man River* in the 1950s (and best, the film *Showboat*), and a leading black film actor whose name I cannot recall. I didn't get a lot out of Sammy but I tried to join in the lively talk, feeling distinctly inferior. It was when we got on to racialism that Sammy said, ina quiet moment, 'I don't care if you're black, white, polka-dot or khaki. Just so long as you're a good neighbour!' And I don't think anyone has put it better.

I was sipping drinks with the dreaded O'Toole in the green-walled lounge of his elegant five-storey Georgian mansion near Hampstead Heath just after his phenomenal performance in *Lawrence of Arabia*, which shot him to international stardom. We were discussing his hell-raising image, and I asked him if there were not corrupting forces in such a swift and early success. At first he laughed and said he hadn't realized his highest hopes yet. Then he added, and I'll never forget the way he said it, nor the look in those electric-blue eyes: 'I tell you this – more people have been butchered by failure than corrupted by success.'

I had done much research into the life of this mercurial, anarchic son of an Irish bookmaker who settled in Leeds when Peter was one year old, as well as having spoken to him on several previous occasions. Long before he was a big name he turned down five lucrative film offers to take up Peter Hall's invitation to act in a Shakespeare season at Stratford-upon-Avon. He didn't just learn his lines and work from within himself. He spent five weeks reading up on Jewish customs and law, and delivered an imperishable Shylock. He spent six days discussing *The Taming of the Shrew* with a university lecturer in English, rented a cottage in the Welsh mountains to ensure complete privacy when learning the part, and delivered a scintillating Petruchio. Critics heaped eulogies on his head, but while serious intellectuals were debating the subtleties of his performances, O'Toole, off duty, downed a yard of ale (two and a half pints) in less than forty seconds to gain another distinction – breaking the Stratford beer-drinking record.

Once, when he was a young actor living in a rather seedy flat, he got a note from the flat opposite: 'Dear Mr O'Toole, would you please draw the curtains when you use the bathroom?' Whereupon Peter wrote back: 'Dear Madam, I'm afraid I have no curtains, would you draw yours?' On the night his first London play opened a gang of thugs attacked some of the cast backstage afterwards. Most of the actors beat a retreat but O'Toole grabbed a chair leg and sailed into the mêlée.

It was when I asked him about his times with one of his best actor mates, Richard Burton, with whom he co-starred in *Becket*, that Peter explained why he was a bit of a hell-raiser. Burton had been quoted as saying, 'That film was fun to make with the terrible O'Toole. We were well matched, though I think I can probably outlast him at a party.' Peter told me: 'Bouts of high spirits always coincide with the ending of a play or film for me. In this business you work under such extraordinary conditions, under a magnifying glass in fact, and I find I have to really let go when at last it's time to stop.' Then he added: 'Unlike Richard Burton, who tends to get wild *during* the time he is working!'

When David Lean wanted to test O'Toole for the role of Lawrence, he put the idea up to the producer, Sam Spiegel, who was highly sceptical and did not like what he had heard about O'Toole's reputation for drinking and being a wild Irishman. Peter said, 'He really believed all the stories about me and we didn't get along at all. It didn't help either when a miniature bottle of whisky tumbled from my pocket during our meeting!' But when Spiegel saw Lean's test he had no more doubts. He had found his Lawrence. For that film O'Toole memorized the gist of the 661 pages of *The Seven Pillars of Wisdom*, spent most of three months in the desert, acclimatizing himself to the awesome silences and the feel of it, much of the time in complete isolation, before a camera went near him. He had to learn the really difficult task of riding a camel like a Bedouin (giving an Oscar-winning performance from its back) and once he was flown to hospital unconscious after being thrown during a charge downhill into the path of oncoming horsemen.

When I reminded him of these things Peter replied in characteristic style, 'Well? I don't fart about when I'm working!'

He then topped up my glass, for the third time, with what he called 'mountain–brewed brandy, very rare'. As I tried to re-collect myself after another mouthful, Peter left the room as his then wife of ten years came in, and I talked to her about their unorthodox marriage. Tall, slim, with deep blue eyes and fiery red hair, Sian Phillips looked less than her thirty-five years. A few quotes:

'Yes, Peter is unpredictable, but to me his wildness springs from his creative nature. We've been married ten years and he's as free and uninhibited as when we first met. Stardom hasn't changed him.' I could hear Peter, who'd just finished making *Goodbye Mr Chips*, playing with their daughters Kate and Pat in the living room at the back of the house, as Sian continued, 'We believe in giving each other complete freedom. We trust each other implicitly. Peter makes up his mind to do extraordinary things on the spur of the moment and I'd never dream of stopping him, particularly as they so often succeed.'

Sian told me of the time Peter desperately wanted Katharine Hepburn to co-star with him in *The Lion in Winter* but on the phone the star actress had been dubious. 'Suddenly Peter said, "Get my passport." I said, "Where are you going?" he replied, "California. I'm going to get that lovely woman in the film if it's the last thing I do." A few minutes later he was at the airport, hopped on a plane, flew to America and arrived unannounced on her doorstep. It was a risky thing to do because above all Kate values her privacy. But it worked – he came home with her signature.'

Back on the theme of their marriage:

'People always say it must be difficult to be happily married when both partners are in the theatrical world, but I can't see how couples manage it if they're *not* in it. Peter may ring up and say, "I'll be home at five." I put on the meal. Then he meets someone important to his work and doesn't arrive until nine. This happens all the time but you forgive quickly enough when it happens to you too. Our marriage seems to work better if we aren't together all the time. We have no career complications *because* we go our separate ways. Peter feels it's monstrous for any man to want to stifle the creative urge in a woman, provided she has some talent and it's genuine and not just ego. He likes me to work and he's enormously generous in that regard. Peter will eat out in restaurants for weeks on end if I'm doing good work, rather than expect me to be just a homebody.'

Nevertheless, she worked less than Peter as she had Kate and Pat to care for, and when she was not working she did most of the chores herself. 'I enjoy cooking complicated dishes. Once I made a very delicious thing where I had to personally stamp about a hundred grapes and cut up a dozen oxtails. It was a French recipe and it took me a whole day. When I served it Peter ate it in complete silence. Afterwards he said, "I would be awfully grateful if you wouldn't make that again." I could have killed him!' She said that Peter couldn't cook at all, 'Not even cut bread or boil an egg. He upholds the honour of the Irish in that regard!'

Well, I spent most of the afternoon and half the evening with the O'Tooles, getting a great deal more fascinating facts and insights about their lives together, so much so that I could write a long piece called 'The Seven Pillars of O'Toole' for one top women's magazine and an even longer piece about life with the star, told from his wife's point of view, for another. As I was about to leave I became aware that Peter was studying me with both a quizzical and critical look. He thought I was a bit unsteady on my feet and he ought to get his chauffeur to run me home! It just so happened I was at the time living in a temporary bedsitter in Fitzjohns Avenue, just a few hundred yards down the road, as I was between flats. I thanked him but said I was sure I could make it on my own. When I got outside, in the cold air of late autumn, I found I was seeing two of everything. To knock back on the O'Tooles' door was unthinkable. It was then that I discovered a ruse that has often stood me in good stead. By closing one eye, my right, I could see just *one* of everything and was able to half-totter home in safety, apart from having to fend off an amorous chap who thought I'd been winking at him.

I was both amazed and disappointed when, after I had been studying rare wildlife in the remotest areas of Canada and the Scottish Highlands for thirteen years, to hear the news in 1979 that after twenty years of marriage, the O'Tooles had divorced. To me it had seemed that theirs was a show-business marriage made in heaven. But I had to laugh some twenty years after *that* when in an interview with Lester Middlehurst in the *Daily Mail*'s *Weekend* magazine, Peter O'Toole admitted he was not cut out for marriage, and having lived alone for almost two decades, he doubted he would ever remarry as 'I wouldn't want to inflict *me* on anyone else again.' It was precisely the answer I have given for years to those who ask *me* why I never married.

While it may seem from the way I've had to foreshorten the time scale for the sake of this narrative that I was dashing from one lucrative star interview to another, by the end of my third year as a freelance my work rate slowed down, and I was lucky if I got one major star interview to sell in a month. This was partly due to my going to my tiny rented attic flat in the country while struggling to finish my novel, but also because it was now clear to the top folk in show business that I no longer had the 'power base' my regular big-circulation weekly magazine columns had given me. I could no longer guarantee publication, that a star's time would not be wasted.

First, the invites to cocktail receptions and film previews began to dry up, so my contacts for ideas dwindled. Then the editors of my main magazines began to change and the new ones no longer commissioned interviews on my say-so – they wanted to see the finished story first before deciding whether to buy it. This sometimes meant I was left trying to sell a rejected article down-market, to American movie fan magazines. I didn't like doing this, and I hated having to give up my big luxury flat and rent a poky little place (one room, kitchenette and bathroom) in the wrong end of St John's Wood so I could cut back on main expenditures and spend more time down in the country on my novel.

Not long after this move my beloved XK 120 Jaguar car went too, to be replaced by a more economical second-hand Mini – but at least it was a Mini Cooper. For all these reasons, and because my efforts to study other writers and philosophers while writing my novel had made me more serious-minded, the long succession of casual lovers came to an end. Another reason for this – and what ironical timing it was – my on-off romance with actress Eva Bartok had been rekindled and she, like Ava Gardner had three years earlier, strongly suggested I ought to be doing something more intelligent with my life than interviewing movie stars for a living. Indeed, it was the influence of these two women that had inspired me to work seriously on a novel in the first place. The fact that my romance with Eva was rekindled just when my economic fortunes had taken a dive did not bode well.

I think I should now tell the story of my relationship with Eva Bartok from the start as her life and mine were interwoven throughout the eight years of my show-business career.

24
Eva

I was dancing with her in a Rome nightclub, one of the most famous women in the world, when suddenly she was up close and asking, 'Why have you never asked me to marry you? Huh? Why, Mike? Tell me. I want to know why!'

I was completely taken aback. I had known Eva Bartok on and off for four years, she had given me some good stories and we'd had minor flirtations, but I'd never thought... The old cliché, 'Well, who am I to presume?' seemed out of place. So I just squeezed her gently and she melted right into me with her fingers in my hair and I wondered if the whole world had gone mad, or was it just me? This sort of scene only happened in movies! I whispered throatily, 'I don't think the possibility ever occurred to me – you were far too remote.'

Eva pushed me away slightly so she could look into my eyes.

'Oh, you silly boy. Why do you think I insisted, insisted it was only you I wanted to write my life story? Why I invited you on this holiday?'

I had a sudden lump in my throat. True, she had invited me, and she had even driven me to Rome from Zurich in her Rolls Royce, but apart from petrol I was paying for everything else, and she certainly liked her luxuries. At the time I had just turned freelance, had even left my large, posh apartment for a pokey little flat in order to save money. I was highly flattered but also a little scared. Our little party of four had been painting Rome red that night and I wondered if it was the drink talking.

'I'm not the man for you,' I said. 'You need so much. You demand so much and I'm no damn millionaire!' I thought I'd said it with just the right light touch.

'Do you think that's what I want? Do you? Do you think I only want money from a man?'

I pressed my cheek to hers and whispered, 'No, darling, of course not.

Good lord... I'll marry you any time you want!'

She gave a long sigh, relaxed into me again and said softly, 'All right... we will talk about it.'

When we returned to our companions, the German actor Karl Adolf and Pino, the guitarist from the Piccolo Mondo whom we'd' 'stolen' when the club closed earlier, we started telling jokes again until Eva said she was tired and we had better leave or she would fall asleep. There was no argument as Eva was our driver! We piled into her Rolls Royce and she dropped us all off at my hotel, from where the other two took taxis to their respective pads.

Naturally, I sort of assumed Eva and I would talk about the possibilities of marriage the following day but although she had told me I could ring her 'any time, day or night' I left it until about 11a.m., so she would have had plenty of time to recover from the rather wild night before. When she answered the phone her voice sounded husky, and I received a shock. Eva said she was feeling strange and didn't want me to come round to her apartment that day as she hated being seen when she was ill. Not even her mother would see her when she was ill, she added.

'I'd like to share your bad and ill times as well as your good and healthy ones,' I said. 'I could come round, help look after Dee Dee (Deana, her daughter) and show off my cooking skills.'

But still Eva declined. As we were saying goodbye and I promised to ring on the morrow, she surprised me by saying that if I went out in Rome that day I had to promise to be good as she was worried about what I might get up to on the Via Veneto! I duly promised to be good, but by now I knew most of Rome's attractions and I was in no mood to go out looking for fun. Instead, after walking up the Via Veneto and having a chance meeting and coffee with British star Anthony Steel, who gave me a nice little story, I spent the afternoon and evening in my hotel room. It was costing a lot, so I thought I might as well make full use of it, and I recalled how I'd first met Eva some four years earlier...

At the time Eva Bartok was at the height of her fame. Born in Hungary, her striking good looks, her weird and extravagant hats and her tangled private life (she had been married four times, lastly to the handsome German star Curt Jurgens with whom she had lived in a romantic Bavarian castle) meant she was famous for just being famous. And yet she had made some thirty films starring opposite the likes of Dean Martin and Peter Finch and even co-starred with the great Burt Lancaster in his hit film, *The Crimson Pirate.* Now she was in London rehearsing for a TV play as well as conducting an on-off affair with the Marquess of Milford Haven, third in line for the British throne, who had been best man at the wedding of his cousin Prince Philip to the then Princess Elizabeth. As Eva had given birth to a baby daughter, Deana Grazia, a year before, the popular press was rife with speculations, pursuing the couple to West End theatres and nightclubs.

I was then working for the *Woman's Sunday Mirror*, and news editor Arthur Redford came over to my desk in his usual jovial jokey fashion, 'Well, Romeo, this looks like a job for you – Eva Bartok…' The upshot was that via her agent I fixed up a tentative interview in a draughty hut in Fulham, where Miss Bartok was rehearsing for a new TV play, by saying I was NOT interested in the Marquess or her private life but in her career and any views she might express about the roles of women in modern society. The agent warned, 'Miss Bartok has agreed to meet you. But she will decide on the spot if she wants to *talk* to you or not.'

Hmm, I like a person who operates on instinct. I do myself. I got togged up in my best gear and went to meet her in the Fulham hut. I was immediately impressed by her natural beauty, for she wore no make-up, not even lipstick, and her dark hair hung loose and straight. I kept the questions purely to her career at first, conscious as we talked that she radiated a kind of inner serenity, her demeanour and movements completely feminine. The actors were on their lunch break, so we gravitated to a nearby pub where we both drank Cokes and Eva clapped a Robin-hood type hat adorned with a long feather on her head.

It was the reaction of some of the pub's customers to her hat as she took it off and put it on the seat beside her that prompted my first personal question.

'You are well known, even rather famous, for wearing outrageous clothes and strange hats. Is that for publicity?'

She gave a merry laugh. 'When I first came to this country I had very little money to buy clothes. I had to make them myself. If they looked extraordinary it was because I was not a good dressmaker! I had only one evening dress, and I often had to use its bolero as a hat.

'The truth is I wear what I think suits me. Very few women wear what's right for them. They worry about being U or non-U but not what is YOU! It's sad in this world that we have little time to be truly ourselves because we are too preoccupied with what other people think. As our concept of their impression is usually wrong, it's a great waste of time – if you get me!'

This was a sign of an original and independent mind and I found myself warming to her conversation. We got talking about her career again but the interview was difficult as the play director and a couple of actors came over for quick chats with Eva. Nevertheless I was both astonished and delighted, when the lunch break came to an end, to feel her hand on my arm and hear her say, 'Look, we can't have a meaningful conversation like this. If you're really interested in my work as an actress, come with me to Frankfurt tomorrow. They are holding the premiere of my newest film, *The Doctor of Stalingrad*, and I think it's the best film I've ever done. Will you come?'

'What a fabulous idea!' I said. Within minutes we had arranged to meet at Heathrow airport on the morrow, and I was racing back to the office to break the good news. Both Arthur Redford and the editor Lee Howard (who later became editor of the *Daily Mirror*) were amazed that a movie star who was currently fending off the world's press would invite a *reporter* to fly to and from Frankfurt with her when we would clearly have hours together. They arranged to buy my return flight ticket and, for once, agreed to my demand for expenses without demur.

As we boarded the plane I was startled when a few photographers leaped in our path and flashed away, and for the first time I realized how bothersome this could be, especially as one of them asked about the Marquess. Sympathizing with her as we settled into our seats gave me the perfect opportunity to talk on a more personal level. Eva said she welcomed publicity and recognition for her work as an actress but not for wearing funny hats or for whom she went out with. She warned that she did not like publicity about her friendship with the Marquess, and it was worse for a man in his position than it was for her.

'But,' I replied, deciding to take a chance, 'it *is* rather obvious that this friendship is more than a casual one. Otherwise, with all the fuss, you'd break it off.'

Eva shot me a cautious glance then said, 'Of course it is obvious to anyone with any sensitivity, but why should I talk about it? Why should I have to say anything to the world if I am in love? It is no one's business.'

I persisted and asked her, 'Would it do any real harm to say if you are in love? People, your public, are interested.'

She replied, 'No, but it is surely a private thing.'

I said, 'Can you keep things secret when you are a celebrity? For instance, people are bound to find out if you get married again. Could you keep that a secret?'

'Yes, I could – until afterwards,' she said. 'No one need know until it is over. Then it will not matter.'

I eased up then as Eva wanted to write a brief speech to read at her film premiere. I noticed she had intense concentration and when she asked my advice about a particular phrase or meaning I tried to help her. When she had finished she snapped her notebook shut and thrust it into a deep pocket in her fur coat, which she was still wearing, and I got on to a more philosophical level by asking her about sources of happiness. To my surprise she responded without hesitation and brought the subject round to one I'd not yet dared to broach – her baby. Deana Grazia had been born only five months before and was now being looked after by Eva's mother and a daily nurse. Eva told me that since the birth she had been happier than ever before, that motherhood meant a great deal to her. I now had another opening and asked her, 'Do you care what the world thinks about you and your baby? Don't the rumours about her father upset you?'

She shot me another cautious glance then said, 'I don't want to talk about my baby really. But look... there are many wrongs in this world. For instance, how many people marry for love? I would like to know. People don't frown on women who marry for money or position. People don't frown on women who marry just because they don't want to be old maids. But I could not marry for any of those reasons.'

She went on: 'Surely, no sensitive woman will frown on a woman who decides with her whole heart that she wants to have and keep her baby?'

Eva had been married four times, two of them rather marriages of convenience. The second one was to American film producer Alexander Paal, which offered her a foreign passport and a means of escape from communist Hungary. She never asked for alimony from any of her husbands, not even Curt Jurgens. 'I do not believe in accepting money from a man I no longer love,' she told me.

I suggested that her rough times had probably made her a better person and therefore a better mother for her baby.

Eva smiled. 'You can keep film premieres, studios, all the receptions and big money. They mean nothing compared with having a baby of your own to love and look after. When I look at Deana and the spring flowers opening in my garden, I have the same sort of feeling of the beauty of new life.'

With all the work and career facts I knew I already had enough to make a first-class human-interest article, and I'd have Eva to myself for the return journey too, so I turned the conversation to a more general philosophical level, discussing her studies with the Subud sect led by fashionable Indonesian guru Pak Subuh. I was going through a Nietszchean period in my spare time just then, and I like to think she thought my ideas were almost as interesting as I found hers.

At Frankfurt two men from Gloria Films whisked us to the Savigny Hotel where Eva was taken to her suite and the make-up experts and hairdresser got to work. In the cinema later I sat between Eva and actor Walther Reyer, who played her lover in *The Doctor of Stalingrad*, and Eva's concentration on her own performance was intense. I had no doubt she had given the most electrifying, compelling performance of her career as a haughty, arrogant woman doctor in a Russian prisoner-of-war camp who falls in love with one of the prisoners. Her love scenes with Reyer rivalled the famous ones between Burt Lancaster and Deborah Kerr in *From Here to Eternity*.

The large audience gave her a great ovation when she walked on to the stage after the film and showered her with flowers. She took five curtain calls, almost unheard of in Frankfurt, and didn't get a chance to read the speech we had so carefully prepared. At a champagne party later Eva sipped a few Cokes, and went to bed before anyone else, certainly me!

In the plane on the way back the following day, apart from now having six film offers to consider, Eva told me she never planned her future. 'In the past, I planned and worried like everyone else, but I have learnt not to do this. Tomorrow or the next day something can happen to change your whole life. But I do think we should provide for the future of our children.'

She revealed more of her personal philosophy and I must admit I was considerably influenced by it. She told me that to her, happiness did not depend on success as an actress, or on the money she earned.

'To me it is entirely serenity of my inner self. It is no good fixing a goal and thinking when you reach it you will be happy. You won't. You must live fully every moment, try to enjoy, to extract the good from the bad. Be aware of yourself all the time.'

For the rest of the journey back I no longer tried to extract facts and our conversation was so animated and absorbing as we exchanged ideas that after we landed we both agreed we'd enjoyed each other's company, exchanged addresses and phone numbers and hoped we would meet again soon. Unfortunately, two days later I was sent to Paris on a four-day assignment to hunt down a couple of major stars. When I got back there was a note from Eva saying that she had been called to Rome to discuss film deals. In it she said she had enjoyed the article, and if and when I was in Rome I must be sure to look her up. She appended her Rome address.

I would like to be able to say that romance blossomed but it did not. The Eva Bartok article was splashed over two pages of the paper and my success with her inspired my editors to assign me to go after the biggest female movie star of the time, the love Goddess Ava Gardner. As I've written, I had worshipped the image of Ava Gardner since my days as a cub reporter in provincial journalism so I set to with a will.

Even so, I kept in touch with Eva Bartok, meeting her once again in London, once in Paris and twice more in Rome over the next four years. We only went out for lunches or dinners, never got more romantic than a cuddle and a pecky kiss, but she always gave me an interesting item for my column. And she also gave me more food for philosophical reflection. I recall once driving down to Rome in my flashy Jaguar XK120 sports car, gleefully sure it would impress and that we would parade along the Via Veneto, hood down, as she waved to her adoring fans. The bloody car broke down in Lerici! It got stuck in first gear, and neither my coaxing nor wrenching would free it. I left it with a local mechanic who said he had no manual handbook but he would take the gear box to bits, find out what was wrong, and reassemble it. Gloomily, I had to hire a tiny affordable Fiat and putter down to Rome in that. Eva's Rolls Royce was back in Zurich being serviced, and I imagined she would refuse to ride in the Fiat. To my surprise she jumped in gaily, even saying she might get one herself as it made more sense for pootling about Rome on non-business trips. On the return drive to Lerici the clutch of the little Fiat broke down and I could only change gear after correctly guessing the relative speeds of the engine and the gearbox cogs. At least the mechanic had my dream car working again.

Eva and I only exchanged a couple of chatty letters in the year that followed, so I was pleasantly surprised one May evening when the phone rang in my little studio flat and I realized it was Eva. She said she was about to drive from Zurich to Rome and there was plenty of room in her Rolls Royce, so did I fancy a drive with her through the Alps, and maybe a week's holiday in Rome itself?

She met me at Zurich airport and when we walked to her gleaming car my first disappointment can be summed up in the words of the old song: 'and mama came too'. Eva was driving her mother to Rome as well! Apart from a smiling introduction her mother spoke no English and I didn't know a word of Hungarian, so conversation between her and me on the trip was non-existent, unless Eva chose to interpret the odd remark.

However, Eva drove boldly and well and I cheered up as whenever I cracked a joke, she would laugh and touch my hand, even my knee. And I was even more delighted to find her looking at me in the mirror from time to time, and when our eyes met she would purse her lips in little kisses. But I felt a bit let down when we stopped for the night in a small lodge house in Lake Como and Eva said her mother was not a good traveller, was not feeling well, and she would have to eat with her in their room. Apart from a brief aperitif together, I was left to dine alone.

I can't recall much of the rest of the drive except that I was secretly pleased and relieved when Eva firmly turned down my offer to take over the wheel. I was none too sure I could handle a Rolls Royce, especially the rare and beautiful Silver Cloud model which she owned. However, when we reached Florence I was concerned that Eva might be overtaxing herself so suggested we take a coffee break. She parked near the pretty main square with its impressive statues, and while Mama said she would stay in the car for a short nap, Eva and I set out to find a nice little café. On the way we did some brief window shopping and were looking through one window at a display of paintings when Eva suddenly said, 'Wait here, Mike,' and dived into the shop. She came out a few moments later clutching a white paper bag containing a picture. She handed it to me, saying, 'Here you are Mike – a present from Eva! It's how you're going to look when you are old!'

I pulled out the picture– a sepia-toned portrait of a benign, handsome old man stuck on hardboard – and felt highly flattered, I asked her if it was of someone special?

'It's Leonardo Da Vinci!'

I knew Eva thought I was a fair amateur philosopher, but to be likened, in any way at all, to one of the greatest thinker-artist-inventors that ever lived was an enormous compliment. I thanked her profusely, kissed her for the first time fully on the lips, and swore I would treasure the portrait for the rest of my life.

We reached Rome in the early evening. I had not really expected to share Eva s apartment with her, certainly not now she was with her mother, and her daughter Deana was also due to join them after staying with friends. So when Eva asked me what hotel I was staying at I made the mistake of trying to show off and replied, 'Well, the Hilton of course.'

Eva drove to the hotel, and while she waited in the car, I booked myself into the cheapest single room available. I was now in my third year as a freelance and financially things weren't going as well as in the first two years (for reasons explained elsewhere) but I told myself, what the hell, live it up for a few days! When Eva heard I was safely booked in she drove to her home, asking me to ring her in the morning. I did just that but had to kick my heels around Rome all day as she couldn't join me until the evening.

She arrived looking marvellous in a dark blue dress and wearing a big smile. We went up to the Roof Garden bar of the hotel for an aperitif before going to somewhere like Bricktops, the Brigadoon or Piccolo Mondo for supper and dancing, and this became our modus operandi over the rather curious evenings that followed.

Once Eva arrived clutching some new photographs taken of her by the top photographer Costa, which made her look at least ten years younger. She wondered if I could get them used in London media but Costa had refused to give her a set. I explained that top photographers don't *give* their best pictures unless commissioned and paid for by the actress, who would otherwise distribute them and they would not get paid. I suggested she just choose the one she liked most and offer to buy the copyright of that one only. Or else just the UK rights as she told me she hoped to relaunch her career in London before too longer.

'I realize my name has sunk over the last three years,' she added. 'But I did it deliberately as I had not wanted to make films or work while Deana was young.'

'Would you like to try the National Theatre?'

'That would be the ultimate hope of all!'

'I know two of the actors there so I could find out the best way to get an audition. You'd probably have to audition for Olivier.'

'I wouldn't mind that at all, but some of the producers here are rude and rubbish. Even Fellini wanted me to make a test – after I'd made thirty-three films! I told him he could look at some of my work at my expense but I didn't want to test as if I was a beginner. But for the National Theatre it would be different.'

Eva then revealed that the other great Italian director, Antonioni, had offered her the part that later went to Monica Vitti, but she had turned it down as 'he couldn't explain to me what *L'Avventùra* was all about'.

I chose my words carefully but opined that she might have been rather silly to turn down directors of such calibre as Federico Fellini and Michelangelo Antonioni for reasons that could have been worked through.

Eva blinked hard a few times, stubbed out her cigarette fiercely, then said softly, 'You're probably right. I wish I hadn't done it now.'

She told me her idea of a film about a modern woman who wants to find the peace of the ancient world and who flies to the Orient and lives a modern-day counterpart to what is known about the lost years of Christ. She had met Walter Wanger, producer of the film *Cleopatra*, at its premiere in London and he had liked the idea, but wondered how to get the money. When Eva offered £10,000 of her own Wanger had laughed: 'She has a million dollar idea and she wants to make a little documentary!' 'But I think it *is* a documentary idea…' she said.

I said, 'So do I. The lost years of Christ have always fascinated me. I'll do some research when I get back to London.'

We talked some more about her career and how I might help her on my return to London. She said I didn't *need* to help her so much. When I said I wanted to she laughed and said maybe I would become too indispensable. I said I hoped so! She asked if I would have enough time to do my work and help her too. I said, 'I have enough energy and strength to help you and do what I have to do as well.'

'I think you have too,' she smiled, and put her hand in mine.

When we were dancing later Eva said she had been attracted to me since that first meeting in the Fulham hut and had felt for years that we might be together one day, but that the time had never been right before. I was not ready. She added that most men were afraid of an intelligent woman. I said that was all I'd ever wanted – and beauty like her's.

'I'm glad you said that.' She gave me a big kiss, then said that Pak Subuh had told her she needed an ordinary man. 'By ordinary I don't mean to denigrate, but a man with his feet on the ground, who was strong and could make his own decisions and stick to them. Someone with a common goal.' I was enjoying the closeness of her body as we danced too much to keep talking and just whispered I was sure we could work it out.

We had some lovely moments on those first meetings, and of course I was falling in love with her, but I was somewhat piqued that I saw relatively little of her and never at all during the day. I had only come to Rome to be with her, and at her invitation after all. On our fourth date Eva was in an exceptionally perky mood, having signed a small film deal that day, and she wanted to celebrate. We went to eat and dance at the Piccolo Mondo until the club closed down. Eva grabbed the guitarist Pino saying, 'Let's take him with us!' She drove Karl Adolf, Pino and myself off in her Rolls. Singing 'Malaguena', 'A Sole Mio' and other Italian ditties, with Pino playing away, we shot off to the Brigadoon. But they wouldn't let us in without Pino wearing jacket and tie. Efforts to borrow these from the establishment proved fruitless. Eva said, 'Never in my life will I go there again. Such snobs. No one would have noticed at all.'

She drove wildly, excitingly, but well. I suggested going to Bricktops. 'Isn't it wonderful to have your own guitarist?' she laughed. 'We must take him everywhere.' It was a Monday night and Bricktop herself was not there but Elsie, the other singer, let us in. We sat, told rude jokes and roared our heads off. But Eva didn't like the band and after half an hour got bored with the place. We left, and she zoomed us off to a baroque little club on the way to Florence. There we sat down and told a few more jokes until Eva suddenly got up.

'Who's going to dance with me?'

All three of us said, 'I will!'

'You were first,' she said to me, and reached for my hands. We danced, and suddenly she was up close. It was then that she sprang her extraordinary question as to why I had never asked her to marry me!

I didn't see her again until the following night when I escorted her to a party given by the Barrymore family. I had resolved not to bring up the marriage question again unless she did, and during that social evening, when both of us were talking mostly to other people anyway, there was no such opportunity.

Suddenly Eva was by my side, wanting to leave early. I assumed she would drive me back to my hotel as usual but she wanted to dump me at the other end of the Via Veneto where I should take a taxi. I argued, wrestling with a sudden paranoid suspicion that she had found someone more interesting at the party and was going back there. But she just smiled, and as I got out offered me her hand and her mouth. I just shook her hand, said, 'Goodnight, Eva' stiffly and walked away. She slammed the door and revved the engine like mad when driving away. I walked all the way back to the Hilton, trying to look casual in case she turned and went past.

In my room I was smitten with remorse, and felt a bit weepy that our relationship might have come to an end. Agonized, I rang her up to apologize. To my surprise she was at home. I said I had been too stubborn, not at all gentlemanly, but I had only come to Rome to be with her. I missed her greatly when kicking my heels around Rome during the day and I added, for the first time, that I loved her very much. Eva started to explain that I'd said I loved Rome and was on a week's holiday whereas she was on business, had to work and see producers and so forth to maintain herself, her mother and daughter, when suddenly she broke off. 'Oh, Mike, don't let's argue any more. Come round and make love to me!' I could hardly believe my ears, but I needed no second bidding, and she gave me some instructions. She would leave her apartment door ajar. I was to be very quiet, close it, ignore the door on the right where her mother slept, and the door on the left where Deana slept. The next door on the right was the bathroom, and the third door was her bedroom. I knew where her apartment was of course but had never been invited to it. I spruced myself up, took a taxi and successfully negotiated her long corridor more silently than a mouse.

Eva was lying back in a large bed, a low light illumining the beauty of her face. As I entered she gave a big smile, whispered 'Sssh,' then unscrewed the top off a half bottle of cognac, took one swallow and handed it to me. Then she opened the bedclothes on her left side to make room for me and I saw she was wearing a lacy black negligee which was unbuttoned all the way down the front. I took one swig of the cognac and put it on the bedside table, where it remained untouched again for the rest of the night.

The loving was wonderful and Eva was utterly feminine. I had been told I could be a rough lover, so with so sensitive a woman I took care to be more gentle, and it was one of the few times in my life I felt I was making love with my mind as much as my body. Even so, I distinctly remember Eva twice hissing in my ear, 'Give me a son! Give me a son!' I did my best to give her triplets! We spent the rest of the night locked in each other's arms, and I enjoyed the feel of Eva's gentle breathing on my cheek so much that I got less sleep than she did. I must have dropped off eventually because I recall Eva waking me up at about 5.30 a.m. saying I ought to leave before Mama and Deana woke up. She promised I *would* now have a day with her: she would pick me up in the Rolls at midday and we would lunch and spend the afternoon at the sandy Lido di Ostia.

I felt selfishly disappointed when Eva turned up with Deana in the Rolls but she proved such a delightful, good-natured child – as well as being beautiful – that I ended up glad that she was with us. I even made her one of my elaborate sandcastles. I prefaced our great day on the beach by fetching a couple of ferne brancas to cure our slight hangovers from the party night. Eva had never heard of the drink but said it bucked her up.

As usual, we got into one of our philosophical discussions. I'd been raising questions about her Subud faith and it seemed to me that while she had imbibed the teachings spiritually she remembered little of them and could not explain them, at least to me. At one point she spoke of the influences of environment upon us all and how no one utters an original thought because all their thinking is coloured by the way others influence them from the time they begin to think. I answered, this by saying, 'How else can one learn but by others? But if you bring upon that learning your own spiritual desires and your own searching reason, you must come up with original thought and progress further beyond all you have absorbed. Such is the way of the creator, and I want to be a creator…'

Eva gave an ironic laugh. 'Well, I don't think flying round the world talking to film stars is very creative!'

I told her I had recently come to much the same conclusion although I'd always tried to get meaningful human interest stories from the biggest names loved by the public and did not write mere gossip. I also told her how I was a quarter way through my first novel, about the spiritual maturing of a young man in the modern world. 'I want to write well, of a truth that I have found and that through my finding, others might find it too.'

Eva gave a little clap of her hands. 'Oh, I'm so glad. That *is* good news. You are far too intelligent, Mike to spend the rest of your life interviewing celebrities. Do perservere with the book.'

'I promise you I will,' I said. Little did I know when I'd made that rather pompous boast that one day I would have seventeen books to my credit, a few of which received considerable critical acclaim.

Eva then said that she did not want me to study Subud because I might leave her and go alone onto a plane where she could not follow. 'You are so ready, and with your reasoning and desire to understand the nature of reality, what is right, what is wrong, what is true, what is false, you will go to the heavens!' One compliment after another from a woman like her... I must say they gave my confidence a huge boost. We were very close that afternoon.

Somehow we got talking about love and I opined that all love was self-love. Human beings could never love unless they wanted to receive love back from the one they love.

Eva pooh-poohed this. 'It is possible to love hopelessly!'

As were talking about receiving, I recalled that apart from petrol, and chauffeuring me around, Eva never paid for anything. As it seemed fairly possible we might end up together, I tried to probe her attitudes to marriage or some other kind of partnership.

'I want a man who doesn't think of the fact that I earn more money than him. I don't *have* to go to smart nightclubs. I don't mind going anywhere *he* wants to go.' She frowned briefly. 'I was going to marry a man in England a few years ago. He wanted me to buy the house, arrange the mortgage, everything. I left him, not only for that but for other reasons…' She looked over at Dee Dee, now 'improving' my sandcastle with a little wooden spade. 'I would put all the money I earned into a fund for Deanna. Why not? It's not her fault she was brought into this world.'

Now I could put a crucial question: 'But what if your husband was earning less than you? Would you expect him to pay for everything while you were stashing away all your money for Deana?'

'Expenses, you mean? Oh, of course I would help to pay rent or buy a house. But as much as I could spare I would put away.' She quoted a Tibetan saying about love which had the phrase 'give and let go' in it, and added, 'I gave and gave to Curt (Jurgens) and made him a film star. He was at a tiny theatre in Budapest when we met and I talked him into doing movies, helped him all I could. Now look at him! I never thought he would become like he is – the big movie star! I would never give to a man like that again. I could never give and give like I did then.'

Well, at least she had given it to me straight. But this didn't quite tally with the wonderful giving of herself last night, I thought.

We paused to watch Dee Dee. She had picked up her little bucket and was toddling towards the sea to fill it with water, presumably to pour over my castle.

'What do you think of Dee Dee?' asked Eva.

'She's lovely – gorgeous in fact. No wonder you're proud of her.'

'Does she remind you of anyone?'

I was astonished at this question as I had already had a distinct impression of whom Dee Dee resembled. I said, 'She has big blue eyes set nicely wide apart in a heart-shaped face. Don't laugh, because I mean it in the best possible sense – to me she looks like the handsome young Frank Sinatra.'

There was a short silence, then a gasp, and I felt Eva's hand clutch my arm. 'Mike, you must swear to keep this a secret but I think you should know.' I duly promised, showing her my crossed fingers to emphasize the point. 'Well,' Eva continued, 'you must be psychic. Frank Sinatra *is* her father!' She went on to explain she had met Sinatra, and the Ratpack, when making the film *10,000 Bedrooms* with Dean Martin. The singer had been divorced for six years and was free to marry again, and they'd had an affair. 'I was very much in love with him but I don't think he really knew it. He walked out one day in a huff and I did not try to explain or repair things because I had to leave America at the same time. Of course I didn't know I was pregnant at the time.

'Then I found I was having Deana. I could have chosen another path but long before this I'd had a premonition that I was going to die the following year, in 1957. This premonition was so strong I was terribly afraid I would die if I had an operation. I also felt I was *intended* to have the child.'

As Dee Dee struggled back towards us with her now-full bucket, Eva said, 'She is growing more and more like him every week. In a year or two it will be easy for many more than you to guess who her father is.'

These were astonishing revelations, and as a freelance journalist I could have made a packet from a big splash story, but I honoured my promise and kept Eva's secret until writing this book many years later. But the secret must have come out in later years for when Eva died in August 1998 at the age of seventy-two, the obituaries mentioned her claim that Frank Sinatra was Deana's father. But at the time she told me I felt almost overwhelmed at the extraordinary trust Eva had placed in me.

We didn't dine out that night as by late afternoon Eva was tired. She drove us back to her apartment, saw Deana safely inside with her mother, then returned to sit in the car for a few moments. By now I'd been in Rome for eight days and not only was money running short but I had some big appointments lined up in Britain. When I told Eva I would have to leave soon, she said, 'I will miss you terribly when you go back to London. I hadn't envisaged this deep involvement but it has happened.' She drew a deep breath. 'I will tend to fight it and withdraw once you have gone, so it will be up to you to keep it alive!'

I felt a slight stab of fear, for how could I do that from such a distance and with my finances? But Eva added we could be together again fairly soon as she still intended to set up in London herself. She said she hoped I would be there and could perhaps help her a little.

'Of course I will. I'll miss you like hell too.'

We had an early supper in the Roof Garden of the Hilton, the head waiter showing us to a romantic nook overlooking the lights of Rome, on the night before my air flight out. Our talk was loving and at the end of our meal I suggested going for a cognac.

'Why not have one here if you want one?'

'I thought we'd go to my apartment, a farewell drink.' (I'd bought a bottle specially.)

'No, not tonight. I'm too tired and I know if I go down there I will not leave till morning. I have these producers coming at nine-thirty. I have to be in good shape!'

As we walked to the lift I felt from the loving way Eva was looking at me that she really did want to come to my room. In the lift I went to press the button for the seventh floor. With a sharp movement Eva beat me to it and pressed T for the ground floor! In her car, as we were about to say goodbye, I said I understood but was still disappointed. Would a ten-minute drink have made much difference?

'I could not be with you in your room for just ten minutes.' She suddenly cupped my face in both hands, her lovely brown eyes staring into mine. 'Oh, Mike, I know you haven't seen me as much as you wanted but I have given you more than any man in the last three years. I did give you almost all my free time and instead of staying in bed after our love night, I kept my promise to you and Dee Dee to take you to the beach.'

'Dear Eva, I'm not complaining. I've had a wonderful time. The most wonderful week of my life. Really, I loved it all, even the little fights – and I love you.'

We called each other darling, promised to meet soon, and after a final kiss and hug, I watched her Rolls until it disappeared up the Via Veneto. In the morning I took a taxi to the airport.

Over the next few months Eva and I exchanged occasional letters but in none of them did either of us mention marriage. By now I was working seriously on my novel. I only did a few celebrity interviews, and tried to sell them to keep my finances ticking over but they were far from healthy. I was hoping the novel would be successful and free me from popular journalism so that I could become what I'd originally wanted to be – a writer.

In early September I received a letter from Eva that caused me to have slight doubts about the future of our relationship. In it she wrote: 'I have thought things over and decided to come to London on or about the 15th of October – just by myself for the time being. Then I'd like to find out about schools for Deana, and try to find suitable accommodation for them to follow me later, so all being well they could come in December ... Now, dear Mike, you said, and I know it to be true, that you are willing to help me. So there is one thing you *can* do for me. Help me to find a flat to come to. I know it is a bore, but with your energy you should be able to do all I need in a couple of hours.' She listed three London hotels she wanted me to investigate and added that she would prefer a service flat: 'Only please keep in mind when you look at them, that there is one thing I cannot cope with – a depressing place, and tiny pokey rooms.' I looked round my shoddy little flat, located in the wrong end of St John's Wood; one room with a kitchenette and a small, narrow bathroom. It *was* pokey, *and* depressing, but, following Robert Mitchum's dictum to his wife, 'I don't care where I live – as long as the roof doesn't leak!' I'd taken it to save money. Any thought of putting Eva up myself, even for the time when she would be alone, fled my mind.

Her letter asked me to find out the exact differences between singles and doubles, whether the word 'service' meant they served meals or just breakfast, and she had to have a sitting room and plenty of cupboard space. It was clear that Eva either hated cooking or couldn't cook, which would explain why she never invited me for a meal in her Rome apartment. She added that if the first two didn't serve food she might take one of the furnished flats in Dolphin Square but didn't want to commit herself to a long let as she would need to rent a bigger permanent flat later so that her mother and daughter could join her. And the location of the bigger flat would depend on her knowing to which private school she would send Deana.

'I am sorry to be so lacking in clarity explaining all this – but the practical side of life, or even talking about it, always confuses me. I hope, though, that you understand.' She added that she was setting off on holiday to Switzerland with Deana by car. 'I am looking forward to this holiday with my child. Who knows, if I find a lovely spot, you may even decide to have a few days away from it all yourself, and will join us. It *would be* nice.' Her last paragraph said: 'I am told October is a difficult time to find flats in London, so please, dear Mike, do not lose time. Thank you very much in advance, and I hope you are not too cross with me for asking you to do this thing for me. All my love, E'

It did not take two hours to check the apartment blocks and everything Eva wanted me to. It took two days. None of them fitted her requirements. When she rang me at the agreed time from Switzerland it took some time for me to convince her of this and for her to agree I should book her into a nice little hotel near the BBC which served meals all day in its own small restaurant, and where she would be within easy reach of many others. We could then look around together for the sort of preliminary flat that would suit her.

When Eva arrived we spent so much time looking at flats there seemed no time for romance. It became clear to me that Mama and Deana came first in Eva's life and any husband would probably come a poor second. It was also obvious that love her though I did, I simply could not afford Eva, never mind her family, not because she was greedy but because of the lifestyle to which she was accustomed.

One day she rang to say she had tickets for a play that night and wanted me to escort her to it. I can't remember much about the play but when we came out and were in the crowded foyer Eva said she felt faint. I saw her head sag and her legs buckle. I clutched her as quickly as I could, but she was wearing her mink coat, which had a silk lining, and she just slid out of it and my grasp, and subsided in a crumpled heap on the floor. I quickly lifted her up and got her coat about her while bystanders called a taxi. I accompanied her to her hotel room where she immediately went to bed.

We usually spent the first few evenings in one or two clubs I knew where the owners were personal friends of mine. I explained Eva's predicament to one of them, who owned a few letting apartments. It turned out he had just the sort of initial flat she was looking for in Notting Hill Gate. It was coming vacant at the end of next week and there was a nice little restaurant right below it which also served takeaway meals. So if Eva didn't want to eat in the restaurant she could take meals up to her flat. It was also a lot cheaper than the hotel.

Two days before she was due to move in I was astonished when Eva rang me from London airport. Her mother had been taken ill, was certainly in no condition to travel, and she had to rush back to Rome to look after her.

'Goodbye, darling Mike. My undying thanks for all you have done. I will write soon,' was her parting shot. Well, we did write over the next few months, by which time it was clear my novel had failed and I was debating the idea of emigrating to Canada to start a new life. I can't recall who stopped writing first, but after eight years of knowing her, my romance with Eva Bartok just fizzled out. Nevertheless, when in August 1998, after I had lived for over thirty years in wild, remote places in Canada, Scotland and Spain, I read that Eva had died I could not restrain tears. She had ended her days in a Paddington hotel. If I had known I would have spent some of those days with or close to her. She was an enormous influence on my life.

25
The Long Walk – and Failure Looms

When my novel was finished I made a few phone calls and delivered it to a leading London literary agent. I gave up the attic flat in the country, which eased the financial outgoings and gave me more time to concentrate on selling show-business interviews. Once I was doing better I moved into a fine two-room flat, a small top floor penthouse in fact, with a nice kitchen and bathroom, in St John's Wood High Street.

My first lucky break now concerned the current musical craze surrounding the most successful pop group ever known in Britain – the Beatles. By chance, I found John Lennon's father down and out in Waterloo station. He wanted to meet his son again after a long absence at sea. I took him to the Stoll Theatre where the Beatles were appearing, but despite a long wait outside, Lennon refused to see him. The father gave me a first-class controversial story of why as a merchant seaman, he had had to leave the family home and he told me all about the family's early years. I sold the story for a good fee, of which I gave a fair percentage to Lennon Sr. A few days later he was at my door wanting more money – he'd blown the lot on the gee-gees!

Oddly, I was next given a difficult job from the prominent Sunday newspaper *The People*, to do a full story about the the Beatles' finances. I had to go all around the houses and make many phone calls but I finally cobbled together a fairly comprehensive story and the features department were pleased with it. The paper's long-time celebrity columnist Arthur Helliwell had retired and I longed to take over his column and escape the increasingly tough task of being freelance. When I handed in my story I saw the features editor and his assistant pulling basketball trainers from their desk drawers and asked what they were for.

'We've entered the Fleet Street London to Brighton Walk Challenge and we're training tonight,' said the features editor, looking intently at me with a wicked twinkle in his eye. Then he added, 'What is more, Mike, if you want to work with us on this paper, you'd better take part too!'

I expressed keenness and was told to buy a pair of trainer boots a size too large, wear thick socks and get into training. The trouble was, the walking race was to be held in only two weeks' time! It was open to all staff on Fleet Street papers who considered themselves fit. The following day I bought the boots and socks and in the evening set off on my first training stint. I did three fast circuits of Regent's Park's inner ring road but gave up after nine miles as I was getting blisters. For the next few nights I just soaked my feet in methylated spirits as I was told this would toughen the skin. I managed one more twelve-mile training stint without getting blisters, and then came the night of the race itself.

My dad agreed to drive the whole fifty miles to Brighton so he could pick me up en route if I wanted to pull out or actually collapsed! A few of the other walkers had wives or relatives driving cars too. We set off from Westminster Bridge and after twenty miles I was in the second small group and getting blisters so felt sure I would not finish the course. After thirty miles I knew my blisters were worse and felt I ought to give up, but when my dad came past me again I couldn't get into the car as it was full of other walkers who had broken down! After briefly cursing my father I kept going. I knew the features editor, his assistant and two others were ahead of me, which I found hard to understand as I had been putting on some fair speed after getting a sort of second wind on Crawley bypass. When Dad next came up I intended to throw a failed walker out of his car and said, 'I don't want to go on. I can't catch that damn group up.'

'What are you talking about?' said one of the walkers. 'They took a rest in the wife's car on the other side of the bypass. You're way *past* them. They're a good half mile behind you.'

That spurred me on and I now felt indifferent to the pain. I then tried out a quickly invented 'heartbreak treatment'. I went slowly up the hills so the features editor's group would think they were catching me up, then when going downhill and out of their sight I walked as fast as possible, so when they next saw me I was further away than ever. By the time I reached the finishing twin pillars on Brighton's London Road my trainer boots were bags of blood; even the hard skin on the soles of my feet had parted from the flesh and I couldn't walk another step without terrible pain. But I had come third, beaten only by a serious semi-pro walker, a member of the Centurions Club which requires would-be members to walk London to Brighton and *back* in under twenty-four hours to qualify, and a younger *People* reporter who had done a lot of training. I wasn't at all tired and but for the blisters could have gone much faster. When the features editor came in with his little group he looked at me briefly, not smiling, and said, 'You fit bastard!'

I never worked for that paper again.

And I learned a valuable lesson: If you want someone to do you a favour – don't beat them at *anything.*

Dad drove me to his cottage near Southwater, Sussex and I spent the next twenty-four hours in bed, with a special contraption from a wooden clothes drying horse that kept the sheets away from my wounded feet. With them heavily bandaged, I managed to drive back to my London flat two days later, get some groceries delivered by a friendly Welsh couple who ran the shop across the street, and lay low for a whole week, just able to write a couple of 'think pieces' for the fan magazines, until I recovered enough to be fully back on my feet.

Soon after that I fell in love with Jilly, a beautiful dancer-showgirl who was unusual in that she had been brought up in a Victorian-type family and had received a classical education. Her ambition to be a ballet dancer had been thwarted when she just grew too big. But, at 5 feet 7½ inches tall she was truly lovely, like a young, blonde Ava Gardner, with huge oval green eyes, masses of thick long blonde hair, and the longest, most shapely legs that seemed to stretch from her dainty feet up to heaven itself. She had just left a long stint as leading dancer-showgirl with both the famous Folies Bergères and Bluebell troupes in Paris, and was now having no trouble in finding well-paid modelling jobs. She had a great sense of humour, seemed to be always laughing, and liked nothing better than to go out to a smart pub or club, have a few drinks and sometimes a meal, then return with me for wild times in my new flat. We even experimented in making love to the rhythms of different kinds of music. She was so very much my type that I wanted to marry her but she resolutely laughed my proposals away saying she was not ready to settle down yet, whereas I, now thirty-six, was. It was a perplexing situation, one I had never experienced before – a fabulous girl who would willingly give me her body but not herself.

After some four months, during which Jilly was getting more glamorous modelling jobs abroad, back in Paris or in Madrid, Athens or Rome, I saw less and less of her and realized the relationship wasn't really going anywhere. Nevertheless, I felt that as I was fifteen years her senior, I should maybe count myself lucky that she would still occasionally, but less frequently, come round for a good bedroom romp! Especially as all my previous girlfriends had melted away.

The biggest blow at this time was my discovery that not only had my novel been turned down by the first publisher the agent sent it to, but the agent had just left it there for three months after it was turned down. By now I'd had some inspirational ideas for rewriting the book, on the same theme but on a far grander scale, so I picked the manuscript up personally from the publisher and put it away on a shelf. I knew I would yet again have to find a more peaceful and inspiring place than a city flat to do the new writing. I was now finding that my once beloved London had become a noisy trap – shortly after moving into each of my last three flats the workmen would arrive with their rattling drills and dig up the road, the water, gas and electricity teams sometimes digging up the same stretch within days of each other.

For a while I tried to find temporary refuge and peace by spending what spare time I had back in the wild woods and fields of Sussex as I had as a boy, even shooting on Jim Adkins's estate, although I had to go round alone as Jim had long retired. But the woods seemed smaller, the rivers muddier, hedges had been dug up and the great variety of wildlife had definitely decreased. My former pastoral haunts no longer held their old allure now I was no longer a boy. Certainly they could not help cure my doubts about the way I was making my living, trying to sell celebrity interviews. These doubts, this new malaise, were bad enough, but far more serious problems loomed when, one by one over a period of several months, major journalistic projects began to fall down.

When Sabrina, who had been a sensation on television as a huge-breasted dumb blonde in the late Fifties, made a return visit to London from Hollywood where she had been living for some years, I persuaded her to tell her potted life story for a popular magazine. I knew her personally from having done a big story on how, at the height of her fame, she had insured her breasts for a million pounds! All went well with the first two interviews in her hotel room, even though I had to fit them in between her work and social dates with her hairdresser boyfriend, who had accompanied her from Los Angeles. When I went to the hotel for the third interview I was shocked to find she had pulled out at short notice and returned to Hollywood with the boyfriend. She hadn't phoned me or even left a note. Annoyed that they had missed out on a promised signed three-part series, the magazine was not interested in printing just an interview piece – nor was any other magazine I tried.

If that was a setback, what happened on my next major project could be termed a minor disaster. Anthony Steel was a leading British star in the Fifties and early Sixties. Handsome and debonair, a former Major in the Parachute Regiment who survived 270 jumps as a wartime Commando, he had worked himself up through small parts to star in films like *Checkpoint,*

The Wooden Horse, The Malta Story and *Where No Vultures Fly.* After falling madly in love with Swedish star Anita Ekberg of *La Dolce Vita* fame, and their romantic wedding in Florence in 1956, Tony had thrown up his career in Britain to try his luck in America where his wife had landed a Hollywood contract.

There had been many problems and adventures over the ensuing years, but the marriage failed and Tony had ended up broke, living in a tiny room in a small *pensione* in Rome, on one occasion going without food for four days. I had met him several times when I was a magazine columnist, and when I heard he was back in England trying to start again at the age of forty-two and had just landed a lead role in the film *The Switch* at Pinewood, I drove up to see him. I convinced him he had a great story to tell, especially if he could describe all the problems and nuances in a marriage between two stars who often had to be in different parts of the world at the same time. I said if I could get it all down and he would sign it in the first person, we would split the proceeds. It would also help put his name back in the public eye after his long absence.

Well, over the next three weeks Tony and I spent a lot of time together, meeting a dozen times, at my flat or where he was staying with aristocratic friends. We went out for meals together, even paid a few visits to pubs and clubs, and after another week writing it all up I had a five-part series we were sure would be easy to sell. To my astonishment, and growing dismay, no one wanted it! No Sunday paper nor any women's magazine, even the ones where I felt I had a good rapport. We did get one derisory offer from a down-market magazine but we decided dignity was more important than pocket money and turned it down. I was more sorry for Tony, and the possible damage to his new-found self-respect, than I was for myself. But this new failure meant I had wasted four weeks' hard work, a considerable misfortune for a freelance.

I thought my luck might have changed when a publicity man with whom I was still friendly gave me a ticket for a preview of the first real James Bond film, *Dr No.* After seeing Sean Connery's magnetic, suave and charismatic performance as Bond I knew he would become a big star. I had a nodding acquaintance with him as we frequented the same few pubs in St John's Wood, and I had once told him I'd admired his performance in the TV play *Requiem for A Heavyweight*, so I approached him with the kind of deal I'd had with Tony Steel. He agreed, and I met him three times over the next three weeks for long interview sessions in his flat. He had some marvellous stories springing from his humble beginnings in a tenement flat on the wrong side of Edinburgh, his jobs as a milkman, a coffin board stacker in a sawmill (as

I had done the same we had something in common), and a temporary nude model, and his early weight-lifting days and struggles to get his first break as one of the sailors in the stage show of *South Pacific.* After typing out copious notes I knew I had a rattling good personal life story, and was offered a substantial deal by a top women's magazine provided it would be told by Sean, in the first person. I was sure he would be pleased.

One can imagine my astonishment, and great disappointment, when the morning before I was due to go round for the fourth interview, Sean rang saying he wanted to pull out of our agreement. He said it was now clear he would be signed up for the next Bond film and maybe the one after that, and his agent had advised him not to tell his story yet. It would be better to wait until the other films came out for if they were also successful his personal story would be worth a great deal of money, certainly a lot more than I had secured.

I protested, but in vain. I pointed out that I had spent a great deal of time doing research, preparing questions, noting and typing out the stories and information he had given me. I said I was an unsalaried freelance and after all that work I could not afford just to forget it all. I can't recall our exact conversation but we soon got into a heated argument. Sean pointed out that it was *his* story, not mine, that he was entitled to gain what he could from it, and that he had been told he didn't need a middle man to tell it, as any leading magazine or newspaper would have a staff features writer who could do it. I kept arguing my point when Sean suddenly said, 'Look, Mike. Don't cross me. People don't – not twice anyway.'

I recall I replied with a line straight from Cyrano de Bergerac, 'That news fails to disquiet me.'

A silence followed as I thought, 'Cripes, how is this going to turn out? Bare knuckles at dawn?' Sean repeated he meant what he said, he *could* not tell his story at this time. I tried a different tack, said I *could* see his point of view but in view of my situation, would he mind if I at least did a normal short interview piece with him? To my relief he agreed to this. I duly wrote the article but of course the magazine didn't want just that and I had to sell it to one of the middle-market general magazines. The fee barely covered my expenses, never mind my time.

The brush with Sean Connery added a new dimension to my increasing disquiet about interviewing stars for a living and the nagging feeling that I ought to be tackling the new novel, making my final stand to be a writer. I could sometimes hear in my mind the urgings of both Ava Gardner and Eva Bartok – so long ago now, it seemed. Sean made me feel like a vulture, that I was battening on to celebrities, teasing their most interesting stories out of them purely for my *own* gain. In a way it was true. I could no longer stay trapped in my earlier days of naivety when the top movie stars of the Forties, Fifties and early Sixties were almost gods to the huge movie-going public, and I'd felt that by writing the most inspirational points from their own lives I could bring some inspiration to that public.

Those gods were slowly dying off, to be replaced by 'accountants who could act', which was my phrase for the new young actors who could act well enough but had colourless personal lives and were prudent technicians. Also, the new 'kitchen sink' concept had crept into entertainment, with heroic themes and adventurous stories replaced by a 'going-under' kind of enquiry, the elevation of the moronic life into drama, and the cult of the anti-hero. Another factor was that the once huge movie-going public had been decimated by the onset of more and more TV sets in people's homes. (I could not possibly have known, as I write this forty years later, that the films those old gods made would become among the most-watched programmes on even more TV sets today.) At the time I'd believed the world of big movie stars was not only dwindling but show business had become more boring, certainly for me. In short, I had not only grown up after behaving like a veritable teenager until I was thirty-six, but had also fallen out of love with myself! Months of near celibacy followed and I even spent every Saturday night jogging round Regent's Park to escape my former pubby/clubby lifestyle.

Society too was changing. The new pop culture did not attract me, the hippie drop-out rebellion of the early Sixties, students demanding more freedom when they'd known nothing else. When the Beatles were each awarded the MBE I was shocked, for what did they ever do but sing silly songs (with a few exceptions) in squeaky voices and get rich? I was also shocked when the Labour government ran to the IMF for a £5 billion loan to bail Britain out of its economic crises. The very noise of London was getting to me, as I've already mentioned, and Britain herself seemed to be degenerating into a land of bingo, brain drain, living on international credit, overworking and underpaying her most essential workforce – doctors, nurses, police, farm workers – and allowing the unions to hold the rest of society to ransom.

I longed to have a life of more basic values, concrete purposes, and to live closer to nature again. If I could find a quiet and peaceful place, I could rewrite the first novel and maybe gain some happiness from real achievement. As the action in the novel was mainly based in London I felt I ought to get away from the city so I could refocus better, and if the Sussex countryside was out – it was too close to the capital – I thought of a move to Spain. I drove all the way to Mazarron in the south-east of the country where my parents had built a large villa by the sea, but not only did I have a quarrel with my stepmother, I found their new lifestyle totally at odds with the one I now sought. They were caught up in a large group of expatriates from many countries who, apart from maintaining the fabric of their villas, had little to do and far too much free time in which to do it. House visits, parties, boozy convivial lunches and meaningless chatter, were the order of the week. I did realize there must be quiet places in so vast a country but at that time I was not confident enough with my poor Spanish to go and look for one on my own.

My other close relatives, my two sisters and half-brother, were now all living in Canada and from time to time urged me to visit. Richard, who was working with commercial film-makers in Vancouver, especially extolled the virtues of the beautiful British Columbian coast, with its still-cheap land and cabins and abundant wildlife, including bears, cougars and bald eagles. I was interested enough to send off for some brochures and although I was not earning very much, if I sold my flat lease, my few nice antiques and my little Mini Cooper, I should have enough to set up for at least a few months in a peaceful place up that coast and concentrate on nothing but writing the new novel. However, I had not yet formulated a final plan for such a big move, and it was just as well I hadn't for there now came a dramatic turn in my life – I fell in love with a truly wonderful girl.

26
Alexandra

One of the few publicity men who were still friendly sent me an invitation to the magazine preview and cocktails reception at the Dorchester Hotel for the Alfred Hitchcock film *The Birds*, which starred newcomer Tippi Hedren. I didn't want to go at first as I knew there was nothing and no one I could write about and sell. Yet it would be a rare night out, and good to chat and drink with a few old former colleagues. I enjoyed the film and at the reception was exchanging jokes at the bar when I saw men's knuckles go white as their fingers tightened on their glasses, and women looked towards the three steps at the room's entrance, then away again, fast. An old workmate said, 'Wow! Mike, will you take a look at *that*!'

I turned, and there, coming down the steps on the arm of an agent I knew, was the most stunningly beautiful creature I'd ever seen, a floating loveliness in a white dress. My heart literally missed a beat! And yet there was surely something familiar about her, the thick, gorgeous blonde hair, the huge, clear blue eyes, the generous mouth. As if drawn by a magnet, I edged into the group with whom she was mingling and then remembered who she was, a girl I'd read about in newspapers and magazines – the up-and-coming actress Alexandra Bastedo. I had recorded her beauty in my mind then, and the fact that she was a Sussex girl and came from my old stamping ground, Brighton and Hove, when I'd worked for the *Evening Argus*. Maybe it would give us some common ground!

As I edged nearer our eyes met – and held. I gave a slight smile. To my delight she smiled back, a dazzling, radiant smile, and it was like being showered with jewels. I soon introduced myself and said I would like to write about her. Her agent said he was sure that would be a good thing and I could arrange the interview through him. Then he turned away to talk to someone else.

Alexandra drew me a couple of paces away from the group and said it would surely be easier if I rang her direct. Would I like her home phone number? I have never taken down a phone number with such alacrity from that day to this! I stuttered my thanks and said we could meet up soon, whenever it was convenient to her, and turned to rejoin my colleagues at the bar when Alexandra stopped me and said, quite directly, 'Can I have *your* phone number?'

'Yes, of course,' I said, adding fatuously, 'I'm up in St John's Wood.'

As I drove home, and tried to get to sleep later, all I could see in my mind's eye was her lovely face and smile, and remember how warmly she had spoken to me. Man, I was smitten! But I told myself it was all wishful thinking. After all, I was thirty-seven years old and she was only twenty. Nothing could come of it, surely. Hard though it would be, I resolved not to ring her straightaway but to leave it for two or three days. I felt it wise not to show over-keenness.

In the morning I half-heartedly started assembling notes for a 'think piece' for a top women's magazine. My idea was that the most successful women in the world were female movie stars, yet most of them had a man behind them and their careers – Sophia Loren had Carlo Ponti; Brigitte Bardot, Jane Fonda and Catherine Deneuve had all had Roger Vadim as husband and director; Melina Mercouri had Jules Dassin; Claudia Cardinale had Franco Cristaldi, and so on. Yes, I reckoned I could 'stand the story up', as the phrase went. Suddenly my telephone rang. To my delight and astonishment it was Alexandra Bastedo – and she was inviting me for tea at her Knightsbridge flat that very afternoon!

I dashed out for a quick haircut, bathed and 'poshed' myself up in my only suit like never before, and reached her elegant flat by the appointed time. As we sat sipping fine China tea and nibbling the odd dainty biscuit I was more interested in trying to get her to like me than anything else, but she did have a nice little story. Her father, Lendon, had been a handsome Canadian stationed in Brighton during the war. Her mother, Riana, also beautiful, was half Italian, half Swiss and had fled to Britain when the Nazis invaded Prague. Alexandra had been brought up in Worthing and Brighton/Hove, which gave us quite a lot in common and plenty to talk about. She won amateur drama awards at Brighton and Worthing festivals before joining the Lewes Little Theatre company.

At sixteen, after a highly publicized national newspaper competition to find the 'Teenage Diplomat For Great Britain', she won the title from 4,000 applicants. The prize was a trip to Hollywood with her mother as chaperone and a part in the Columbia Pictures film *The Candy Web*.

'It wasn't exactly a classic – I had to scream decorously and show wide-eyed terror when encountering corpses hanging from meat hooks!' Alexandra laughingly told me.

She met stars like Charlton Heston, Sandra Dee, Bobby Darin and Tab Hunter and was having a fine time, but her mother decided that even stylish 'old' Hollywood was not the place where her daughter should grow up, and whipped her back to Hove.

'I was livid!' Alexandra remembered.

She had recently played her first role in a British film, as a Bond girl in *Casino Royale*, enjoying a 'delightful' scene with the spoof James Bond, David Niven, who had been charming to her. She was now going to acting and singing classes and attending auditions for new parts. I made her laugh with some stories of my boyhood in Sussex and a few amusing anecdotes about top stars I'd met and my exploits in Hollywood. We seemed to be getting on so well that I plucked up courage to invite her out to dinner that night and was even more chuffed when she accepted. We had a great meal and conversation at my favourite new club, The Village, near Sloane Square, started by the extraordinary entrepreneur Alex Sterling. He was on top form and enhanced our chat.

Well, I do not believe in 'kiss and tell', especially if one or both members of a romantic partnership is still living, so suffice it to say we soon embarked on an intimate relationship and we clearly loved each other. It was not a wildly physical romance as it had been with Jilly. Alex was virtually a teetotaller, not only because she was serious about her career and couldn't afford to look even slightly out of sorts at auditions, but because, as she told me, she had a slight weakness of the liver. She could last a whole evening on a single glass of white wine. Mind you, that had its advantages too, with my present earning capacity! Our loving was cooler, more genteel, more dignified in a way – as was Alex herself, for she was well brought up, well spoken and, I sometimes thought, just a bit too good in all respects for the likes of me! I do remember one night in my flat, however – maybe I'd managed to get her to drink *two* glasses of white wine – when I persuaded her to wear a suspender belt and black stockings. I can recall the scene vividly today, as I looked down at her, blonde hair flowing like a golden mane over the pillow, gorgeous blue eyes looking lovingly into mine, arms extended to embrace me, and I had thought: 'All that beauty – and black stockings too!'

Unlike many beautiful actresses, Alexandra never expected or asked for expensive presents, but when her Pisces birthday was approaching I insisted I buy her something, and asked her what she would like. She had often told me she had kept various animals as a child and missed their company, and now replied without hesitation, 'A dog. A *little* dog I can take round with me, as a companion.'

I felt like saying *I* could fulfil that role! But of course I could not. When I was not actually interviewing a star I needed to be near a phone almost as much as she did. I bought some doggy magazines and eventually located some pedigree Yorkshire terrier puppies up in Hertfordshire whose parents were farm-working dogs. This made it likely the puppies would be brighter and better balanced than most little mutts. I drove to the farm and bought a puppy and by the time I got back to my flat I was more than tempted to keep him myself as he seemed to have a quite captivating character.

Alexandra was delighted when I handed him over, and soon christened him Huston, after the great director John Huston, who had directed her in *Casino Royale*.

The only trouble was that occasionally now I had to compete with Huston for Alexandra's affections; he tried to bite my bottom at one embarrassing moment. However, on my birthday in May, it was my turn to be delighted – she presented me with an exquisite real gold Dupont lighter, so much nicer for lighting my pipe than my usual boxes of messy and bothersome matches.

One phenomenon in our relationship, and one I'd never met before even when dating actresses, were the continual demands on Alexandra's time. We spent as much time in our flats as in going out because she felt she had to be near the phone – to hear the results of auditions and be available to talk to directors and producers her agent put in touch with her. (Mobile phones had not been invented then.) The phones seemed to ring at all times, when we were in the middle of a meal or even during loving moments, and if she was expecting a vital call she felt compelled to dash off and answer it. Quite often our small private arrangements had to be broken – for example when I was looking forward to driving her down to my favourite country club near Ockley in Surrey, to spend a relaxing afternoon in the lovely arboretum with its flowing brook, followed by a candlelit dinner. Almost at the last minute Alexandra would ring up and cancel as she had to meet some important film-maker or other. These men seemed to come from all over – Rome, Paris, New York, even Hollywood – and sometimes they invited her to impromptu parties to meet other associates or just be part of their group, and she felt obliged to go.

These were minor irritations but they coincided with my increasing difficulty with the way I made my living, compounded by my new dislike of it, and my nagging conscience that I ought to be getting on with my new novel. Even so, I was very much in love with Alexandra and after about three months, while I don't remember actually going down on one knee, I made it clear I wanted to marry her, feeling that if we operated from a single base we would make a great team. She didn't say yes but she didn't say no – she just felt we should wait a while longer.

It was at this time that another major project of mine fell down. I had just had a long and marvellous interview with Sophia Loren on the set of *Arabesque* in which she was co-starring with Gregory Peck. She had gone into great detail about her early life and struggle, how despite all her success she had lost a child in miscarriage but still longed to have children, her views on aspects of motherhood and stardom, and her emotions through the most eventful times of her life. In fact it was the best interview I'd ever had with a star and just from the rough draft alone *Woman's Own* magazine promised a substantial fee. I was into the third day of writing it all up when the magazine's editor rang me. They had heard from Sophia Loren and Carlo Ponti's lawyers that they did *not* want the magazine to proceed with my story, as unknown to Sophia, Carlo had sold exclusive rights to her full life story to a top American magazine (*Ladies' Home Journal* or *Cosmopolitan*, I can't remember which now). My shattered feelings were slightly relieved the following day when the editor rang me again, to say they were buying the UK rights to the American series, but in view of my good work, and the hope of more to come (could I get Brigitte Bardot, for instance?), they were paying me a fee anyway. It was only a quarter of what I would have received but it kept me afloat a while longer.

Even so, I felt this really was the beginning of the end of my show-business writing life. This was the fifth major project of mine to have failed in a row. I now knew that somehow, *somehow* I had to go somewhere more peaceful and write that new novel, for which more notes were being made every day. I thought again of Canada – but then I thought of Alexandra. Although she had family and theatrical connections in Canada I could hardly expect her to go there with me, especially as I would be writing most of the time. It was three more days before I saw her again – and it was to receive the biggest shock of all.

She was in an excited, exhilarated mood for she had just signed a contract to make a TV series called *The Champions* at Elstree Studios, in which she would play the heroine of a trio of fighters with abnormal out-of-the-world powers who fought against spies and other evil-doers. It would take well over a year to shoot the projected thirty hour-long episodes. I was delighted for her, and just a little bit for me, because I was sure it would mean she no longer had to stick by phones or dash about meeting possible employers or doing auditions. If we married and moved in together it would give her a really stable base where I would hold the fort, take messages, be her 'fast call' chauffeur when necessary, and do my writing while she was away all day working at the studios. But when I hinted at this I was astonished at her reply: 'Mike, I can't marry you, or anyone else. Not yet! There is a clause in the contract that stipulates I can't get married for three years.'

Talk about a heart sinking! I felt momentarily stunned and just heard myself say something feeble like, 'Crickey, you might have asked... discussed it with me at least. You signed that contract without even...?'

My voice trailed off as the truth dawned. Alexandra had obviously decided not to marry me. And as the next few weeks passed it was clear she had even less time for a social life. She had to shampoo her hair every morning at 6 a.m., be at the studios by 7.30 a.m. for an hour of make-up, then be filming on the set or location all day. All she wanted to do when she got home was sleep. She was so busy she couldn't even take little Huston to the studios and handed him to her parents in Hove to look after.

I now thought seriously of making that break from London and finding a place in Canada, to be far away from all I'd known and to make that last stand to be a writer. The idea was compounded when I drove up to Nottingham to see my grandmother, my last surviving relative in Britain. My father had told me that her husband, his dad, had travelled all over Canada for some years before he married her. As I recorded in my book *Alone in The Wilderness*, she told me an incredible story.

Before she had married my grandfather David Tomkies, he had wanted to go to Canada but she had refused to go with him. One night he arrived outside her house and threw gravel at her window. 'I'm off to Canada,' he told her. After working as a waiter on the Trans-Canadian Express he had settled down in Calgary, Alberta, as a cowpoke. One day, returning from a beer parlour with friends, he had been ambushed by a group of stone-throwing Indians and his right eye was knocked out of its socket so that it rested on his cheek. Patched up by local doctors, he was sent to a specialist in Vancouver who told him the best eye surgeon in the world was a Dr Watts, who lived in Nottingham! Back he had come, had his eye treated and visited my grandmother again, who this time accepted him. She told me he had been full of stories of how great a land Canada was, of its vast, untouched wild places. As she spoke I remembered with a slight shock that as a boy it was the book *Animal Heroes* by the great Canadian naturalist Ernest Thompson Seton that had helped inspire my own first love of nature. As I drove back to London I not only realized that but for a stone-throwing Indian I would not be alive, but perhaps my grandad's desire for the great free wilderness of Canada had been reborn in me.

I chose the right moment during my next meeting with Alexandra and broached the idea that I might fly out to Canada and write my novel there. It would take at least a year. She thought for a few moments, then said she knew I would never be happy until I got the book out of my system, and as I could not work on it in noisy London and she had so little free time from her hectic filming schedule, maybe it *was* a good idea. She didn't really want me to leave but once the novel was finished I should come back – I'd probably have to anyway, to sell it – and as my return would probably coincide with the end of her filming we could see how things stood between us then. She reminded me she could not marry anyone else, either, for three years.

I felt a little better then, but still dithered about making the final commitment to sell up and go. It took a visit to Paris, another meeting with Brigitte Bardot, and a remarkable film to tip me over the edge.

27
Brigitte, Zorba – and Farewell to My Old Life

After *Woman's Own* asked me to get a major interview with Brigitte Bardot in Paris I decided to try because if I pulled it off, it would give a much needed uplift to my coffers, especially if I did decide to go to Canada. Also, if my show-business writing life was over, then I couldn't end it with a bigger or better name than that of Brigitte Bardot. Better to go out with a bang…

I hardly expected her to remember me from our encounter at her beachfront villa outside St-Tropez eight years before but I wrote a diplomatic letter to her via her secretary in Paris. I was more than gratified when less than a week later the secretary rang me to say Brigitte *did* remember me and would be pleased to see me in her home in the Avenue Paul Doumer in four days' time. If my luck had changed at the last minute it was probably a little too late, I reflected. My flight to Paris was slightly delayed, so I had to take a taxi from the airport immediately after landing, and even so was a few minutes late.

There was no name on her front door and I had to ask a woman in the ground-floor apartment which was Bardot's. She made it clear she was tired of having to direct yet another caller but pointed to a rickety, creaky wooden lift only big enough for two, and said I had to go up to the seventh and top floor, all of which was Bardot's.

The door, opened by a Spanish maid, led into an oddly rococo apartment, for the modern, swinging Bardot obviously eschewed the contemporary. The furniture was antique, the sofa was Louis Quatorze, the table lampshades were in dull red and white vellum, and there were both modern abstract and Impressionist pictures on the walls. Bardot, wearing no make-up but black eye-liner, sat on the sofa, her gold slippers making a bold splash against the plush red carpet. If I was surprised at the warm cosiness of her home, I was even more so to see that at thirty-one she looked only two years, and not the eight years, older since I had last met her.

She gave me a sensational interview, revealing a constant sort of Peter Pan personality in that she deliberately preserved an innocence in her approach to her life and career, admitting, 'I'm not out of childhood in many ways.' There is no room for the long interview here, just a few extracts:

Did she not regret that Roger Vadim had projected her as an amoral sex kitten at the start of her career? Would she not have preferred to make her name by sheer acting talent like, say, Jeanne Moreau?

'No. This way has made me famous. She has her personality and I have mine. I am very happy to be like I am, natural. I don't try to change myself. I have always acted myself, played myself on the screen. Vadim did not make me act or behave in a certain way. That was the secret of the success of *And God Created Woman*. It was the first time I was free to be myself on the screen… I am not doing the same kind of parts any more. I have now made comedies and dramas but I have not changed in *character*. She is still free, still natural, and she does what she wants to do without hypocrisy. Yes, she is older but I don't think I *look* older, but this is not important. It is what is inside you that matters.'

Well, how did she feel inside?

'Inside I am very immature,' Bardot replied. 'I don't really care about time or age. I don't think that because I am thirty-one now I have to be a respectable lady with a Rolls Royce and a chauffeur to drive it.'

I asked her if after two divorces, she missed a happy marriage.

'Marriage! But I am against marriage! I do not regret not being what you call "happily married", not at all. I am very happy to be free. I don't know if I will ever marry again. Marriage is only important for *other* people in society. It's not a question of me having enough money to indulge my attitudes. Even if I had no money I would probably be able to live with someone without being married.'

Perhaps her career, the demands of it, had spoiled her chances of a successful marriage?

'It's an impossible situation, surely. If you are married you have to be at home and be there for your husband and for your children. Yet I have to be free – to go to Mexico for a movie or to London or New York. That is difficult for a marriage. Perhaps many people do it. But do they do it *well*? Many women of course stop acting when they get married. If you want to succeed in your marriage you have to be free for your husband, and if you want to succeed in your career you have to be free for *it*. What do I want most? Obviously, my career of course. You see, I am honest.'

Had she never met a man who was more important to her than her career?

'Every time when I meet a man and love him he is more important than everything in the world – and after, I prefer my career!'

I said she was a monster! She devoured men!

'Oh Mike, I am not a monster. Love, you see, is not a thing which is possible for long, long years. At first there is physical attraction, tenderness and affection and nothing else matters. Then I think after two or three years it is no longer the same thing, it becomes a habit. I think no love can last longer than three years.'

And so the interview went on, with some quite surprising revelations, even confessions. I will never forget the expression on her face – the sadness, the seriousness, the *strength* – when I reminded her she had once said, 'I am alone – everyone is alone.' Was this how she really felt?

'Yes, I still feel that. I always feel I am on my own. Everyone is alone. Even if you are with friends, even if you are in love, even if you adore your parents, even if you have a child, you are always alone because when you are born you are alone and when you die you are alone and all your life you are alone. I don't say that because I think it's very sad. To me it is normal.'

As I was leaving and we were shaking hands, Bardot presented her face for a quick continental peck on each cheek, and made me promise to send her a copy of the printed story. As I wandered along the Champs-Elysées a little later, feeling slightly depressed by Bardot's deadly accurate analysis of *aloneness*, I decided to cheer myself up with a touristy night out in Paris, maybe a visit to the Folies Bergères or the Bluebell girls' cabaret, in both of which Jilly had once danced. However, I never made it to either.

Quite by chance, I bumped, almost literally, into an old girlfriend, Barbara, with whom I'd enjoyed a romantic interlude some years ago in my second (and best) bedsitter and her own artistic garret on Paris's Left Bank. She was an unusual girl, not only because she was a blonde Berber Arab (her friends told me she was a Berber princess, although she always denied it to me) but because she had founded a semi-political magazine in Paris which was a sort of Who's Who of the governments in Europe and the Orient. She figured that as many of such governments changed personnel quite often she would have a regular sale of who is/was who magazine updates. Pretty smart reasoning, I felt. In the end I had just let her go after finding her (apparently surreptitiously) injecting herself with a syringe. I was horrified that I obviously had a drug addict as a girlfriend but said nothing to her about it. Over a year later I met a friend of hers in Paris who told me she was merely a diabetic who needed regular jabs of insulin. Of course, I had known nothing about diabetics at the time but I sent her an apologetic note, to which she did not reply.

As we now sat and sipped coffee at one of the pavement cafés on the Champs-Elysées, Barbara soon talked me out of going to any cabaret clubs. She was on her way to see a new film about a Greek peasant with a heroic spirit which her friends in the elite intellectual circles she frequented were all talking about. It was, she thought, called *Sorba, El Greco*, and by all accounts it was the kind of film a free spirit like me would appreciate. She suggested that after the film we could go ten-pin bowling with two friends of hers. I'd never done any ten-pin bowling so it promised to be an interesting night.

As Barbara drove me to the arts theatre on the other side of Paris to see the movie I wondered if it was the one I'd heard about some three years ago when I had been driving my open-top XK 120 Jaguar through the Alps near Gap on my way to interview two stars at the Cannes Film Festival. I was zooming along the high mountain roads at a good speed when I saw a sports car appear in my mirror. It kept annoyingly close to my tail, then roared past on a long bend, the driver brandishing a fist as if in triumph once past me. What fun! I gave chase and soon caught up to the car, which had Italian plates and a male passenger. As we swept round bend after bend the tail of the Alfa Romeo swished slightly from side to side, the car almost seeming to curve as it came out of a bend. Finally it pulled over and I swept past, sensing the driver's anger before raising my own victorious fist to return *his* salute. After a few more miles they were behind and out of my sight but, feeling peckish, I pulled into an attractive-looking roadside café which had tables outside. I locked some documents into the glove compartment and was climbing out of the car when the Italian car drew up beside me. The two men, who were well dressed, were laughing.

'Hey,' said the driver, 'you drive good! But… you drive like that too many times you will get into much trouble, you could lose your *life*!'

My instant reply, without thinking, was: 'It's *life* that's trouble – death is not. Death is peace!'

Both men laughed again, and the passenger said, 'That's good. That's very good. I'll remember that one.'

They asked me what I did for a living, so I told them. They said that they were in show business too and were about to make a film in Crete about a simple Cretan peasant who was a rebel with a unique view of life and way of living it. They invited me to visit the location. Knowing my show-business writing was coming to an end, I expressed only polite interest but did gather that the film was based on a book by someone called Kazakis, and the driver introduced his passenger as the film's director, called, to my ear, Miguel Kyanis, but both names meant absolutely nothing to me. They invited me to join them at the bar but as I didn't drink during the day, I sat at a table for a quick omelette and was soon on my way, the incident already out of my mind.

Sitting now with Barbara and watching the credits, the first marvellous scenes and Anthony Quinn's incredible performance as *Zorba The Greek* unfolded on the screen, I instantly recalled that meeting. The passenger in the sports car had clearly been Michael Cacoyannis, the film's producer/director, and I was soon brought up with a shock – but a pleasant shock. In the scene where Zorba is urging Alan Bates, the young English intellectual, to visit the island's beautiful widow, Bates, reluctant, says, 'No, I don't want any trouble.' Instantly Zorba seizes him and says: 'Boss, life *is* trouble. Only death is not! To be alive is to undo your belt and *look* for trouble!'

Cacoyannis, I thought, had a very good memory indeed. And he didn't pay me! But of course, it could have been coincidence. I felt like writing to him though, but not about that. I felt he ought to rewrite Zorba's second line. No one who has any experience of street fights would undo his belt and look for trouble. He would do up his belt, tighten it. One can't fight if one's trousers fall down.

I loved the film and still cannot understand why, although he was nominated for an Oscar, Quinn didn't actually win it. But it was in the very last scene that there came a line that affected me deeply, in fact it helped change my life. Zorba's dream overhead log 'railway' to take trees off a mountain has just collapsed totally. The attending crowds and monks have run away, and Zorba and Bates are left alone on the beach, tucking into chunks of the whole roast lamb turning on a primitive spit over a wood fire. Suddenly Zorba clutches Bates by the knee. 'Dammit, boss! I like you too much not to say it. You've got everything except one thing – madness! A man needs a little madness or else…'

Bates lowers his chunk of lamb, stares seriously at Zorba and repeats, 'Or else?'

And Zorba replies, 'He never dares cut the rope – and be *free*!'

That line has stayed with me for the rest of my life. A man needs a little madness, or else he never dares cut the rope – and be free. I've found it a permanent inspiration whenever I've had to face a tough decision.

I hardly remember the rest of that evening. Barbara drove me to the outskirts of Paris to the bowling rink and we met her two male French pals but when I was taking my turn, I looked up to find the three of them had gone. Barbara had dumped me out in the sticks, no doubt in revenge for my virtually doing the same to her years ago! I just took a taxi back to my hotel.

I didn't mind for I was grateful to her for taking me to see such a memorable film, which has inspired me ever since. I never suspected then that in the years to come I would be even more grateful to Zorba's author, the great Cretan writer Nikos Kazantzakis, for even stronger inspiration.

When I returned from Paris I was horrified to find that workmen had erected scaffolding around my apartment building and were drilling into the roof, all without due notice from the landlord. It was the last straw. *Now* was the time for madness, the time to cut that rope! I was so disillusioned with everything that I didn't even write up the Bardot interview myself. I gave the notes to a freelance colleague who had done a lot of work for *Woman's Own*, and we split the fee. Over lunch one Saturday I told Alexandra I'd made the final decision. Again, she seemed to think it was the right one – I could come back when I had finished the novel, after all.

Within two weeks I sold the flat lease, my few antiques and the Mini Cooper for less than their real value, got my immigration permit from Canada House, and delivered one large crate of my personally valuable gear to London docks for shipping to Vancouver.

On the evening before the day I was due to fly from Heathrow to Vancouver, Alexandra rang to say she was ill in bed and could I visit her tomorrow? Accordingly, I set off early so I could visit and comfort her and say what I hoped would be a temporary goodbye. It was a rather short, tearful meeting and Alexandra said she wished I wasn't going after all.

'So do I, darling,' I replied. 'But I can't do anything about it now. All my gear is in a crate on the high seas, and I'm on my way to the airport!'

We kissed, promised to write, and I left by taxi to catch my plane. Later, as the jumbo's jet engines burst into life and the plane lumbered along the runway, I leaned back in my uncomfortable seat knowing I was at last on my mission to try to retrieve the possibly irretrievable shallow man in me. I was off into the great unknown.

Well, Zorba, I cut the rope.

VHS Videos from Mike Tomkies

EAGLE MOUNTAIN YEAR (125 minutes, £15)
This tape tells the story of a magical Highland mountain through all four seasons. There are golden eagles at the nest, their glorious courtship 'air dances', and a female eagle hauling a deer carcass uphill on her own. Rare black-throated divers are seen diving, courting and, for the first time on film, at their nest. Pine martens are shown hunting, at their den, even feeding from my hands. Hunting and nesting peregrine falcons are shown in detail, as is all the comic-tragic sibling rivalry at buzzard nests. There are courting mergansers, ospreys, ravens, foxes and even a hunting wildcat. Throughout all, I show the lives of the red deer herds.

AT HOME WITH EAGLES (102 minutes, £10)
Shown in incredibly intimate detail, this is the story of three pairs of courting, hunting and nesting golden eagles – one pair exchanging incubation duties, a second pair trying against the odds to hatch infertile eggs, and a third pair who are successful in raising their chick from egg to flying stage. Never before have the secret lives of the king of birds been revealed in such fascinating detail. Two eminent naturalists have described it as *probably the greatest eagle film ever made.*

FOREST PHANTOMS (60 minutes, £6)
This tape takes six barn owls through a full year, from chicks to hunting adults. Also starred are the forest phantoms of the day – rare goshawks at the nest, as well as nesting buzzards, long-eared owls, foxes, and, yes, even *eagles* again.

MY BARN OWL FAMILY (52 minutes, £6)
A tape of my barn owls Blackie and Brownie, and how they finally raised four youngsters to flying stage. We see them incubating eggs, hunting the woods and pastures, perch hunting from my garden fence, and taking prey back up to the loft. Intimate glimpses of their complicated behaviour inside the loft and nest box; and all the growing stages of the chicks are recorded in loving detail. Also shown are the daytime 'invaders' of their world – a badger who was unusually tame, a fox who used my sheep walls to spy prey, a beautiful female kestrel who came for any food the owls left on the table – not to mention chaffinch hordes, bellicose siskins, cheeky jays and other entrancing characters.

RIVER DANCING YEAR **(92 minutes, £10)**
A celebration of the superb wildlife of Scottish rivers – from the raging upper waterfalls where salmon leap heroically to reach their spawning grounds; through serene reaches where swans, herons, moorhens, mallards, dippers, goosanders, gulls and kingfishers go about their lives and finally to where the river enters the sea and the estuary kingdom of the great sea eagles. We see foxes playing in a riverside garden, a vixen giving suck to her four cubs ...a boisterous badger family, digging, playing hilarious judo games, and even taking food from my hands ...a grooming, prowling and hunting wildcat ...otters fishing and in their holt ... peregrines guarding their chicks ...herons catching fish and even swallowing a duckling, a young golden eagle preparing to leave its nest...ospreys catching and bringing fish to their grown young ...and a host of other species. Above all, it is a long insight into the world of the rare white-tailed sea eagles, as a pair guard their flown youngster, exchange beak-to-beak greetings, and provide glorious flight sequences when they hunt for prey in their kingdom at the end of the river.

WILDEST SPAIN **(77 minutes, £7)**
A tape about Europe's finest wildlife. It tells of successful treks and adventures all over Spain in pursuit of wild bear, wolf, lynx, wild boar, ibex, black stork, very rare vultures and eagles, plus many other species in a magical European country not hitherto known for its often excellent wildlife conservation.

WILDEST SPAIN REVISITED **(52 minutes, £6)**
This updates the previous video, with totally new material, concentrating on rare wild brown bear and wild wolves. Some extraordinary and hitherto unknown behaviour is captured.

LAST EAGLE YEARS **(75 minutes, £8)**
This tape covers the five wilderness years since all the previous videos ended. I show three pairs of hunting, courting and nesting golden eagles, a veritable feast of red kites competing with ravens, buzzards and crows for food, and goshawks and peregrine falcons at the nest. There are wild goats (and a fight between two males), brown hares, courting curlews, red and rare black-throated divers, and a long sequence of ospreys hunting for fish and feeding young at two nests. On my way to the kingdom of the rare white-tailed sea eagles, I show huge Atlantic seals and dolphins somersaulting in the sea, and finally the great sea eagles soaring to and from their island nest as they tend their single youngster.

MY BIRD TABLE THEATRES (80 minutes, £6)
This tape showing the fascinating behaviour of the myriad hordes of birds who visited bird tables at my last four homes, ranging from the wild Scottish hills near Ullapool, to the Borders and deepest Sussex. Shown through the four seasons, all the normal garden birds are here plus nuthatches, linnets, goldfinches, ring doves, colourful jays, green woodpeckers, comical squirrels, a flock of pheasants who became tame, and even a kestrel and a barn owl. At night foxes and a pair of badgers come for the food I set out, including a huge semi-albino boar weighing over 30lbs who pulls down a Victorian pedestal a man can hardly lift, to get at some meat.

MY WILD 75th SUMMER (80 minutes, £6)
My last season filming peregrine falcons, red kites and goshawks feeding chicks at the nest; the roe deer, foxes and cubs, and a badger pair at my new wildlife reserve in deepest Sussex. It shows how I set up the reserve, planted a wild flower meadow and the butterflies it attracted. I show the playful and courting behaviour of rabbits, foxes, squirrels, pheasants, plus jays feeding flown chicks, a frolicking weasel and colourful woodpeckers. The film ends with fabulous footage of rare white-tailed sea eagles soaring to and from their tree nest on Mull with prey, and how they cooperate to feed their twin chicks. This 11-minute sequence, shot on my 76th birthday, is my 'swan song' to wildlife filming.

Book
GOLDEN EAGLE YEARS (£7)
The reissue of the book long out of print, which contains more and better colour pictures than the first edition. It tells of my first five years studying Scotland's magnificent golden eagles. The treks, the pitfalls and defeats, the joys and triumphs, are fully described.

(*All the above prices include post and packing, and please indicate if and how you want them signed. Cheques payable to Mike Tomkies*)
Please send your remittance and delivery address to:
Whittles Publishing Ltd., Dunbeath Mains Cottages, Dunbeath, Caithness, KW6 6EY, Scotland.

ANOTHER WEEKEND EXCLUSIVE

The Rock 'n' Roll idol opens his heart

This is MY

What was he like before that sizzling voice . . . those swivelling hips . . . made him one of the world's top stars? What is he like now? Frankly and sincerely, Elvis tells all to MIKE TOMKIES

● hun we All hav

☆ ★ ☆

I REMEMB into the Aaron. H he was born i

I remember stay here for e all else, sobbing ber my mothe sacrificed her h the rough times

These are th I recall when p of fans who s

Please forget self-appointed young behavio talk about tha

I don't forg days now I h limousines, a sion, and ha records than living.

SURE, I've b live like lucky tha all over the w had to offer—t material thing

I thank God But there w whe have M were mar 19 so o I born